COMPREHENSIVE ENGLISH GRAMMAR

COMPREHENSIVE ENGLISH GRAMMAR

(WITH ANSWERS)

VERY USEFUL FOR

- ❒ ALL SCHOOL STUDENTS (ALL CLASSES)
- ❒ ASPIRANTS FOR ALL COMPETITIVE EXAMINATIONS
- ❒ COLLEGE STUDENTS
- ❒ THOSE ASPIRING TO LEARN ADVANCED ENGLISH GRAMMAR
- ❒ TEACHERS AND SCHOLARS

By

MADAN SOOD

GOODWILL PUBLISHING HOUSE

B-3, RATTAN JYOTI, 18, RAJENDRA PLACE

NEW DELHI-110008 (INDIA)

Published by

Rajneesh Chowdhry
for
Goodwill Publishing House
B-3, Rattan Jyoti
18, Rajendra Place
New Delhi-110008
Tel : 25750801, 25755519, 25820556
Fax : 91-11-25763428
E-mail : goodwillpub@vsnl.net
Website : www.goodwillpublishinghouse.com

Typeset at
Radha Laserkraft
R-814, New Rajinder Nagar
New Delhi-110060 • Tel : 28742031

Printed at : Kumar Offset Printers, Delhi-110092

Preface

There is no denying the fact that the knowledge of English langauage is becoming an inevitable necessity each day. No student can claim to be an expert in any language unless he has mastered the rules of grammar of that language. This book has been written with a view to make the rules of English Grammar easy to understand. There is no doubt that there are innumerable books of grammar in the market but the fact also cannot be denied that in spite of the best books of grammar, some students do not understand the rules without the help of an expert English teacher.

This book caters to the requirement of those students who find the rules of grammar difficult to grasp and assimilate. While studying this grammar book, students will feel as if an expert English teacher is sitting beside them and explaining the rules of grammar to them.

The traditional as well as modern concepts of grammar find their due place to facilitate easy comprehension. The book contains comprehensive and exhaustive details of different Parts of Speech, Writing correct Sentences and topics such as Tenses, the Voice, the Reported speech, Analysis, Synthesis, Transformation, Punctuation, Determiners, Prepositions, Modals, Articles, Non-finite, etc.

A comprehensive chapter on Transformation of Sentences and Idioms and Phrases would prove to be a boon for those who want to acquaint themselves with idiomatic and ornate learning of the English language. Several solved and unsolved exercises on all topics of grammar have been incorporated and answers have been provided to all unsolved exercises in order to enable the students to evaluate their grasp of the rules.

To write more about the usefulness and quality of this book will be an exaggeration and the book will speak for itself. Public School students, College students and those preparing for competitive examinations can derive immense benefit from this book, besides, it will serve as a reference book for teachers and scholars.

My thanks are due to my Publishers for their keen interest, co-operation, motivation and confidence reposed in me for my being involved in the writing and teaching of English language, literature, conversation and writing skills for over twenty five years. My published books are — Art of Precis Writing, Current Affairs Informa, Probable Essays, English Grammar with a difference with answers. Precis writing for College and Competitive Examinations and Unique Comprehension—2 Volumes.

MADAN SOOD

Contents

Introduction

English is one of the many languages which are spoken and written in the world. Before one studies the fundamantals of grammar, it is important to know what a language is and why and how one should learn a particular language. Firstly, a language is learnt for the purpose of communication which is followed by the immense pleasure one derives in learning and speaking a language.

A. **Language.** Language is the medium of communication through which one expresses one's emotions, ideas, thoughts and feelings to other human-beings.

B. **Alphabet.** The letters in a language are treated as the alphabet of the language of which it is composed. The alphabet of English is composed of twenty six letters which are known as the alphabet and are used for printing and writing.

C. **Division of the Alphabet.** The Alphabet of English is divided into two classes — (i) Vowels, (ii) Consonants.

   (i) The five letters —a, e, i, o u — are called vowels. It is not possiblle to write even a single word without the use of a vowel.

   (ii) Consonants : The remaining twenty one letters are called consonants. They are — b, c, d, f, g, h, j, k, l, m, n, p, q, r, s, t, v, w, x, y, z.

D. **Syllable.** A part of a word which consists of a vowel sound, is called a Syllable; i.e., En-cyclo-paedia. There are three syllbles in the word encyclopaedia.

E. **Grammar.** Grammar is a systematic study of scientific method providing essential information and guidance to learn a language. The knowledge of grammar teaches one to write and speak a language accurately. Hence, no one can claim to be an expert in any language unless he has mastered the rules of grammar of that language.

Importance of Grammar

As grammar deals with the linguistic problems and plays a very significant role in practical life, its important cannot be underestimated. One cannot write or speak flawless English unless one has mastered the rules of grammar. Without acquainting oneself with the rules of grammar, one cannot speak or write correct English.

Since grammar is primarily concerned with the study of language, it clarifies the difficulties experienced in learning a language and guides us as to how language is effectively used in our practical life. Grammar also teaches us how words are formed and when and where they are used. Grammar also familiarises us with the sentence structure and patterns and it surveys and defines various parts of speech, thereby providing adquate information as to when and where these parts of speech are used in written and spoken Engligh.

The need of grammar is also realised by those who desire to perfect their written English as it teaches us how paragraphs, essays and letters are written in simple and ornate style. It also equips us with perfect communication aids and abilities. Thus, grammar is very essential for communication and correspondence and its importance is undeniably unprecedented.

1

The Sentence

A group of words that make complete sense is called a **sentence**. A sentence must always begin with a capital letter and end with a full stop (.) as,

1. This dog has a long tail.
2. The crowd is very large.
3. Cows give milk.
4. The elephant has great strength.
5. We all love honesty.

KIND OF SENTENCES

Sentences are of five kinds :

(1) A sentence which makes a statement or declares something is called **Assertive** or **Declarative**; as

1. The sun sets in the west.
2. Humpty Dumpty sat on a wall.
3. The boys are playing cricket.
4. He received a present.

(2) A sentence which asks a question is called an **Interrogative sentence**; as,

1. Where do you live ?
2. Have you completed your work ?
3. Why were you late yesterday ?
4. Did you give him the message ?

(3) A sentence that expresses a command, request, order or entreaty is called an **Imperative sentence**; as,

1. Have mercy on the poor.
2. Don't make a noise.
3. Open the door.

4. Please type this letter now.
5. Move forward.

(4) A sentence that expresses sudden feelings of joy, sorrow or surprise is called an **Exclamatory sentence**; as,

1. What a beautiful weather !
2. What a clever boy you are !
3. Bravo ! they have climbed.
4. Hurrah ! we have won the series.
5. What a shame !

(5) A sentence that expresses a sudden wish is called **Optative sentence**; as,

1. May she live long !
2. May you be blessed with a son !
3. If only you had been present !
4. May you be blessed with a good health !

EXERCISE 1

State the kind of the following sentences :

1. The sun rises in the east.
2. The boys are making a noise.
3. Sit down.
4. Where do you live ?
5. Don't make a noise.
6. What a wonderful weather !
7. May you live long !
8. Work hard.
9. Please come here.
10. How beautiful the lotus is !
11. Let him come in.
12. Don't park your car here.
13. All that glitters is not gold.
14. How horrible the sight was !
15. Have you solved all the sums ?
16. Where have you kept my purse ?
17. Stand up.
18. Take care of your health.
19. Switch on the lights.
20. There were no casualties.

2

Subject and Predicate

Every sentence has two parts – The part that names the person or thing we are speaking about is called the **subject** of the sentence. The part that tells something about the subject, is called the **predicate** of the sentence.

In order to find the subject of a sentence put the question 'who' ? or 'what' after the verb; as,

Sohan climbed the hill (put the question – who climbed the hill ?) The answer is Sohan. So Sohan is the *subject.*

The moon shines brightly (put the question – what shines brightly ? The answer is – the moon. So the 'moon' is the *subject.*

Note. Verb is the part of the predicate.

In imperative sentences, the subject is understood and hence not expressed; as,

Switch off the light. (here the subject '*you*' is understood).

Study the following sentences :

1. I met you yesterday.
2. The sun rises in the east.
3. Barking dogs seldom bite.

In sentence 1, '*I*' is the subject and the remaining part of the sentence – '*met you yesterday*', is the predicate.

In sentence 2, '*the sun*' is the subject and '*rises in the east*' is the predicate.

In sentence 3, '*barking dogs*' is the subject and '*seldom bite*' is the predicate.

Note. The subject and the predicate may consist of a single word each or more than a single word; as,

We elected Sonu captain.

The boys of our school elected Sonu captain.

In the first sentence '*we*' is the subject. In the second sentence '*the boys of our school*' is the subject.

EXERCISE 2

Separate the subject and the predicate in the following sentences :

1. They have completed their homework.
2. She knows me.
3. The boys are playing.
4. The Himalayas are the highest mountains in the world.
5. Sweet are the uses of adversity.
6. A thing of beauty is a joy forever.
7. The naked everyday he clad.
8. Nature is the best physician.
9. Stones wall do not a prison make.
10. Borrowed garments never fit well.
11. No man can serve two masters.
12. He is a man of might.
13. A barking sound the shepherd heard.
14. The sun sets in the west.
15. Rising early can keep your body and mind fit.
16. Here are your clothes.
17. Boys are flying kites.
18. In the corner sat the hunter waiting for the prey.

3

Parts of Speech

The words are divided into different kinds according to their use or the work they do in a sentence. These kinds are called **parts of speech**.

There are eight parts of speech.

1. Noun
2. Pronoun
3. Adjective
4. Verb
5. Adverb
6. Preposition
7. Conjunction
8. Interjection

(1) **Noun :** A noun is the name of a person, place, animal or a thing; as,

1. The *sun* rises in the *east.*
2. *Kolkata* is on the *Hooghly.*
3. *Ram* is a brave *boy.*

In the above sentences—sun, east, Kolkota, Hooghly, Ram and boy—are Nouns.

Note. The word thing includes all objects which we can see, hear, taste, touch or smell.

There is one type of noun (abstract Noun) which we can only think of but we can not feel by our senses.

(2) **Pronoun :** A pronoun is a word that is used in place of noun; as,

1. Johan is a boy. He studies in our school.
2. Jayshree is a girl. All like her.

In the above sentences, 'He' and 'Her' are pronouns as they are used in place of nouns—(John) in the first sentence and (Jayshree) in the second sentence.

(3) **Adjective :** An adjective is a word that says more about a Noun or a pronoun.

1. Shana is a clever girl.
2. Chirag is a nice boy.

In the above sentences 'clever' and 'nice' are adjectives as they say more about the nouns 'girl' and 'boy'.

(4) **Verb :** A verb is a doing word. Through a verb, an action is conveyed; as,

1. We saw a movie.
2. You typed a few letters.
3. They watched a cricket match.

In the above sentences 'saw', 'typed' and 'watched' are verbs since they convey actions.

(5) **Adverb :** An adverb is a word that says something more about :

A verb
An adjective
Another adverb

1. I spoke politely.
2. This building is very beautiful.
3. I spoke quite politely.

In the above sentences, words 'politely', 'very' and 'quite' are adverbs.

In the first sentence, the word 'politely' is adverb because it is telling more about the verb 'spoke'.

In the second sentence, the word 'very' is adverb as it is telling more about the adjective 'beautiful'.

In the third sentence, the word 'quite' is adverb as it is telling more about another adverb 'politely'.

(6) **Preposition :** A preposition is a word used with a noun or a pronoun to show how the noun or pronoun stands in relation to something else; as,

1. The books are on the table.
2. The sky is above us.
3. He is fond of reading.
4. There is a spider on the wall.
5. We rested under a tree.

In the above sentences, the words 'on', 'above', 'of', 'on' and 'under' are prepositions.

(7) **Conjunction :** A conjunction is a word that is used to join two words, two phrases, two clauses or two sentences; as,

Home and office

In the above phrase 'and' is a conjunction because it is joining two words — 'home' and 'office'

at home but not in the office.

In the above phrase 'but' is a conjunction because it is joining two phrases — 'at home' and 'not in the office'.

If you work hard and if you are sincere.

In the above clauses 'and' is a conjunction because it is joining two clauses — 'if you work hard' and 'if you are sincere'.

I went to the market but I could not get the books.

In the above sentence 'but' is a conjunction because it is joining two sentences — 'I went to the market' and 'I could not get the books'.

(8) **Interjection :** An interjection is a word which expresses sudden feelings of joy, sorrow or surprise; as,

1. Hurrah ! we have won the match.
2. Alas ! her only son is dead.

In the above sentences — the words 'Hurrah' and 'Alas' are interjections.

EXERCISE 3

(A) ***State the part of speech of each italicized word in the following sentences :***

1. She *won* a *prize*.
2. This *class consists* of forty *students*.
3. We have *heard* this before.
4. He is an *honest person*.
5. *Kolkata* is a *big* city.
6. *Hurrah ! they* have *won* the series.
7. *You* should *obey* your *parents*.
8. I can not *teach you* today.
9. The *tiger* has *great strength*.
10. A small *leak* may sink a *great* ship.

THE NOUN : KINDS OF NOUN

Words which are used as names of persons, animals, places or things are called **nouns**. Thus we can say that all naming words are nouns — John, boy, military, honesty, wood etc.

(1) A **Proper noun** is the special name of a particular person or place. For example, Sohan is a proper noun, for it is the name of one particular person. Similarly, Delhi is a proper noun, because it is the name of a particular city.

Note. A proper noun always begins with a capital letter.

(2) A **Common noun** is a noun which does not point out any particular person, place or thing but is common to all persons, places or things of the same class or kind; as boy, girl, city.

(3) A **Collective noun** stands for a collection of persons, or things considered as one complete whole; as,

Fleet, jury, class, bunch, army, contingent, team, herd, committee, family etc.

(4) A **Material noun** is the name of the material of which things can be made; as,

gold, wood, iron, etc.

(5) An **Abstract noun** denotes a thing which we can neither see nor touch. An abstract noun is the name of something that we can only think of; as,

knowledge, hope, honesty, courage, pity, sleep, death, sincerity, joy, sorrow etc.

EXERCISE 4

Pick out the nouns in the following sentences and say whether they are common, proper, material, collective or abstract :

1. The jury found the prisoner innocent.
2. I hear a strange noise.
3. Pen is mighter than sword.
4. Wisdom is better than strength.
5. Ornaments are made of gold.
6. I saw a herd of cattle grazing in the field.
7. There is no happiness without health.
8. The soldier lost an arm in the battle field.
9. Hardwork, discipline and sincerity are good qualities.
10. There are thirty students in this class.
11. Each soldier was given an award.
12. I bought a bouquet for his birthday.
13. The police used tear-gas shells.
14. Health and happiness go together.
15. Cleanliness is next to godliness.

EXERCISE 5

Put these collective nouns in the blanks given below :

(Team Jury Swarm Regiment Flock Fleet Committee Mob Crew Herd)

1. The .... of soldiers is marching away.
2. A .... of sheep is grazing in the field.
3. A .... of cattle is being chased.
4. The .... was dispersed by the police.
5. The prisoner was found guilty by the ....
6. We appointed a .... of ten members.
7. A .... of bees is flying in the sky.
8. The ship sank with all the ....
9. I saw a .... of ships anchored in the harbour.
10. Our cricket .... has performed very well.

EXERCISE 6

Fill in the blanks with the Abstract Nouns formed from the words given in brackets.

1. Dara Singh is famous for his .... (strong)
2. The old men often think of the happy days of their .... (child)
3. He was given .... for not doing his home work. (punish)
4. The Managing Committee accepted the .... of the members. (propose)
5. Solomon was known for his .... (wise)
6. We should always speak the .... (true)
7. The slavery system did not allow any .... (free)
8. Everyone believes in her .... (innocent)
9. There is no .... without health. (happy)
10. The soldier was praised by all for his .... (brave)

4

The Noun : Gender

A noun has four genders — **Masculine Gender, Feminine Gender, Common Gender** and **Neuter Gender**.

A noun that denotes a male is called **Masculine Gender** and a noun that denotes a female is called **Feminine Gender**.

All living beings are either of the male or the female sex.

A noun that denotes either a male or a female is of the **Common Gender**; as,

Baby, person, thief, child, parent etc.

A noun that denotes a thing which is neither male or female is called **Neuter Gender**; as,

book, house, pencil

Some of the Masculine and Feminine Nouns are given below.

By using a different word; as,

Masculine	**Feminine**	**Masculine**	**Feminine**
Bachelor	Spinster	Hart	Roe
Boy	Girl	Horse	Mare
Brother	Sister	King	Queen
Buck	Doe	Lord	Lady
Bullock	Heifer	Man	Woman
Cock	Hen	Monk (frier)	Nun
Colt	Filly	Nephew	Niece
Dog	Bitch	Papa	Mamma
Drake	Duck	Ram	Ewe
Drone	Bee	Sir	Madam
Earl	Countess	Son	Daughter
Father	Mother	Stag	Hind
Gander	Goose	Uncle	Aunt
Gentleman	Lady	Wizard	Witch

By adding a syllable (-ess, ine, -trix, -a

Masculine	Feminine	Masculine	Feminine
Author	Authoress	Mayor	Mayoress
Baron	Baroness	Patron	Patroness
Count	Countess	Peer	Peeress
Giant	Giantess	Poet	Poetess
Heir	Heiress	Priest	Priestess
Host	Hostess	Prophet	Prophetess
Jew	Jewess	Shepherd	Shepherdess
Lion	Lioness	Steward	Stewardess
Manager	Manageress	Viscount	Viscountess

In the following –ess is added after dropping the vowel of the masculine :

Masculine	Feminine	Masculine	Feminine
Abbot	Abbess	Preceptor	Preceptress
Benefactor	benefactress	Prince	Princess
Conductor	Conductress	Seamster	Seamstress
Enchanter	Enchantress	Songster	Songstress
Founder	Foundress	Tempter	Temptress
Hunter	Huntress	Tiger	Tigress
Instructor	Instructress	Traitor	Traitress
Master	Mistress	Waiter	Waitress
Negro	Negress		

The suffix –ess is the commonest suffix used to form feminine nouns from the masculine.

Masculine	Feminine	Masculine	Feminine
Administrator	Administratrix	Marquis	Marchioness
Czar	Czarine	Murderer	Murderess
Duck	Duchess	Signor	Signora
Emperor	Empress	Sorcerer	Sorceress
Executer	Executrix	Sultan	Sultana
Fox	Vixen	Testator	Testatrix
Hero	Heroine		

By placing a word before or after; as,

Masculine	Feminine	Masculine	Feminine
Bull-calf	Cow-calf	Jack-ass	Jenny-ass
Cock-sparrow	Hen-sparrow	Land-lord	Land-lady
Grand-father	Grand-mother	Man-servant	Maid-servant
Great-uncle	Great-aunt	Milkman	Milkmaid
He-bear	She-bear	Peacock	Peahen
He-goat	She-goat	Washerman	Washerwoman

EXERCISE 7
(NOUNS : GENDER)

Write the Feminine Genders of the following Masculine Genders :

Masculine	Feminine	Masculine	Feminine
1. Boy	....	19. Host	....
2. Girl	....	20. Count	....
3. Lion	....	21. Giant	....
4. Cock-sparrow	....	22. Drake	....
5. Hero	....	23. Manager	....
6. Brother	....	24. Jew	....
7. Dog	....	25. Duke	....
8. Buck	....	26. Uncle	....
9. Colt	....	27. Wizard	....
10. Gentleman	....	28. Steward	....
11. Sir	....	29. Tiger	....
12. Ram	....	30. Negro	....
13. Son	....	31. Heir	....
14. Stag	....	32. Conductor	....
15. Father	....	33. Prince	....
16. Gander	....	34. Poet	....
17. Baron	....	35. Waiter	....
18. Author	....	36. Peacock	....

5

The Noun : Number

A noun that denotes one person or thing is **Singular Number**; as,

Boy, book cow, pencil

A noun that denotes more than one person or thing is **Plural number**; as,

Boys, books, cows, pencils

Some of the Singular and Plural Nouns are given below :

Singular	Plural	Singular	Plural
Boy	Boys	Hero	Heroes
Pen	Pens	Solo	Solos
Book	Books	Ratio	Radios
Cow	Cows	Stereo	Stereos
Girl	Girls	Story	Stories
Dish	Dishes	Pony	Ponies
Watch	Watches	Thief	Thieves
Potato	Potatoes	Life	Lives
Negro	Negroes	Loaf	Loaves
Volcano	Volcanoes	Leaf	Leaves
Photo	Photos	Chief	Chiefs
Desk	Desks	Roof	Roofs
Class	Classes	Gulf	Gulfs
Brush	Brushes	Grief	Griefs
Branch	Branches	Hoof	Hoofs
Match	Matches	Strife	Strifes
Tax	Taxes	Man	Men
Box	Boxes	Goose	Geese
Buffalo	Buffaloes	Foot	Feet
Mango	Mangoes	Tooth	Teeth
Cargo	Cargoes	Ox	Oxen

Singular	Plural	Singular	Plural
Echo	Echoes	Dwarf	Dwarfs
Baby	Babies	Safe	Safes
Army	Armies	Serf	Serfs
Lady	Ladies	Brief	Briefs
City	Cities	Proof	Proofs
Wife	Wives	Belief	Beliefs
Calf	Calves	Woman	Women
Knife	Knives	Mouse	Mice
Wolf	Wolves	Louse	Lice
Shelf	Shelves	Child	Children

Some nouns have the **Singular** and the **Plural** alike; as,

Singular	Plural	Singular	Plural
Swine	Swine	Pair	Pair
Sheep	Sheep	Dozen	Dozen
Dear	Dear	Score	Score
Cod	Cod	Gross	Gross
Trout	Trout	Hundred	Hundred
Salmon	Salmon	Thousand	Thousand
		(When used after Numerals)	

Some nouns are used only in the plural; as

Spectacles, pincers, tongs, scissors, bellows, trousers, drawers, breeches, measles, mumps, billiards, draughts (games) annals, thanks, proceeds (of a sale) tidings, environs, nupitals, obsequies.

Some nouns originally singular are now generally used in the plural; as,

Alms, riches, eaves

The following plural forms of nouns are commonly used in singular :

News, innings, politics, mechanics, physics, mathematics

'Means' is used either as **Singular** or **Plural**, but when it has the meaning of 'wealth' it is always plural; as,

I have succeeded by this means (or by these means) in accomplishing the task.

My means are meagre but I have incurred no debt.

Certain **Collective Nouns** though Singular in form, are always used in **plural**; as,

Gentry, people, vermin, cattle, poultry

'People' as a **Common Noun** means a 'nation' and is used in both Singular and Plural; as,

There are many different peoples in India.

Koreans are a hard-working people.

A **Compound Noun** generally forms its plural by adding –s to the principal word; as,

Singular	**Plural**
Commander-in-chief	Commanders-in-chief
Coat-of-mail	Coats-of-mail
Son-in-law	Sons-in-law
Step-son	Step-sons
Step-daughter	Step-daughters
Maid-servant	Maid-servants
Passer-by	Passers-by
Looker-on	Lookers-on
Man-or-war	Men-or-war

Nouns taken from foreign languages

Singular	**Plural**	**Singular**	**Plural**
Bandit	Banditti/bandits	Crisis	Crises
Madame	Mesdames	Basis	Bases
Monsieur	Messieurs	Analysis	Analyses
Erratum	Errata	Parenthesis	Parentheses
Index	Indices	Hypothesis	Hypotheses
Radius	Radii	Phenomenon	Phenomena
Formula	Formulae/formulas	Criterion	Criteria
Memorandum	Memoranda	Cherub	Cherubim/cherubs
Terminus	Termini/terminuses	Seraph	Seraphim/seraphs
Axis	Axes		

Sc· nouns have two forms for the plural, each having somewhat different meaning;

Singular	Plural
Brother	Brothers : sons of the same parent Brethren : members of a society or a community
Cloth	Cloths : pieces of cloth Clothes : garments
Die	Dies : stamps for coining Dice : small cubes used in games
Fish	Fishes : taken separately Fish : collectively
Genius	Geniuses : persons of great talent Genii : spirits
Index	Indexes : tables of contents to books Indices : signs used in algebra
Penny	Pennies : number of coins Pence : amount in value

Some nouns have two meanings in the singular but only one in the plural.

Singular		Plural
Practice :	1. habit (exercise of a profession)	Practices : habits
Light :	1. radiance 2. a lamp	Lights
People :	1. nation 2. men and women	Peoples : nations
Powder :	1. dust 2. a dose of medicine; fine grains like dust	Powders : doses of medicine

Some nouns have one meaning in the singular and two in the plural.

Singular	Plural	
Manner (method)	manners	1. methods 2. right behviour
Colour (hue)	colours	1. hues 2. the flag of regiment
Custom (habit)	customs	1. habits 2. duties levied on imports

Singular	Plural	
Effect (result)	effects	1. results 2. property
Moral (a moral lesson)	morals	1. moral lessons 2. conduct
Number (a quantity)	numbers	1. quantities 2. verses
Pain (suffering)	pains	1. sufferings 2. exertion
Premise (proposition)	premises	1. propositions 2. buildings
Quarter (fourth part)	quarters	1. fourth parts 2. lodgings
Spectacle (sight)	spectacles	1. sights 2. eye-glasses
Letter (1) letter of the alphabet (2) epistle	Letters	1. letters of the alphabet 2. epistles 3. literature
Ground (1) earth (reason)	Grounds	1. enclosed land attached to house 2. reasons 3. dregs

Some nouns have different meaning in the singular and in the plural.

Singular	Plural
Advice : counsel	Advices : information
Air : atmosphere	Airs : affected manners
Good : well-being/benefit	Goods : merchandise
Compass : range/extent	Compasses : an instrument for drawing circles
Respect : regard	Respects : compliments
Physic : medicine	Physics : natural science
Iron : a kind of metal	Irons : fetters
Force : strength	Forces : troops

Figures, letters and other symbols are made plural by adding an apostrophe and s, as,

There are more u's and p's in this letter
Dot your m's and cross your n's
Add five 2's and six 3's

Abstract nouns do not have plurals; as,

joy, love kindness, hope

When such words appear in the plural, they are used as common nouns; as,

kindnesses = acts of kindness
Provocations = instances of provocation

Material nouns are also used as singular; as,

wood, cotton, tin, gold, silver, copper

When these nouns are used in the plural, they become common nouns with changed meanings; as,

Irons : fetters

Tins : cans made of tin

Coppers : copper coins

Woods : forests

6

The Noun : Case

When a noun or pronoun is used as the subject of a verb, it is said to be in the **Nominative Case.**

When a noun or pronoun is used as the object of a verb, it is said to be in the **Objective** or **Accusative Case**.

Note. To find the nominative, 'who' ? or 'what' ? should be put before the verb and its subject; as,

Boys flew kites.

Scorpion bit the boy.

In sentence 1, the noun 'boys' is the subject. It is the answer to the question 'who flew kites ?'. What did the boys fly ? — kites. 'kites' is the object which the boys flew. The noun 'kites' is therefore called the object.

In sentence 2, the noun 'scorpion' is the subject. It is answer to the question — 'who bit the boy ?'. The noun 'boy' is the object. It is answer to the question 'Whom did the scorpion bite ?'. A noun which comes after a preposition, is also said to be in the Accusative case; as,

The books are on the table.

Here the noun 'table' is in the Accusative case governed by the preposition 'on'.

Note. The nouns in English have the same form for the nominative and the accusative. The nominative generally comes before the verb and the accusative after the verb. They are thus distinguished by the order of the words or by the sense.

The Possessive case. The possessive case of a noun answers the question 'whose' ? as,

This is Ram's shirt.

Ram's shirt = the shirt belonging to Ram.

The form of the noun Ram is changed to Ram's to show possession or ownership. The noun Ram's is therefore said to be in the possessive case.

Note. The possessive case does not always denote possession. It is also used to denote kind, origin, authorship etc.; as,

The jury's verdict = the verdict given by the jury.

Professor's speech = the speech given by the professor.

Charles Dicken's novels = the novels written by Charles Dickens.

Rama's temple = the temple dedicated to Lord Rama.

Birla's temple = the temple built by Birlas.

Formation of the Possessive Case

When the noun is singular, the possessive case is formed by adding 's to the noun; as,

The girl's skirt : the boy's shirt

Note. The letter 's is omitted in certain words where too many hissing sounds come together; as,

For goodness' sake, for Jesus' sake, for conscience' sake

When the noun is plural, and ends in s, the possessive case is formed by adding only an apostrophe; as,

Boys' school; Girls' hostel

When the noun is in plural but does not end in 's' the possessive is formed by adding 's; as,

Men's room; Children's playground

When a noun or a title consists of several words, the possessive sign is attached only to the last word; as,

The Prince of Wale's coronation.

When two nouns are in apposition, the possessive sign is put to the latter only; as,

These are Shakespeare, the playwright's plays.

Each of two or more connected nouns meaning separate possession must take the possessive sign; as,

Dicken's and Austin's novels.

Use of the Possessive Case

The possessive case is used with the names of living things; as,

The girl's books, The Governor's car

So we may say

The grill of the door (not the door's grill).

The page of the diary (not the diary's page).

However, the possessive is used in the names of Personified* objects; as,

At death's door; nature's laws

The possessive is also used with nouns denoting time, space or weights; as,

A pound's weight, a week's holiday; in a year's time.

The following use of possessive is also common :

To my heart's content; at my wit's end, at your fingers' end for mercy's sake.

Note. Whenever there is a doubt whether to use a noun in the possessive case or with the preposition 'of', it is to be remembered that the possessive case is used to denote possession or ownership. Therefore it is better to say 'The victory of the army' than the army's victory.

Declension of Nouns

When the various cases of a noun or (Pronoun) are given in order in the two numbers, we are said to give its Declension. The full Declensions of the noun 'Girl' and 'man' are given below :

	Singular	**Plural**
Nominative case	girl	girls
Genitive case	girl's	girls'
Accusative case	girl	girls
Nominative case	man	men
Genitive case	man's	men's
Accusative case	man	men

Nominative of Address or the Vocative Case

A Noun used to name a person or thing addressed is in the vocative case; as,

Ramu, come here

In the above sentence, Ramu is the name of a person spoken to or addressed to. The following are the other examples of Nominative of Address :

Eat, my child, eat
Come on, friends
Come into my room, Sonu

---

* When a non-living thing is treated as a living thing, it is said to be personified.

Dative Case

The indirect object of a verb is said to be in the Dative Case; as,

The chief quest gave a present.

The chief guest gave Sohan a present.

In each of the above sentences, the noun 'present' is the object of the verb 'gave'.

In the second sentence, 'Sohan' is the person to whom the chief guest gave a present. The noun 'present' which is an ordinary object is called the direct object and is in the Accusative case. The noun 'Sohan' is called the indirect object of the verb 'gave' and is said to be in the Dative Case. The position of the Indirect object is immediately after the verb and before the Direct object.

Nouns in Apposition

When one noun follows another to describe it, the noun which follows is said to be in 'Apposition' to the noun which comes before it.

Study the following sentence :

Ankur, our English teacher, teaches us grammar.

In the above sentence, 'Ankur' and our English 'teacher' are one and the same person. The noun 'teacher' follows the noun 'Ankur' simply to explain which teacher is referred to.

Note. A noun in Apposition is in the same case as the noun which it explains.

7

Kinds of Adjectives

An **adjective** is a word that is used to add something to the meaning of a noun; as,

He is an *honest* person
Ashoka was a *great* king.
Delhi is a *polluted* city
Kolkata is a *big* city

KINDS OF ADJECTIVES

Adjectives may be divided into the following classes :

Adjective of Quality : These adjectives show the kind or quality of a person or a thing; as,

1. Rita is a *clever* girl.
2. Ashok is an *intelligent* boy
3. She is a *poor* woman.
4. The sky is *cloudy*.
5. Ramu is an *honest* servant.

In the above sentences, clever, intelligent, poor cloudy and honest are adjectives of quality because they are telling about the Quality of nouns (girl, boy, woman, sky, servant).

Note. Adjective of Quality answer the question — 'of what kind' ?

Adjectives of Quantity; These adjectives show the quantity of a thing; as,

1. You have *much* money.
2. I want *some* money.
3. He takes *enough* exercise.
4. The saint gave *sufficient* advice.

In the above sentences, much, some, enough, and sufficient are Adjectives of Quantity.

Note. Adjectives of Quantity answer the question — 'how much' ?

Adjectives of number : These adjectives show how many persons or things are meant; as,

1. *Several* members came to attend the meeting.
2. *All* men are mortal.
3. I have *ten* rupees in my pocket.
4. There are *many* toys in the almirah.
5. He is the *first* boy to enter the class.

In the above sentences, several, all, ten, many and first are the adjectives of number.

Note. Adjectives of Number answer the question — 'How many ?' or (In what order) ?

Demonstrative Adjectives : These adjectives point out which person or thing is meant; as,

1. I don't like *such* things.
2. *This* boy is intelligent.
3. *That* shirt is yours.
4. I like *these* mangoes.
5. *Those* hills are beautiful.

In the above sentences, such, this, that, these, and those are Demonstrative adjectives.

Note. Demonstrative adjectives answer the question — 'Which' ?

Possessive Adjectives : These adjectives show the possession of a thing; as,

1. These are *your* shoes.
2. This is *my* house.
3. It is *his* bicycle.
4. It is *their* flat.

In the above sentences, your, my, his and their are possessive adjectives.

Interrogative Adjectives ; which, what and whose — when they are used with nouns to ask questions — are called interrogative Adjectives; as,

1. *What* topic is being discussed ?
2. *Which* hobby do you have ?
3. *Whose* pen is this ?

In the above sentences, what, which and whose are interrogative adjectives.

Distributive adjectives : These adjectives refer to each one of a number; as,

1. *Each* member was given an award.
2. *Every* student must obey the rules.
3. *Either* dictionary will do.
4. *Neither* blame is true.

In the above sentences, each every, either, and neither are Distributive adjectives.

FORMATION FOR ADJECTIVES

Many adjectives are formed from nouns

Noun	Adjective	Noun	Adjective
Boy	boyish	Pardon	pardonable
Fool	foolish	Laugh	laughable
Care	careful	Outrage	outrageous
Play	playful	Courage	courageous
Hope	hopeful	Glory	glorious
Shame	shameful	Envy	envious
Gold	golden	Man	manly
Silk	silken	Trouble	troublesome
Sense	sensible	Venture	venturesome
Dirt	dirty	King	kingly
Storm	stormy	Gift	gifted

Some adjectives are formed from verbs

Verb	Adjective	Verb	Adjective
Tire	tireless	Cease	ceaseless
Talk	talkative	Move	moveable

Some adjectives are formed from adjectives

Adjective	Adjective	Adjective	Adjective
Tragic	tragical	Black	blackish
Whole	wholesome	Sick	sickly
Three	threefold	White	whitish

EXERCISE 8

Pick out the adjectives in the following sentences and say to which kind each of them belongs :

1. The storm caused a heavy damage to the crop.
2. He is a funny person.
3. An empty vessel makes much noise.
4. The soldier fell down from great height and lost his precious arm.
5. We should not waste our precious time in useless talk.
6. The sea is stormy and rough.
7. There were many sheep grazing in the green field.
8. Every man must do his duty.
9. I like these mangoes.
10. This is a heavy box.
11. These are your shirts.
12. Which book do you like ?
13. Whose pens are these ?
14. The soldier died a heroic death.
15. She is an honest and sincere woman.

EXERCISE 9

Supply suitable adjective to each blank in the following sentences :

1. A .... person does not give a ....reply.
2. Lemon is .... but sugar is ....
3. This knife is not ....
4. Ramu is an .... servant.
5. A .... enemy is better than a .... friend.
6. An .... man is liked by all.
7. A .... leak may sink a great ship.
8. I know the .... way.
9. She likes .... food.
10. He brought .... mangoes.
11. There is .... sugar in the vessel.
12. The teacher gave .... advice.
13. .... men must suffer.
14. .... mountains are high.
15. .... matter is being discussed.
16. It is .... car.
17. .... student should bring his own pen.
18. The principal gave .... advice to the students.

COMPARISON OF ADJECTIVES

Adjectives change in form to show comparison. They are called the three Degrees of comparison — Positive Degree, Comparative Degree and Superlative Degree.

The Positive Degree of an adjective is the adjective in its simple form. It is used when no comparison is made; as,

My mango is sweet.

The comparative degree of adjective tells about a higher degree of quality than the positive; as,

Your orange is sweeter than Ram's.

The Superlative Degree of an Adjective tells about the highest degree of quality; as,

My orange is the sweetest of all.

Some of the comparative and superlative degrees of adjectives are given below :

Positive	**Comparative**	**Superlative**
Great	greater	greatest
Young	younger	youngest
Kind	kinder	kindest
Small	smaller	smallest
Brave	braver	bravest
Able	abler	ablest
Wise	wiser	wisest
Happy	happier	happiest
Easy	easier	easiest
Big	bigger	biggest
Hot	hotter	hottest
Fat	fatter	fattest
Good	better	best
Bad	worse	worst
Much	more	most
Beautiful	more beautiful	most beautiful
Proper	more proper	most proper
Difficult	more difficult	most difficult

Note. Some words like proper and beautiful etc. are tongue-twisting in their 'er' and 'est' form and take 'more' and 'most' in their Comparative and Superlative forms.

EXERCISE 10

Write the Comparative and Superlative Degrees of the following adjectives :

	Positive	Comparavite	Superlative		Positive	Comparavite	Superlative
1.	Brave	....	....	22.	Tall	....	....
2.	Heavy	....	....	23.	Bold	....	....
3.	Beautiful	....	....	24.	Clever	....	....
4.	Ugly	....	....	25.	Kind	....	....
5.	Noisy	....	....	26.	Young	....	....
6.	Light	....	....	27.	Great	....	....
7.	Timid	....	....	28.	Proper	....	....
8.	Wise	....	....	29.	Learned	....	....
9.	Noble	....	....	30.	Difficult	....	....
10.	Able	....	....	31.	Splendid	....	....
11.	Large	....	....	32.	Good	....	....
12.	White	....	....	33.	Much	....	....
13.	Fine	....	....	34.	Many	....	....
14.	Happy	....	....	35.	Old	....	....
15.	Easy	....	....	36.	Black	....	....
16.	Wealthy	....	....	37.	Bad	....	....
17.	Big	....	....	38.	Able	....	....
18.	Red	....	....	39.	Dry	....	....
19.	Hot	....	....	40.	Merry	....	....
20.	Thin	....	....	41.	High	....	....
21.	Small	....	....	42.	Sad	....	....

EXERCISE 11

Point out the adjectives in the following sentences and name the degree of comparison :

1. Ram is a better singer than Sonu.
2. Ramesh is the best boy of our school.
3. This sword is sharper than yours.
4. This milk is less hot.
5. Reeta is the idlest girl of our class.
6. The unhappy man has seen happier days.
7. Dara Singh was the strongest wrestler of India.
8. Let us hope for the better days.
9. The Himalayas are the highest mountains in the world.
10. Africa is the hottest country in the world.
11. The patient has mild fever.

12. Sonu is the most intelligent boy of our class.
13. He received the best prize.
14. Your handwriting is untidy.

EXERCISE 12

Supply the appropriate Comparative and Superlative Degrees in the following blanks :

1. Are you feeling .... today ?
2. June is .... than any other month.
3. Masses are the .... judge.
4. This is .... beautiful place.
5. Silver is .... than gold.
6. He is the .... friend, I know.
7. He knows me .... than you.
8. Sita and Geeta are my classmates, Sita is .... intelligent.
9. I am feeling .... today.
10. The Himalayas are the .... mountains in the world.
11. Climbing Mount Everest was the .... moment of Tenzing Hillary.
12. Sonu's work is bad, Suresh's is .... but yours is the ....
13. She brought the .... news.
14. These are the .... mangoes.

8 Kinds of Pronouns

A **Pronoun** is a word that is used instead of a Noun; as,

Look at the painting. It is very beautiful. Many people have come to see it. They are enjoying the painting.

In the above sentences, 'it' and 'they' are pronouns because they are used for the nouns 'painting' and 'people'.

(1) **Personal Pronouns** : I, we, you, he, she, it, and they — are called Personal Pronouns because they stand for three persons; as,

The person speaking
The person spoken to
The person spoken of

The pronouns, I and We which denote the person or persons speaking are the personal pronouns of the **First Person**.

The pronoun 'you' denotes the person or persons spoken to, is the personal pronoun of the **Second Person**.

The pronouns, 'he' 'she' and 'they' which denote the person or persons spoken of, are the personal pronouns of the **Third Person**.

(2) **Reflexive Pronouns** : When 'self' is added to my, your, him, her, it, and 'selves' to our, your, them, they become Reflexive Pronouns; as,

1. I enjoyed myself.
2. You enjoyed yourself.
3. He enjoyed himself.
4. She enjoyed herself.
5. We enjoyed ourselves.
6. They enjoyed themselves.

In the above sentences myself, yourself, himself, herself, ourselves and themselves are Reflexive Pronouns.

(3) **Emphatic Pronouns** : When 'self' and 'selves' are added for emphasis, they become Emphatic Pronouns; as,

1. I myself gave him money.
2. You yourself said so.
3. He himself gave you money.
4. They themselves accepted my invitation.

In the above sentences, myself, yourself, himself and themselves are used for emphasis and thus they are called Emphatic Pronouns.

(4) **Demonstrative Pronouns** : These pronouns are used to point out the objects to which they refer; as,

1. This is the pen she gave me.
2. That is a very beautiful valley.
3. Both pens are good, but this is better than that.

In the above sentences, 'this', 'that' and 'this' are Demonstrative Pronouns.

(5) **Indefinite Pronouns** : All those Pronouns which refer to persons or things in a general way, but do not refer to any person or thing in particular are called Indefinite Pronouns; as,

1. Do not insult others.
2. Some body has visited this place.
3. One must do one's duty.

In the above sentences, others, somebody and one are Indefinite Pronouns.

(6) **Relative Pronouns** : Relative pronoun refers to some noun going before; as,

1. I have found the pen which I had lost.
2. We met the director who was present in the office.
3. She has returned the book that she borrowed.

In the above sentences, 'which', 'who', and 'that' are Relative Pronouns.

(7) **Interrogative Pronouns** : These pronouns are used to ask questions; as,

1. What does he want ?
2. Which is the herb ?
3. Who is he ?
4. What is the matter ?

In the above sentences, 'what', 'which' and 'who' are Interrogative Pronouns.

Note. Here the Pronouns are similar in form to Relative Pronouns, but the work they do is different.

(8) **Distributive Pronouns** : These Pronouns refer to persons or things one at a time. They are always singular and are followed by a singular verb; as,

1. Each of the boys has been given a prize.
2. Either of you can do the work.
3. Neither of the girls was present.

In the above sentence, 'each', 'either' and 'neither' are Distributive Pronouns.

EXERCISE 13

Fill in the blanks with suitable Pronouns :

1. This is the book ....you gave me.
2. He is the boy .... stood first in the class.
3. I know .... you mean.
4. The teachers like the students .... work hard.
5. No one can lose .... he never got.
6. This is the instrument .... they installed.
7. This is the snake .... bit the cow.

EXERCISE 14

Fill in the blanks with suitable Pronouns :

1. The students went to the examination hall but .... were late and the examiner did not allow .... to enter the hall.
2. The aeroplane flew over the house, did you see .... ?
3. 'No', ... did not see ....
4. The teacher said to the monitor, "Please ask all the boys to come inside as .... want to teach ....".
5. The students said to the teacher, "Sir .... want .... to teach .... the use of tenses".
6. The manager said to Sonu, why are .... late again ?"
7. The CBI inspector said to the soldier, "Please take these files and put .... in a box and lock .... properly. Then come back to .... and .... shall tell .... why .... keep them under a lock and key.

EXERCISE 15

Fill in the blanks with the correct Reflexive Pronouns or Emphatic Pronouns :

1. I .... gave you money.
2. The prisoner hanged ....
3. They enjoyed ....
4. She .... gave this statement.
5. The Director .... was present.

EXERCISE 16

Pick out the Demonstrative Pronouns and Demonstrative Adjectives in the following sentences :

1. These are your books.
2. This house is for sale.
3. This is a present for you.
4. These books are costly.
5. These are the letters typed by her.
6. This book is mine and that book is yours.
7. This is the book given by him.
8. I don't like such persons.
9. Such was his behaviour that no body liked him.

EXERCISE 17

Pick out the Demonstrative Pronouns in the following sentences :

1. This is her book.
2. These are your shoes.
3. This a very sweet mango.
4. Both houses are good, but this is better than that.
5. This is the present given by him.
6. Those are the hills covered with snow.
7. Such is his method of counselling.
8. That is the house, I believe.

EXERCISE 18

Pick out the Indefinite Pronouns in the following sentences :

1. I don't like any of these almirahs.
2. Some are born great, some acquire greatness.
3. All were saved.
4. None but a fool will believe it.
5. One is not sure of one's future.

EXERCISE 19

Pick out the Distributive Pronouns in the following sentences :

1. Each of the members was present in the meeting.
2. Either of these boys will help you.
3. Neither of these blames is true.
4. Either of you can join.
5. Each of them was given a warning.

EXERCISE 20

Fill in the blanks with suitable Interrogative Pronouns :

1. .... of you has not done your home work ?
2. .... are you waiting for ?
3. .... is better, pen or sword ?
4. By .... were the awards distributed ?
5. .... do you prefer, vegetarian or non-vegetarian ?
6. .... of these toys will you buy ?

EXERCISE 21

Pick out the Relative Pronouns in the following sentences :

1. The man who is sincere and honest is liked.
2. I have read the novel which you gave me.
3. This is the man whom we met in the party.
4. The question which you asked was not logical.
5. Ashoka was one of the greatest kings who have ever lived.
6. All that glitters is not gold.
7. Is this the book which we saw in the other book-store ?
8. God helps those who help themselves.
9. This is the boy who stood first in the class.
10. This is the jug which you gifted me.

EXERCISE 22

Fill in the blanks with suitable Relative Pronouns :

1. God helps those .... help themselves.
2. The man .... is honest is trusted.
3. He is the only person .... can help you.
4. Here is the purse .... you had lost.
5. He .... is content, leads a perfect life.
6. This is the girl .... stood first.
7. You can pick up any toy .... you like.
8. He .... loves all, is loved by God.

9

Verb

A **Verb** is a doing word. Through verb, an action is conveyed. The Principal parts of a verb in English are — the present tense, the past tense, and the past participle.

They are so called because from them we can form all other parts of verb. The three forms of some of the verbs are given below. The following verbs ending in d or t and called weak verbs :

Present tense	Past tense	Past participle
Abide	abode	abode
Arise	arose	arisen
Bear (bring forth)	bore	born
Bear (carry/tolerate)	bore	borne
Beat	beat	beaten
Become	became	become
Beget	Begot	Begotten
Begin	Began	Begun
Behold	beheld	beheld
Bid	bade	bidded
Bind	bound	bound
Bite	bit	bitten
Blow	blew	blown
Break	broke	broken
Chide	chid	chidden
Choose	chose	chosen
Cling	clung	clung
Come	came	come
Dig	dug	dug
Do	did	done
Draw	drew	drawn
Drink	drank	drunk

Present tense	Past tense	Past participle
Drive	drove	driven
Eat	ate	eaten
Fall	fell	fallen
Fight	fought	fought
Find	found	found
Fling	flung	flung
Fly	flew	flown
Forbear	forbore	forborne
Forbid	forbade	forbidden
Forget	forgot	forgotten
Forsake	forsook	forsaken
Freeze	froze	frozen
Get	got	got
Give	gave	given
Go	went	gone
Grind	ground	ground
Grow	grew	grown
Hide	hid	hidden
Hold	held	held
Know	knew	known
Lie	lay	lain
Ride	rode	ridden
Ring	rang	rung
Rise	rose	risen
Run	ran	run
See	saw	seen
Shake	shook	shaken
Shine	shone	shone
Shoot	shot	shot
Shrink	shrank	shrunk
Sing	sang	sung
Sink	sank	sunk
Sit	sat	sat
Slay	slew	slain
Slide	slid	slid
Sling	slung	slung

Present tense	Past tense	Past participle
Smite	smote	smitten
Speak	spoke	spoken
Spin	spun	spun
Spring	sprang	sprung
Stand	stood	stood
Steal	stole	stolen
Stick	stuck	stuck
Sting	stung	stung
Stink	stank	stunk
Stride	strode	striden
Strike	struck	struck
String	strung	strung
Strive	strove	striven
Swear	swore	sworn
Swim	swam	swum
Swing	swung	swung
Take	took	taken
Tear	tore	torn
Throw	threw	thrown
Tread	trod	trodden
Wear	wore	worn
Weave	wove	woven
Win	won	won
Wind	wound	wound
Wring	wrung	wrung
Write	wrote	written

The following verbs have two forms — one strong and one weak :

Awake	awoke (awaked)	awoke (awaked)
Crow	crew (crowed)	crowed
Hang	hung (hanged)	hung (hanged)
Thrive	throve (thrived)	thriven (thrived)
Wake	woke (waked)	woke (waked)

Note. When the verb 'hang' refers to the hanging of a person the past tense is hanged; otherwise both past tense and past participle are hung.

Following are those weak verbs which do not include verbs which form their past tense and past participle by adding –d or –ed :

Present tense	Past tense	Past participle
Bereave	bereft	bereft
Beseech	besought	besought
Bleed	bled	bled
Breed	bred	bred
Bring	brought	brought
Build	built	built
Burn	burnt	burnt
Burst	burst	burst
Buy	bought	bought
Cast	cast	cast
Catch	caught	caught
Cost	cost	cost
Creep	crept	crept
Cut	cut	cut
Deal	delt	delt
Dwell	dwelt	dwelt
Feed	fed	fed
Feel	felt	felt
Flee	fled	fled
Have	had	had
Hit	hit	hit
Hurt	hurt	hurt
Keep	Kept	kept
Kneel	knelt	knelt
Lay	laid	laid
Lead	led	led
Learn	learnt	learnt
Leave	left	left
Lend	lent	lent
Let	let	let
Lose	lost	lost
Make	made	made
Mean	meant	meant
Meet	met	met
Pay	paid	paid
Put	put	put
Read	read	read
Rid	rid	rid
say	said	said

Present tense	Past tense	Past participle
Seek	sought	sought
Sell	sold	sold
Send	sent	sent
Set	set	set
Shed	shed	shed
Shoe	shod	shod
Shut	shut	shut
Sleep	slept	slept
Slit	slit	slit
Smell	smelt	smelt
Spell	spelt	spelt
Spend	spent	spent
Split	split	split
Spread	spread	spread
Sweep	swept	swept
Teach	taught	taught
Tell	told	told
Think	thought	thought
Thrust	thrust	thrust
Wed	wed/wedded	wed/wedded
Weep	wept	wept

Note. Verbs that form their past tense by adding –ed, -d, or t, to the present, with or without any inside vowel-change, are called weak verbs. Verbs that form their past tense by merely changing the vowel in the body of the present are called strong verbs.

Auxiliary Verbs

Auxiliaries are the 'helping verbs' which are used to make the form of another verb. The following are the auxiliary verbs :

Be	may	might	ought
do	will	would	need
have	shall	should	used
can	could	must	dare

These verbs are also called special verbs because they are the only verbs which are used before the subjects in questions.

The Auxiliaries, can, could, may, might, shall, should, will, would, must, ought, used, need, dare — are called Modal Auxiliaries or Modals because they express attitudes, like permission, necessity, obligation etc.

TRANSITIVE AND INTRANSITIVE VERBS

Transitive Verbs are those which are incomplete without objects; as,

She brought	They killed
The boys carried	I made

All the verbs in the above sentences — brought, killed, carried and made are Transitive verbs because they do not make sense unless objects are provided to them.

Intransitive Verbs are those which need not have objects and they make complete sense even without objects; as,

The dog barked	The birds fly
The old man died	She laughed

In the above sentences — barked, fly, died, and laughed are Intransitive Verbs because they give complete meaning even without the objects.

Note. Some verbs can be used both transitively and intransitively as,

Used Transitively	**Used Intransitively**
The driver stopped the bus	The bus stopped
The birds fly	The pilot flies a combat aeroplane
Ring the bell	The bell rang
The storm sank the ship	The ship sank

EXERCISE 23

Write Past Tense and the Past Participle of the following verbs :

	Present	Past	Past Participle		Present	Past	Past Participle
1.	Write	....	....	15.	Flow	....	....
2.	Read	....	....	16.	Find	....	....
3.	Speak	....	....	17.	Get	....	....
4.	Bathe	....	....	18.	Choose	....	....
5.	Know	....	....	19.	Begin	....	....
6.	Tell	....	....	20.	Beat	....	....
7.	Hear	....	....	21.	Arise	....	....
8.	Play	....	....	22.	Bear (to bring forth)	....	....
9.	Dance	....	....				
10.	Give	....	....	23.	Bear (to carry)	....	....
11.	Grow	....	....	24.	Kneel	....	....
12.	Hide	....	....	25.	Win	....	....
13.	Forget	....	....	26.	Put	....	....
14.	Fly	....	....	27.	Feel	....	....

	Present	Past	Past Participle		Present	Past	Past Participle
28.	Cut	....	....	54.	Become	....	....
29.	Breed	....	....	55.	Tear	....	....
30.	Shut	....	....	56.	Sell	....	....
31.	Creep	....	....	57.	Teach	....	....
32.	Spread	....	....	58.	Learn	....	....
33.	Lose	....	....	59.	Buy	....	....
34.	Telecast	....	....	60.	Bring	....	....
35.	Broadcast	....	....	61.	Catch	....	....
36.	Come	....	....	62.	Seek	....	....
37.	Lend	....	....	63.	Refuse	....	....
38.	Quit	....	....	64.	Make	....	....
39.	Smell	....	....	65.	Feed	....	....
40.	Spend	....	....	66.	Carry	....	....
41.	Think	....	....	67.	Run	....	....
42.	Weep	....	....	68.	Shoot	....	....
43.	Burst	....	....	69.	Shine	....	....
44.	Hurt	....	....	70.	Shake	....	....
45.	Let	....	....	71.	Shrink	....	....
46.	Meet	....	....	72.	Strive	....	....
47.	Pay	....	....	73.	Take	....	....
48.	Say	....	....	74.	Swear	....	....
49.	Sing	....	....	75.	Throw	....	....
50.	See	....	....	76.	Swim	....	....
51.	Hold	....	....	77.	Wear	....	....
52.	Ring	....	....	78.	Build	....	....
53.	Blow	....	....	79.	Have	....	....

EXERCISE 24

Say whether the verbs in the following sentences are Transitive or Intransitive :

1. The child is sleeping.
2. He brought a good news.
3. Birds fly in the air.
4. The children made a great noise.
5. Each of the boys received a prize.
6. The ship sank.
7. I met an old friend.
8. They spoke loudly.
9. This man killed a tiger.
10. The girls were dancing.

11. The robbers ran away quickly.
12. We played tennis.
13. The lion roared in the cage.
14. The children go to school daily.
15. I saw him in the party.

EXERCISE 25

Separate the Main Verbs and the Auxiliary Verbs in the following sentences :

1. The girls are singing.
2. The boys were flying kites.
3. He did not return my money.
4. He will receive an award.
5. He does not like non-vegetarian food.
6. The wind is blowing hard.
7. The waiter laid the table.
8. Columbus discovered America.
9. I hung the painting.
10. He is making a noise.
11. He won a medal.
12. The cat caught the mouse.
13. They killed a tiger
14. The hunter fired a shot
15. The principal was delivering a speech

EXERCISE 26

Choose the right words from brackets to complete each sentence :

1. I (hung/hanged/put) the painting on the wall.
2. The sun (awoke/rose/raised) in the sky.
3. Columbus (invented/explored/discovered) America.
4. The wind (flew/blew/moved) strongly.
5. A rivulet (flows/swims/floats) near this house.
6. The maid (lain/lay/laid) the table.
7. The robbers stole/carried/robbed) the house.
8. A cork (floats/sails/flows) on the water.
9. Ducks (caw/cackle/quack).
10. Geese (cackle/quack/crow).
11. Sirons (wail/blow/sound).
12. An ass (neighs/brays/bleats).
13. Owls (hoot/scream/shout).
14. Snakes (hum/murmur/hiss).

10

Adverb

An **Adverb** tells more about (a) a verb (b) an adjective (c) another adverb.

KINDS OF ADVERBS

(1) Adverb of time (they show 'when'); as,

1. He will arrive tomorrow.
2. She arrived early.
3. He formerly worked in Indian Air Force.
4. They will come soon.
5. I have come here before.
6. She met me yesterday.

In the above sentences — tomorrow, early, formerly, soon, before, yesterday are adverbs of time.

(2) Adverbs of Frequency (they show 'how often').

1. You have come here twice.
2. We often go to temple.
3. The manager has come again.
4. He always does his best.
5. He seldom came here.

In the above sentences, twice, often, again, always and seldom are adverbs of frequency.

(3) Adverb of place (they show 'where').

1. She lives here.
2. The aeroplane landed there.
3. We looked for him everywhere.
4. Mother has gone out.
5. Look forward.
6. Don't sit here.

In the above sentences here, there everywhere, out forward and here are Adverbs of place.

(4) Adverb of Manner (they show 'how' or 'in what manner').

1. I spoke politely.
2. They ran fast.
3. The child is crawling slowly.
4. The students worked hard.
5. You have acted wisely.
6. He behaved foolishly.
7. The warriors fought bravely.
8. He has done well.

In the above sentences, politely, fast, slowly, hard, wisely, foolishly, bravely and well are adverbs of manner.

(5) Adverbs of Degree or Quantity (they show 'how much' or 'in what degree').

1. The food is almost ready.
2. He was fully right.
3. They were quite wrong.
4. He is very intelligent.
5. The building was partly demolished.

In the above sentences, almost, fully, quite, very, partly are adverbs of Degree.

(6) Adverbs for Affirmation or Negation (they show 'yes' or 'no').

1. He will certainly pass.
2. I do not know him.
3. You surely ran fast.

In the above sentences, certainly and surely are the adverbs of Affirmation and 'not' is Adverb of Negation.

(7) Adverbs of Reason (they show 'the cause').

1. He therefore resigned his job.
2. You are hence eligible for the post.

In the above sentences, 'therefore' and 'hence' are adverbs of Reason.

(8) Interrogative Adverbs (They 'ask questions').

1. When did you meet her ?
2. How did you go there ?

3. Why do you disturb him ?
4. How did you reach this place ?

In the above sentences, when, how, why, and how are Interrogative Adverbs, as they are used in asking questions.

EXERCISE 27

Identify the Adverbs in the following sentences :

1. She spoke softly.
2. This athlete runs fast.
3. He often visits this area.
4. You have been badly treated.
5. He hit the ball strongly.
6. The old man slipped and fell down.
7. He is very intelligent boy.
8. You never stole anything.
9. Come now.
10. Don't go there.
11. Luckily, all escaped unhurt.
12. He is certainly expected today.
13. The soldier fought bravely.
14. We hope you will soon be well.
15. You did badly in the test.
16. The bull attacked angrily.
17. The Commandos moved silently.
18. He was brutally murdered.
19. They entered the Parliament house noisily.
20. We should not treat any one cruelly.

EXERCISE 28

Insert suitable Adverbs in the following sentences :

1. They came ....
2. You closed the door ....
3. The students fared .... in the examination.
4. The birds sing ....
5. You should not go ....
6. I can .... believe it.

7. The girl is .... shy.
8. I left the house .... today.
9. I don't decide anything ....
10. The principal spoke ....
11. We can .... guess.
12. The patient is .... better.
13. I .... go to his house.
14. The boys ran ....

11

Preposition

Preposition is a word placed before a Noun or a Pronoun to show in what relation the person or thing denoted by it stands in regard to something else.

1. There is a flower in the garden.
2. The sky is above us.
3. She came with me.
4. I am fond of tea.

In the first sentence, the preposition 'in' shows relation between two things — flower and garden.

In the second sentence, the preposition 'above' shows the relation between 'sky' and 'us'.

In the third sentence, the preposition 'with' shows the relation between the action expressed by the verb 'came' and 'me'.

In the fourth sentence, the preposition 'of' shows the relation between 'fond' and 'tea'.

The meaning of the word preposition is 'that which is placed before'. The noun or pronoun which is used with a preposition is called its object. A preposition may have two or more objects; as,

The river flows under the bridge and valley.

In the above sentence, the preposition 'under' has two objects — 'bridge' and 'valley'.

KINDS OF PREPOSITION

Simple prepositions : at, by, for, with, up, to, till, out, through, on, off, in from — are the simple prepositions.

Compound prepositions : These prepositions are generally formed by prefixing a preposition to a noun, an adjective or an adverb; as,

About, above, across, without, within, along, amidst, among, amongst, around, before, below, behind, beside, beneath, between, beyond, inside, outside underneath.

Phrase prepositions : These prepositions are group of words used with the force of a 'single' prepositions' as,

in order to
in lieu of
in front of
in favour of
in course of
in consequence of
in compliance with
in comparison to
in case of
on behalf of
in addition to

for the sake of
by way of
by virtue of
by reason of
by means of
by dint of
because of
away from
along with
according to
with an eye to

with regard to
in response to
in place of
in regard to
in spite of
in the event of
on account of
owing to
with a view to
with reference to
in accordance with

Study the use of prepositions in the following sentences :

1. You must agree with me on this matter.
2. I do not agree to your proposal.
3. The students acted upon the teacher's advice.
4. He is addicted to alcohol.
5. You should feel ashamed of your behaviour.
6. Do not be afraid of death.
7. I am fond of travelling.
8. The God is kind to all of us.
9. I prefer milk to tea.
10. Be careful about your health.
11. The principal was angry with the student for his misconduct.
12. He died of malaria.
13. He is proud of his son.
14. You should beg for mercy from the teacher.
15. The boss was displeased with his secretary.
16. Nehru was born of rich parents.
17. I take delight in reading.
18. I am busy with my work.
19. She is ill with fever.
20. I was astonished at her conduct.
21. We were alarmed at this news.

22. The dog is faithful to his master.
23. This pen is different from Johan's.
24. He will not excuse you for coming late.
25. The house is full of gas.
26. Fill the vessel with water.
27. She invited us to dinner.
28. We should pray to God daily.
29. You should not quarrel with any one over trivial matters.
30. He was not satisfied with your work.
31. I am tired of this person.
32. The accused was charged with murder.
33. We should have pity for the poor.
34. My father prevents me from coming to this place.
35. You are ignorant of the facts.
36. The players were rewarded with medals.
37. He was anxious about his daughter's return.
38. One should not laugh at any one.
39. It is my pleasure to deal with you.
40. Fortune will certainly smile on you.
41. Be free from worries.
42. She arrived in Delhi at noon.
43. Please introduce me to your father.
44. We supplied the poor with blankets.
45. The son complained to the father.
46. You should not complain against me.
47. I am surprised at your success.
48. Some one has parted with this pen.
49. One day we must part from our friends.
50. The child depends on parents' help.
51. We deal in electronic goods.
52. Do not borrow money from relations.
53. He has failed in mathematics.
54. I have applied for leave.
55. Many people are suffering from diarrhoea.
56. I am sorry for my mistakes.

57. Sonu is married to Rita.
58. He comes of a noble family.
59. One should be true to one's word.
60. He is related to me.
61. You were accused of theft.
62. I am annoyed with you.
63. He congratulated me on my success.
64. The committee objected to your proposal.
65. I am obliged to him for his kindness.
66. You should bathe in luke-warm water.
67. Do not hide anything from your physician.
68. We must sympathise with others in their adversity.
69. One must always be prepared for the worst.
70. He called on us last week.
71. You should wait for him.
72. Try to explain everything to me.
73. One should be contented with one's lot.
74. I am annoyed at your behaviour.
75. Be obedient to your teachers and parents.
76. She is blind in the left eye.
77. I have no taste for painting.
78. You should listen to what your teachers say.
79. He was accompanied by the chief guest.
80. We should not rejoice at others' sorrows.
81. Drugs are injurious to health.
82. This book is superior to that.
83. Trust in God.
84. Do not be negligent in your work.
85. You should save yourself from such people.
86. Do not lean against the railing.
87. Is she acquainted with you ?
88. She has no affection for her children.
89. This grammar book is useful for the students.
90. The robbers broke into their house.
91. I was grieved to hear this news.

92. She was grieved at the news.
93. She is insisting on going there.
94. He has recovered from illness.
95. You are always short of money.
96. The terrorists set the house on fire.
97. She was robbed of her money.
98. My uncle presented a watch to me.
99. The president of India is popular with the children.
100. You should look after your aged parents.
101. She was inquiring after my health.
102. This face seems to be familiar to us.
103. Do not prove false to any one.

EXERCISE 29

Fill in the blanks with suitable prepositions :

1. She prefers milk .... tea.
2. The committee agreed .... your proposal.
3. This computer differs .... that.
4. I am very fond .... reading.
5. You are always in need .... money.
6. She has no taste .... music.
7. She is related .... me.
8. The conference hall is full .... members.
9. I am ever obliged .... you.
10. He is married .... Geeta.
11. Mother is .... home.
12. The guard is .... duty.
13. She met a stranger .... the way.
14. He was talking .... his friend.
15. Many people died .... cholera.
16. He died .... his country.
17. She is proud .... her beauty.
18. I was congratulated .... my success .... the examination.
19. She is not acquainted .... me.
20. The chairman agreed .... me .... all points.
21. One should be kind .... the poor.
22. You should have warned me .... the danger.

23. She is famous .... her learning.
24. The examinees were provided .... pens and paper.
25. You complained .... me .... the principal.
26. One should not be afraid .... death.
27. You should take care .... your health.
28. He is going to compete .... the prize.
29. I was glad .... my son's success.
30. She parted .... her children .... a heavy heart.
31. This book is full .... errors.
32. The train is .... time.
33. Beware .... pick pockets.
34. I take delight .... my studies.
35. You should feel ashamed .... your behaviour.
36. Kailash was senior .... me in Indian Air Force.
37. This pen is inferior .... that.
38. This ritual is practised .... the Hindus.
39. I always start .... eight .... the morning.
40. He does not leave his home .... eight O'clock.
41. They cycled .... Delhi .... Mumbai.
42. She will soon recover .... illness.
43. I am tired .... walking.
44. She bought the newspaper .... a rupee.
45. We have been living here .... 2003.
46. Children are afraid .... darkness.
47. On hearing shouts, he rushed .... my room.
48. They cut down a tree .... an axe.
49. The steam engine was invented .... James Watt.

12

The Conjunction

Conjunction is a word that joins two words, two phrases, two clauses and two sentences.

KINDS OF CONJUNCTIONS

Coordinating Conjunction : A Coordinating Conjunction joins together clauses of equal rank; as,

Whether ...... or	I do not bother whether you come or not.
Not only ...... but also	Not only is she stupid but arrogant also.

Compound Conjunctions : Many compound expressions are also used; these are called Compound Conjunctions.

In order that	I studied hard in order that I might get good marks.
On condition that	I can teach you on condition that you study seriously.
Even if	You can not be pardoned even if you repent.
So that	We walked fast so that we could reach in time.
Provided that	You can go providéd that you come back soon.
As though	She walks as though she is slightly lame.
Inasmuch as	I can not accept your proposal inasmuch as I find it irrelevant.

The chief coordinating conjunctions are — and, but, for, or, nor, also, either, or, neither, nor.

Coordinating conjunctions are of four kinds.

(1) **Cumulative** or **copulative** : This merely adds one statement to another; as,

They carved not a line, and they raised not a stone.

(2) **Adversative** : This expresses contrast between two statements; as,

You are slow, but you are sure.

He is annoyed, still he keeps quiet.

(3) **Disjunctive or Alternative** : This expresses a choice between two alternatives; as,

Neither a borrower nor a lender be

Walk quickly or else you will miss the train

(4) **Illative** : This expresses inference; as

All precautions must not have been taken, for the cholera spread fast.

Any of the coordinating conjunctions, with the exception of *or, nor* may be omitted and its place taken by a comma, semi colon, or colon; as,

I went to meet my uncle, my wife stayed at home.

Some conjunctions are used in pairs; as,

Either—or	Either he will come or he will inform.
Neither—nor	It is neither attractive nor useful.
Both—and	I both respect and love him.
Though—yet	Though he is poor, yet he is happy.
As well as	Sohan as well as Mohan was present in the meeting.
As soon as	All stood up as soon as the principal entered the class.

Subordinating conjunctions : Subordinating conjunctions join a clause to another on which it depends for its full meaning.

The chief subordinating conjunctions are — after, because, if, that, though, although, till, before, unless, as, when, where, while.

1. You will not pass *unless* you work hard.
2. *Since* he says so, I must believe it.
3. He said *that* he would come.
4. I shall wait for you *until* you come.
5. I do not know *where* he has gone.
6. Switch off the lights *before* you go home.
7. *After* the rain stopped we went out.
8. Make hay *while* the sun shines.
9. I do not know *how* he came so early.
10. *When* I was young, I played a lot of tennis.
11. I do not understand *why* he has come again.
12. He ran away *because* he was a coward.

Certain words are used both as prepositions and Conjunctions; as,

Preposition	**Conjunction**
He stayed with me *till* Sunday.	I shall stay here *till* she returns.
We have not met *since* last week.	I shall accompany you *since* you insist.
The soldier died *for* his country.	You must meet me, *for* I so desire.
The cop ran *after* the thief.	I left *after* the bell had gone.
Every body *but* Sheela was present.	I tried *but* failed.
She is standing *before* the house.	Meet me *before* you go

EXERCISE 30

Point out the conjunctions in the following sentences and state whether they are coordinating or subordinating :

1. Unless you work hard you can not pass.
2. The aeroplane landed after we had left.
3. I do not know where he lives.
4. You will get the job if you deserve it.
5. Do not go before I come.
6. You will be punished if you are late.
7. I got in the bus before the rain started.
8. You should stay until I return.
9. He said that he would come in time.
10. I run faster than you.
11. You are richer than I am.
12. He asked whether he could go.
13. Bread and milk is a wholesome food.
14. I went to market but it was closed.
15. I shall attend the meeting since you insist.
16. He entered the house after I had left.
17. He put the best efforts but failed.
18. Walk slowly lest you should fall.

EXERCISE 31

Fill in the blanks with appropriate conjunctions :

1. I have succeeded better .... I hoped.
2. Do not light a match, ... the room is full of gas.
3. Make haste, ... you will be late.
4. Wait .... I return.

5. I finished first .... I began late.
6. A open rebuke is better .... secret love.
7. The soldier fled, ... he was coward.
8. Be just .... fear not.
9. I remained at home ....I was ill.
10. Two .... two make four.
11. Is your name Sonu .... Monu ?
12. We shall not go .... it rains.
13. .... you work hard, you will not succeed.
14. You are rich .... you are not happy.
15. You will be punished .... you are guilty.
16. I wonder .... she will come.
17. He is honest .... sincere.
18. Man proposes .... God disposes.
19. He will not get the prize .... he deserves.
20. Catch me .... you can.
21. .... I were you, I won't do it.
22. Tell him .... you have understood.
23. It is hoped .... all will go well.
24. You are latter .... I (am).
25. He studied so hard .... he spoiled his heath.
26. He knows me better .... you (do).
27. How can I buy it ....I have no money.
28. I don't know .... he will come.
29. Do .... you are bidden.
30. He tried hard .... he could not succeed.
31. I will come, ... it rains .... not.
32. It has been a long time .... we last met him.
33. I am better, ... I do not feel very strong.
34. Grouses can not be redressed .... they are known.

EXERCISE 32

Join each pair of the following sentences by means of a suitable conjunction. Make other necessary changes :

1. Ram works hard.	Sham works hard
2. He will come.	He is not ill.
3. Sohan sells bananas.	He sells apples.
4. Chirag played well.	Hari played well.
5. Sonu plays for pleasure.	Monu plays for money.

6. My father is not here. My mother is not here.
7. He is rich He is not happy.
8. I respect him. He is an honest person.
9. I could not pass. I worked hard.
10. He is slow. He is sure.
11. I shall sit. I shall draft a letter.
12. You must start at once. You will be late.
13. My brother went to office. My sister stayed at home.
14. You do not write fast. You write well.
15. He is seriously wounded. He met with an accident.
16. I came in. The rain stopped.

13

Tense

The word **tense** comes from the Latin, tempus, which means time. There are three main Tenses — The present, the past, the future.

A verb that refers to present time is said to be in the present tense; as,

1. He gets up early in the morning.
2. The sun sets in the west.

A verb that refers to the past time, is said to be in the past tense; as,

1. He met me in the party yesterday.
2. The boys were flying kites.

A verb that refers to the future time, is said to be in the future tense; as,

1. The children will play.
2. He will be teaching the class.

All the three tenses — present, past and future have four forms each.

Simple Present Tense : This tense is used :

1. To express a habitual action' as,
   (i) She takes exercise every day.
   (ii) I go to bed at ten O'clock.
2. To express general truths; as,
   (i) Two and two make four.
   (ii) The sun rises in the east.
   (iii) Man is mortal.
3. To indicate a future event; as,
   (i) The Prime Minister visits the U.S.A. next week.
   (ii) I leave for Bombay tomorrow.
   (iii) When does the school reopen ?

Rules. While using this tense, the following rules should be observed :

(i) Present form of the verb.

(ii) 's' or 'es' with the main verb if the subject is Third person Singular Number (he, she, it).

(iii) Auxiliaries 'do' and 'does' are used to make Negative and Interrogative sentences.

(iv) 'Does' is used with Third person singular Number (he, she, it) and 'do' is used with all other subjects (I, you, they, we).

(v) If 'does' is used, 's' or 'es' is not used with the verb.

Following are the examples of Simple Present Tense :

1. She takes bath everyday.
2. My father goes to office at nine O'clock.
3. This magazine appears twice a week.
4. The sun sets in the west.
5. People take tea every morning.
6. The hunters shoot wild animals.
7. The birds fly in the air.
8. He runs fast.
9. The judge punishes the accused.
10. All men worship God.

Present Continuous Tense : This tense is used :

(1) To express an action which is going on at the time of speaking.

(i) The children are playing.

(ii) Mother is cooking food.

(iii) He is doing his home work.

(2) To express an action that is planned to take place in the near future; as,

(i) She is going to her aunt's house in the evening.

(ii) My son is arriving tomorrow.

Rules :

(i) 'is' or 'are' or 'am'

(ii) Present form of the verb+ing

(iii) 'are' is used with all plural subjects

(iv) 'am' is used with I

Following are the examples of present continuous tense :

1. He is learning grammar.
2. The girl is playing with dolls.
3. Mother is washing clothes.
4. The birds are singing.
5. The woman is cutting grass.
6. The farmers are sowing seeds.
7. The teacher is teaching the class.
8. I am doing my home work.
9. The hawker is selling bangles.
10. I am going to London next week.

Present Perfect Tense : This tense is used :

(1) To indicate an actions just completed; as,

(i) I have taken my breakfast.

(ii) My father has left for office.

(2) To express those past actions whose time is not definite; as,

(i) She has already passed this test.

(ii) I have seen this movie.

(3) To express an action which began at some time in the past and is continuing up to the present moment; as,

(i) She has so far written me four letters.

(ii) I have lived here for five years.

Rules :

(i) 'has' or 'have'

(ii) Past participate form of the verb.

(iii) 'has' is used with third person Singular Number and 'have' with all other persons.

Following are the examples of Present perfect tense :

1. My mother has cooked food.
2. The students have written their answers.
3. The aeroplane has taken off.
4. You have so far written me four letters.
5. I have read Shakespeare's Hamlet.

6. She has returned my book.
7. We have worked here for many years
8. The driver has stopped the train.
9. The child has broken the toy.
10. The gardener has trimmed the hedge.

Present Perfect Continuous Tense : This tense is used :

To denote an action which began in the past and is still continuing.

Rules :

(i) 'has been' or 'have been'

(ii) Present form of the verb+ing

(iii) 'has been' is used only with third person singular number (he, she, it 'have been' is used with all other subjects (I, you, we they).

(iv) Since or for

Note. 'Since' is used to denote *point of time* and 'for' is used to denote *period of time.*

Following are the examples of present perfect continuous tense :

1. We have been studying for five hours.
2. The girls have been dancing since two O'clock.
3. The teacher has been teaching the class for forty minutes.
4. The boys have been playing since afternoon.
5. Sita has been knitting for one hour.
6. I have been travelling for five days.
7. The boys have been flying kites since morning.
8. The Prime Minister has been speaking for three hours.
9. She has been helping me for a long time.
10. We have been living here for ten years.

PAST TENSE

Simple Past : This tense is used :

1. To indicate an action completed in the past; as,

(i) She met me in the party yesterday.

(ii) I visited my home town last month.

2. To indicate past habits; as,
   (i) She saw a movie once a week.
   (ii) We practised mathematics for hours.

Rules :

(i) Past form of the verb
(ii) 'did' for making Negative and Interrogative sentences.
(iii) Present form of the verb in negative and interrogative sentences (when 'did' has already been used).

Following are the examples of the past simple tense :

1. The Prime Minister gave a long speech.
2. I wrote him a letter yesterday.
3. A film star inaugurated the function.
4. The chief guest distributed the prizes.
5. She typed all the letters.
6. I met him in the party last week.
7. She went abroad last month.
8. They purchased a new house.
9. India defeated Pakistan in Kargil war.
10. He brought a good news.

Past Continuous Tense : This tense is used :

1. To denote an action going on in the past; as,
   (i) The children were playing.
   (ii) The teacher was evaluating the answer sheets.
2. To denote a continuous/persistent habit in the past; as,
   (i) He was always disturbing me.
   (ii) She was always listening to the music.

Rules :

(i) 'was' or 'were'
(ii) 'was' is used with all singular subjects and 'were' is used with all plural subjects.
(iii) Present form of the verb+ing

Following are the examples of past continuous tense :

1. The girls were dancing.
2. I was doing my home work.

3. The maid was washing the utensils.
4. They were listening to the music.
5. The students were solving their sums.
6. The boys were playing cricket in the park.
7. The farmers were ploughing their fields.
8. She was making clay models.
9. I was ironing my clothes.
10. The physician was examining the patient.

Past Perfect Tense : This tense is used :

To describe that action in the past which was completed before another action of the past.

If two actions happened in the past, it is essential to show which action happened earlier than the other action. The action which happened earlier, is conveyed through a clause of past perfect tense and the action which happened later, is put in a clause of past simple tense; as,

(i) I had reached home when the rain started.
(ii) I had completed my class work when the teacher came.

Rules :

(i) 'had' with all the subjects.
(ii) Past participle form of the verb.
(iii) Another clause of past simple tense to show the action which happened later.

Following are the examples of past perfect tense :

1. The students had done their work when the teacher entered the class room.
2. The train had left before we reached the station.
3. The aeroplane had taken off before we reached the air port.
4. The gardener had planted the saplings when the chief guest arrived.
5. She had cooked the food when the guests arrived.
6. The pilot had baled out when the engine caught fire.
7. The fishermen had caught the catch when the storm came.
8. The driver had jumped off the bus before it collided with a tree.
9. The patient had recovered when the doctor came.

Past Perfect Continuous Tense : This tense is used.

To describe an action that began before a certain point in the past and continued up to that time; as,

(i) The boys had been playing since afternoon.
(ii) She had been cooking for half an hour.

Rules :

(i) 'had been' with all the subjects.
(ii) Present form of the verb+ing.
(iii) 'since' or 'for'

Following are the examples of past perfect continuous tense :

1. She had been studying in Doon Public School since 1998.
2. The labourers had been working since morning.
3. The students had been writing for a long time.
4. We had been waiting for the bus for half an hour.
5. The cashier had been counting the cash since morning.
6. The students had been doing their home work for two hours.
7. The baby had been crying since morning.
8. He had been doing hard work since boyhood.
9. The cook had been cooking since morning.
10. She had been learning guitar for one year.

FUTURE TENSE

Simple Future Tense : This tense is used :

To describe an action that will take place in future; as,

(i) We shall play a match tomorrow.
(ii) They will come back next week.

Rules :

(i) 'shall' or 'will'
(ii) present form of the verb
(iii) 'shall' is used with first person singular number and plural number (I, We).
(iv) 'will' is used with all other subjects (you, he, she, it, they)

Note. 'will' can also be used with First person Singular number and plural number but that use is restricted to Modal Auxiliaries.

Following are the examples of Simple Future Tense :

1. I shall meet him tomorrow.
2. The boys will clean their room.
3. The girls will go to the beauty parlour.
4. They will help us in our difficulties.
5. The girls will sing national anthem.
6. He will come back next month.
7. We shall take lunch in a restaurant.
8. The teacher will give my report card.
9. He will obey the teachers.
10. The hawker will sell his wares.

Future Continuous Tense : This tense is used :

1. To denote an action which will be going on at some time in future; as,
   (i) The teacher will be teaching the class.
   (ii) The boys will be studying.
2. To denote future events that are planned; as,
   (i) He will be staying with me for one month.
   (ii) She will be joining us next week.

Rules :

(i) 'shall be' or 'will be'
(ii) present form of the verb+ing.

Following are the examples of Future Continuous tense :

1. The child will be sleeping then.
2. Father will be reading the newspaper.
3. The teacher will be teaching the class.
4. Mother will be cooking food.
5. The doctor will be examining the patient.
6. The girls will be rehearsing for the function.
7. We shall be taking our food.
8. The chief guest will be giving speech.

9. The students will be doing their home work.
10. The children will be watching television.

Future perfect tense : This tense is used :

To describe the completion of an action by a certain time in future; as,

(i) We shall have solved our sums by five O'clock.

(ii) My mother will have cooked food.

Rules :

(i) 'shall have' or 'will have'

(ii) past participle form of the verb.

(iii) 'shall have' is used with first person singular number and plural number (I, we) and 'will have' is used with all other subjects (you, he, she, it, they)

Following are the examples of Future perfect tense :

1. I shall have completed my graduation by 2007 A.D.
2. We shall have dug the earth by then.
3. The aeroplane will have taken off (before we reach the air port).
4. The soldiers will have crossed the river.
5. The players will have withdrawn the stumps before sunset.
6. The Prime Minister will have finished his speech.
7. The fishermen will have come back from the sea before the storm comes.
8. I shall have taken my dinner by 9 p.m.
9. The All India Radio will have switched off the transmission.
10. The chief guest will have inaugurated the function.

Future Perfect Continuous Tense : This tense is used :

To denote that action which will begin in future and will be continuing in future at a particular time; as,

(i) We shall have been studying in DPS International since 2005.

(ii) They will have been preparing for their examinations for a long time.

Rules :

(i) 'shall have been' or 'will have been'

(ii) present form of the verb+ing

(iii) 'since' or 'for'

Following are the examples of Future perfect continuous tense :

1. I shall have been studying since morning.
2. The driver will have been driving the bus for twelve hours.
3. The child will have been playing since morning.
4. They will have been working for a long time.
5. The spectators will have been watching the match for six hours.
6. You will have been working in this company for six years.
7. She will have been evaluating the answer sheets for one week.
8. I shall have been doing my home work for two hours.
9. The boys will have been playing since morning.
10. The cook will have been cooking for two hours.

EXERCISE 33

Use the correct form of the tense (verb) given in brackets :

1. I .... him in the party yesterday. (meet)
2. She .... English for six months. (learn)
3. He .... me for a long time. (know)
4. The sun .... in the east. (rise)
5. My father .... ten minutes ago (leave)
6. I .... my home work by 6 P.M. (complete)
7. This newspaper .... twice a week. (appear)
8. She .... me this week. (not meet)
9. My uncle .... next week (arrive)
10. The students .... their lessons now. (learn)
11. .... you .... him ? (know)
12. .... you .... since morning ? (work)
13. I .... home when the rain started. (reach)
14. The train .... when we reach the station (leave).
15. My father .... home at 9 P.M. but he .... yet (come, not come).
16. You .... for a long time. (rest)
17. The baby .... just now. (sleep)
18. He ....to Bombay yesterday. (go)
19. He .... of going to the U.S.A. (think)
20. I .... a lot of work today. (do)
21. My uncle .... for Calcutta tomorrow. (leave)
22. She .... half an hour ago (go)

23. I .... at the a station for you for two hours. (wait)
24. You are always .... (grumble)
25. She .... from fever since last night. (suffer)

EXERCISE 34

Rewrite the following sentences putting all the verbs in the past tense :

1. We win almost every match.
2. She drinks tea every morning.
3. Water freezes in winter.
4. He forgets what he says.
5. You always get up first of all.
6. The waves rise high and the ships sink.
7. The birds fly in the air.
8. He comes of a good family.
9. My friend writes to me every month.
10. This swimmer swims very well.
11. The teacher punishes the guilty students.
12. I have been waiting for him for a long time.
13. She comes home very late.
14. Sonu knows the work very well.
15. She has been sleeping for a long time.
16. He makes clay models.
17. You generally forget my name.
18. The athlete runs down the road.
19. He feels sorry for his misconduct.
20. I go for a morning walk every day.

EXERCISE 35

Change the following sentences into Present Tense :

1. You made many mistakes in your composition.
2. He knew me.
3. She wrote to her mother every week.
4. My gum bled profusely.
5. She cut the vegetables.
6. The boys flew many kites.
7. She drank the tea very fast.
8. The people held him in high esteem.
9. She knew her job well.

10. The sun was shining brightly.
11. He was taking a morning walk.
12. I had been waiting for you for a long time.
13. It took three days to reach Shillong.
14. The baby clung to her mother.
15. The bird flew very high in the sky.
16. The sky grew dark.
17. The dog lay on the floor.
18. She worked the sum correctly.
19. They tried hard and succeeded.
20. She hid her face.
21. The boys were playing football.
22. I heard a strange noise.
23. He met me in the party.
24. This hen laid two eggs.

EXERCISE 36

Fill in the past tense or past participle of the verb given in the following sentences :

Go :	The price of vegetables .... up.
	He .... home after the work.
	The judgement .... against him.
See :	I .... him in the party yesterday.
	I have already .... this movie.
	We .... a tiger in the zoo.
Begin :	The movie had .... when I reached the cinema hall.
	The programme .... at 9 A.M.
	He .... to speak nuisance after consuming alcohol.
Fall :	She .... from the high roof.
	The old man .... down while walking.
	The price of diesel has ....
Bite :	He was .... by a dog.
	A scorpion .... him.
	This monkey has .... the baby.
Run :	On seeing the tiger, he .... for his life.
	When we reached the spot, he .... five kilometres.
	I have .... fifteen kilometres.
Bid :	I .... him good bye.
	You should do as you are ....
	The jokey .... five thousand rupees for the horse

Tear :	He .... the letter in a fit of anger. Your shirt is .... I am mentally ....
Forget :	Surprisingly, he has .... my name. He .... to bring his bag. The student realised that he .... to bring his pens.
Catch :	All the robbers were .... by the police. We .... sight of a new animal in the zoo. The fishermen .... fish.
Give. :	The teacher .... the students a test. She .... me a beautiful present on my birthday. You never .... me a chance to speak.
Know :	He has never .... sickness. The judge .... the past history of the accused. He .... me for a long time.
Teach :	The principal .... English to the students. My tutor has .... me this lesson. The teacher .... the class when I reached the class room.
Ring :	I .... her up on telephone. The bell was .... by the peon. Who has .... the bell ?
Steal :	My purse was .... by this man. The burglars .... money from this almirah. Your heart was .... by her.
Sow :	One must reap one has .... The farmers .... the seeds
Write :	I have .... this letter. He ....me a letter last week.
Eat :	Food was .... in haste. I .... my dinner in time.
Say :	Who .... these words ? I have .... what I wanted to say.
Fly :	Where has the bird .... Many birds .... in the sky.
Find :	I have .... my lost pen. She has .... the correct answer.
Shoot :	Who .... the animal ? The poachers .... down the elephant.
Teach :	Who .... you English last year ? The teacher has already .... this lesson.

14

Active and Passive Voice

A verb is said to be in Active Voice when the person or thing denoted by the Subject does the action; as,

(i) I am doing my home work.
(ii) He gave me a message.

A Verb is said to be in the passive Voice when something is done to the person or thing denoted by the subject; as,

(i) The students are being taught by the teacher,
(ii) The road will be repaired by the labourers.
(iii) The letters have been typed by the typist.

When the verb is changed from the Active Voice to the Passive Voice, the object of the verb in the active voice becomes the subject of the verb in the passive voice; as,

(i) The boy kicked the ball (active).
(ii) The ball was kicked by the boy (passive)

Thus, the word 'ball' which is the object of the verb 'kicked' in Active Voice, becomes the subject of the verb 'was kicked' in the passive voice.

Note. Sentences having Transitive Verbs can only be changed into Passive Voice. Sentences having Intransitive Verbs can not be made passive.

TRANSITIVE AND INTRANSITIVE VERB

A **transitive verb** is a verb that denotes an action which passes over from the subject to the object; as,

The boy kicked the football.

In the above sentence, the action 'kicked' denoted by the subject 'boy' passes over to the object 'football'.

Intransitive Verb : An Intransitive Verb is a verb that denotes an action which does not pass over to the object; as,

(i) The birds fly.
(ii) He came.

In the above sentences, the verbs 'fly' and 'came' do not need any object.

THE USE OF ACTIVE AND PASSIVE VOICE

1. The active voice is used when the 'doer' of the action (i.e. agent) is to be made prominent and the passive voice is used when the person or thing acted upon is to be made prominent. The passive voice is generally used when the active form would involve the use of vague pronoun or noun; as

(i) English is spoken all over the world.

(ii) I was invited to the party.

(iii) Kalidas is considered the Shakespeare of India.

(iv) The road is being repaired.

In such cases, the agent with 'by' is generally avoided as in such sentences, action is given prominence and not the doer of the action.

2. The passive voice is also used when the doer of action is not known; as,

(i) The house has been burgled.

(ii) The purse has been stolen.

3. Passive voice is also used while reporting an experiment; as,

The water was taken. It was put in a tube, the tube was heated etc.

Rules for Changing Active to Passive Voice

Tense	Active	Rules	Passive
Simple Present	He visits us	is/are/am Past Participle by	We are visited by him
Present Continuous	He is visiting us	is/are/am being Past Participle by	We are being visited by him
Present Perfect	He has visited us	has been/have been Past Participle by	We have been visited by him
Present Perfect Continuous	This tense does not change into passive voice		
Past Simple	He visited us	was/were Past Participle by	We were visited by him
Past Continuous	He was visiting us	was/were being past Participle by	We were being visited by him
Past Perfect	He had visited us	Had been Past Participle by	We had been visited by him
Future Simple	He will visit us	Shall be/will be Past Participle by	We shall be visited by him
Future Continuous	This tense is usually used in the Active Voice		
	He will have visited us	shall have been/will have been past participle by	We shall have been visited by him

EXERCISE (SOLVED) ASSERTIVE SENTENCES

Active : The children are flying kites.
Passive : Kites are being flown by the children.

Active : I have done my home work.
Passive : My home work has been done by me.

Active : She likes vegetarian food.
Passive : Vegetarian food is liked by her.

Active : He bought apples.
Passive : Apples were bought by him.

Active : They will help us.
Passive : We shall be helped by them.

Active : He is learning English grammar.
Passive : English grammar is being learnt by him.

Active : I shall have completed my M.B.A. by next year.
Passive : My M.B.A. will have been completed by next year by me.

Active : Children love animals.
Passive : Animals are loved by children.

Active : The mad dog bit the beggar.
Passive : The beggar was bitten by the mad dog.

Active : They elected him king.
Passive : He was elected king by them.

Active : He named his son Chirag.
Passive : His son was named Chirag.

Conversion of Interrogative sentences into Passive Voice.

The same rules are observed while changing Interrogative Sentences into passive voice except that when an Interrogative Sentence is changed into Passive Voice or Vice Versa, it remains interrogative. Thus, the auxiliary (the helping verb) of the particular tense is put in the beginning of the sentence; as,

Active : Does he help you ?
Passive : Are you helped by him ?

Active : Do you like this painting ?
Passive : Is this painting liked by you ?

Active : Will he attend the function ?
Passive : Will the function be attended by him ?

Note. While changing sentences which have two objects, into Passive Voice, or vice versa, either of the objects can be picked up and brought to the place of subject; as,

Active : I gave him a book.
Passive : A book was given to him by me
or
He was given a book by me.

Active : She taught us English.
Passive : English was taught to us by her.
or
We were taught English by her.

Active : Did you tell him a story ?
Passive : Was a story told to him by you ?
or
Was he told a story by you ?

Note. Some intransitive verbs with prepositions, used as Transitive verbs, can be changed into passive Voice; as,

Active : She laughted at him.
Passive : He was laughed at by her.
Active : All agreed to her proposal.
Passive : Her proposal was agreed to by all.

If an interrogative sentence begins with 'wh' words and 'how', these words are put before the helping verbs; as,

Active : How did you solve such sums ?
Passive : How were such sums solved by you ?

Active : Where do you keep your books ?
Passive : Where are your books kept by you ?

Active : Who teaches you English ?
Passive : By whom are you taught English ?
or
By whom is English taught to you ?

Active : When does he take exercise ?
Passive : When is exercise taken by him ?

Active : When will you help me ?
Passive : When shall I be helped by you ?

Active : Why did you keep the money here ?
Passive : Why was the money kept here by you ?

Conversion of Imperative sentences into Passive voice.

While changing Imperative sentences into passive voice the use of 'let' is made; as,

Active : Switch on the light.
Passive : Let the light be switched on.

Active : Don't close the door.
Passive : Let the door not be closed.

Note. While changing imperative sentences with intransitive verbs, into passive voice, 'let' can not be used; as,

Active : Go there.
Passive : You are requested/ordered to go there.

Active : Come here.
Passive : You are requested/ ordered to come here.

As the above sentences have Intransitive verbs — 'go' and 'come', they do not have objects. The complete sentences in Active Voice will be — 'I order/ request you to go there' and 'I ask/order you to come here'.

EXERCISE 37

Name the verbs in the following sentences and say whether they are in the Active Voice or in the passive voice :

1. He has been dismissed from the service.
2. She is doing her home work.
3. All the letters have been posted.
4. She knew all the guests.
5. She is writing a letter to her mother.
6. Are you telling the truth ?
7. Do all the boys bring their books ?
8. The party was given in honour of the chief guest.
9. No alcohol was consumed in the party.
10. Sonu was given an award.
11. He flew many kites.
12. The fields were being ploughed.
13. Let the lights be switched off.
14. Don't go there.
15. He has done this work.
16. Was the work done in haste ?
17. Is he given his salary in time ?

18. Has the money been returned ?
19. Will you be obeyed by your children ?
20. She is making paper boats.

EXERCISE 38

Change the following sentences into passive voice :

1. Do you obey your teachers ?
2. She bought many toys.
3. Storm felled many trees.
4. Where did you keep my money ?
5. Are you doing your home work ?
6. Will she type all the letters ?
7. I can lift this heavy box.
8. You may get a short leave.
9. Did you cut the vegetables ?
10. Who taught you English ?
11. Where do you keep your clothes ?
12. How did you cross the river ?
13. They sell radios here.
14. Could you get your money back ?
15. I can not solve this sum.
16. She can solve all the difficult sums.
17. Will you accompany me ?
18. Has the commander alerted the soldiers ?
19. Don't open the door.
20. Obey the rules.
21. Are you watching a popular serial on television ?
22. Who attacked Naga Saki ?
23. Did our army defeat the enemy forces ?
24. He wishes to see your house.
25. Did he want to attend the meeting ?
26. Will you attend the meeting ?
27. The students had solved the sums when the teacher came.
28. Do not waste your time.
29. Children love animals.
30. We elected him captain.

EXERCISE 39

Change the following sentences into Active voice :

1. He is known to me.
2. What can not be cured must be endured.
3. The poor have been given woollen clothes.
4. How can this problem be solved ?
5. By whom was the work done ?
6. The poor should not be deprived of their dues.
7. Am I not always disturbed ?
8. He was presented a new television.
9. Different medicine was prescribed by the doctor.
10. This news was broadcast on All India Radio.
11. All the wrong-doers were punished.
12. Was the work completed in time ?
13. The door is being knocked at.
14. Where will the meeting be held by them ?
15. Can I be helped in this juncture ?
16. Was he hanged for no crime of his ?
17. All the telephone wires were cut.
18. He was ruined by gambling.
19. By whom were you taught English ?
20. All the robbers have been caught by the police.
21. They were called cowards.
22. By whom was the computer dismantled ?
23. He was appointed Mayor.
24. Let the door not be shut.
25. You are requested to come here.

EXERCISE 40

Change the voice in the following sentences :

1. All desire wealth but some acquire it.
2. Who broke this jug ?
3. He was seen stealing the purse.
4. He was accused of various offences.
5. Do not insult the poor.
6. Why did he not type this letter ?

7. We were refused admission.
8. They elected him captain of our school team.
9. Who is making a noise ?
10. What can not be cured must be endured.
11. Shall I forget that unhappy period of my life ?
12. You must listen to your teacher.
13. By whom was the T.V. switched off ?
14. He was given a beautiful present.
15. The food was cooked in time.
16. No letter was written by me during the last fortnight.
17. The new ministers were administered the oath of office and secrecy.
18. Post this letter.
19. The rumours were being spread.
20. Many terrorists have been arrested.
21. Can this sum be solved by you ?
22. Let the rules be obeyed.
23. He is being led by dishonest persons.
24. No room was left unattended.
25. Have you informed him of the flash news ?
26. Do you know him ?
27. A message was left for you by him.
28. You will be obeyed by every one.
29. Did you give him the message ?

15

Direct and Indirect Speech

When we repeat the actual words of a speaker, we use **Direct Speech**. When we say or report what the speaker said without quoting his exact words, we use **Indirect Speech** or **reported speech**; as,

Direct : He said, "I am tired."
Indirect : He said that he was tired.

In **Direct Speech**, we use Inverted Commas " " to use the exact words spoken by the speaker. In **Indirect speech**, the inverted commas " " are removed.

In the first sentence, 'said' is called the **Reporting Verb** and 'I am tired' is called the **Reported Speech**. The Reported speech is introduced by the conjunction 'that'.

The tense of the verb in the reported speech is changed from the Present to the past.

Rules for changing Direct Speech into Indirect Speech.

Rule 1. If the reporting verb is in the present or future tense, the verb in the reported speech is not changed at all; as

Direct : He says, "I am tired."
Indirect : He says that he is tired.

Direct : The teacher says, "Ram will not pass".
Indirect : The teacher says that Ram will not pass.

Direct : The boys say, "We have done our best."
Indirect : The boys say that they have done their best.

Rule 2. If the reporting verb is in the past tense, the reported speech in one sentence or different clauses changes into past tense.

(i) The simple present becomes the Simple past; as,

Direct : He said, "I go for a walk."
Indirect : He said that he went for a walk.

Direct : Ram said, "Sonu studies daily."
Indirect : Ram said that Sonu studied daily.

(ii) The present continuous becomes the past continuous; as,

Direct : Ram said, " I am studying."
Indirect : Ram said that he was studying.

Direct : You said, "The boys are playing cricket."
Indirect : You said that the boys were playing cricket.

(iii) The present perfect becomes the past perfect; as,

Direct : The student said, "I have done my home work."
Indirect : The student said that he had done his home work.

Direct : The typist said, "I have typed all the letters."
Indirect : The typist said that she had typed all the letters.

(iv) The present perfect continuous becomes the past perfect continuous; as,

Direct : He said, "I have been studying since morning."
Indirect : He said that he had been studying since morning.

Direct : The teacher said, "I have been teaching since morning."
Indirect : The teacher said that she had been teaching since morning.

(v) The simple past becomes the past perfect; as,

Direct : He said, "I went there in the morning."
Indirect : He said that he had gone there in the morning.

Direct : She said, "Ram returned at noon."
Indirect : She said that Ram had returned at noon.

(vi) The past continuous becomes the past perfect continuous; as,

Direct : The teacher said, "The boys were doing their sums."
Indirect : The teacher said that the boys had been doing their sums.

(vii) The past perfect remains the past perfect.

Direct : The teacher said, "I had been teaching for half an hour."
Indirect : The teacher said that she had been teaching for half an hour.

(viii) In future Simple, future continuous, future perfect and future perfect continuous tenses 'shall' and 'will' change into 'would'; as,

Direct : He said, "I shall pass."
Indirect : He said that he would pass.

Direct : You said, "Ram will come."
Indirect : You said that Ram would come.

(ix) 'Shall' changes into 'should', if it is used for permission.

Direct : He said, "Shall I go ?"
Indirect : He asked if he should go.

(x) The pronouns of the first person in Direct speech are changed in indirect speech to the same person as the subject of the introductory verb; as,

Direct : He said, "I have completed my work."
Indirect : He said that he had completed his work.

(xi) Pronouns of the second person in Direct Speech are changed in Indirect Speech to the same person as the noun or pronoun which comes after the Introductory verb; as,

Direct : Ram said to me, "You are sincere."
Indirect : Ram told me that I was sincere.

Direct : The teacher said to Sohan, "You have not done well."
Indirect : The teacher told Sohan that he had not done well.

(xii) Pronouns of the third person in direct speech remain the same; as,

Direct : Hari said to me, "She is not well."
Indirect : Hari told me that she was not well.

Note. In the above examples, the verb 'said to' in Direct Speech becomes 'told' in Indirect Speech and the preposition 'to' is omitted.

(xiii) Words expressing 'time' or 'nearness' are generally changed into words expressing 'distance' in indirect speech; as,

this	changes into	that
these	changes into	those
tomorrow	changes into	the next day or 'the day after
yesterday	changes into	the previous day or the day before
may	becomes	might
can	becomes	could
must	remains	must
last night	becomes	the night before
now	becomes	then
here	becomes	there
ago	becomes	before
thus	becomes	so

Note. If the speech is reported during the same period, or at the same place, these changes do not occur; as,

Direct : You say, "I am glad to be here this evening."
Indirect : You say that you are glad to be here this evening.

Exception to Rule 2

If the reported speech contains some universal or habitual fact, the simple present is not changed into the corresponding Simple past in Indirect Speech but remains unchanged; as,

Direct : The teacher said, "Honesty is the best policy."
Indirect : The teacher said that honesty is the best policy.

Direct : He said, "Two and two make four."
Indirect : He said that two and two make four.

Direct : The teacher said, "The sun rises in the east."
Indirect : The teacher said that the sun rises in the east.

Conversion of Interrogative Sentences into Indirect speech

While changing interrogative sentences into indirect speech.

(i) The verb 'asked' should be used in place of 'told'.

(ii) Conjunction 'if' or 'whether' should be used in place of 'that'.

Note. As all interrogative sentences become Assertive when they are changed into Indirect Speech, the 'noun' or 'pronoun' should be used before the helping verb or the main verb; as,

Direct : I said to him, "Have you done your home work ?"
Indirect : I asked him if he had done his home work.

Direct : He said to his mother, "Is food ready ?"
Indirect : He asked his mother if food was ready.

Direct : I said to him, "Do you take this route to your office ?"
Indirect : I asked him if he took that route to his office.

Direct : She said to me, "Will you help me ?"
Indirect : She asked me if I would help her

Direct : The interviewer said to me, "Do you speak good English ?"
Indirect : The interviewer asked me if I spoke good English.

Direct : The teacher said to the students, "Have you solved the sums ?"
Indirect : The teacher asked the students if they had solved the sums.

Direct : You said to me, "Will she attend the party ?"
Indirect : You asked me if she would attend the party.

Direct : I said to my daughter, "Has Sonu returned your money ?"
Indirect : I asked my daughter if Sonu had returned her money.

Direct : I said to my sister, "Did you meet your friend last night"
Indirect : I asked my sister if she had met her friend the night before.

Conversion of Interrogative sentences with Interrogative Words into Indirect speech

While changing interrogative sentences with interrogative words — who, whom, what, where, which, when how — all the rules as used in changing other forms of interrogative sentences are used except 'if' or 'whether' is not used but the same interrogative word is used; as,

Direct : He said to me, "Where do you live ?"
Indirect : He asked me where I lived.

Direct : I said to him, "How do you go to office ?"
Indirect : I asked him how he went to office.

Direct : My father said to me, "Who teaches you English ?"
Indirect : My father asked me who taught me English.

Direct : He said to me, "What are you doing?"
Indirect : He asked me what I was doing.

Direct : I said to a stranger, "What do you want ?"
Indirect : I asked a stranger what he wanted.

Direct : He said to his mother, "When will the food be ready ?"
Indirect : He asked him mother when the food would be ready.

Direct : He said to his servant, "Why have you disturbed me ?"
Indirect : He asked his servant why he (servant) had disturbed him.

Conversion of Imperative sentences into Indirect speech

While changing Imperative sentences into Indirect speech, the Introductory verb is changed to ordered/requested/recommended/advised/ or some other word suiting the sense; as,

Direct : He said to his servant, "Bring a glass of water."
Indirect : He ordered his servant to bring a glass of water.

Direct : The teacher said to me, "Work hard."
Indirect : The teacher advised me to work hard.

Direct : He said to me, "Please close the door."
Indirect : He requested me to close the door.

Direct : The commander said to the soldiers, "Move forward."
Indirect : The commander commanded the soldiers to move forward.

Direct : The teacher said to the students, "Do not make a noise."
Indirect : The teacher ordered/asked the students not to make a noise.

Conversion of Exclamatory sentences and wishes into Indirect Speech

(i) While changing Exclamatory sentences and Optative sentences into indirect speech, the Introductory verb is changed into wished/exclaimed with joy/exclaimed with sorrow or some other similar verb.

(ii) Interjections — the words showing exclamation such as Alas, Hurrah etc. are omitted.

(iii) The tense is changed as done in the case of Assertive sentences.

(iv) Exclamatory mark is omitted; as,

Direct : They said, "What a fine weather !"
Indirect : They exclaimed with joy that it was a very fine weather.

Direct : The boys said, "Hurrah ! we have won the match."
Indirect : The boys exclaimed joyfully that they had won the match.

Direct : The saint said, "May you live ling !"
Indirect : The saint wished that he (somebody) might live long.

Direct : He said to me, "May God bless you !"
Indirect : He prayed that God might bless me.

EXERCISE 41

Change the following sentences into Indirect speech (Assertive) :

1. He said to me, "I have given you much trouble."
2. The students said, "We have done our home work."
3. The child said to the mother, "I want to go out."
4. The teacher said to the students, "I am giving you a small home work."
5. "I shall meet you tomorrow", she said to me.
6. The boys said, "We have completed the work."
7. He said to me, "I met you in the party yesterday.
8. My father said to me, "I gave you some home work yesterday."
9. Mother said to the child, "I can not allow you to play outside."
10. He said, "It may rain today."
11. The principal said, "I am busy."
12. The soldiers said, "We shall do our best."
13. Sonu said, "I went to the cinema last night."
14. He said, "I shall come back tomorrow."
15. He said, "I take exercise every day."
16. I said to my father, "It may not be possible for me to solve this sum."
17. The students said to the teacher, "We have done our class work, sir."
18. My mother said to me, "I am going out and shall return after two hours."

19. The teacher said to the student, "You have not taken serious interest in your studies."
20. The announcer said, "The train is likely to be late by four hours."
21. The principal said, "The examinations are likely to be postponed for a fortnight."
22. I said to him, "I went to your house yesterday."
23. The examiner said, "Any examinee who takes help of books shall be disqualified for five years."
24. He said, "Most of the educational institutions have become business centers these days."
25. You said, "I have had my lunch."

EXERCISE 42

Change the following sentences into indirect Speech (Interrogative) :

1. I said to him, "When will you come back from the tour ?"
2. Mother said to her daughter, "Did you give him my message ?"
3. I said to my mother, "May I go out to play ?"
4. He said to me, "Are you going to market ?"
5. The student said to the teacher, "May I come in, sir ?"
6. I said to a passerby, "Can you tell me the way to the nearest inn ?"
7. She said to me, "Can you accompany me to the market ?"
8. He said to me; "Where do you live ?"
9. My friend said to me, "What can I do for you ?"
10. "How do you go to your office ?" I said to him.
11. He said on telephone, "Am I speaking to Mr. Anil ?"
12. My friend said to me, "Do you want to come with me for a walk ?"
13. My mother said to me "Who teaches you English ?"
14. She said to the guests, "What would you like to have ?"
15. I inquired, "Will you come back from London by next month ?"
16. I said to him, "Do you like vegetarian food ?"
17. He said to me, "Where do you come from ?"
18. The doctor said to me, "How do you feel today ?"
19. She said to me, "Which is your book ?"
20. The mother said to her daughter, "Why are you so late tonight ?"
21. The employer said to Rakesh, "Why are you sitting idle ?"
22. The poor woman said, "Will no one help me ?"
23. "Do you like this place ?" I said to the guest.
24. I said to my mother, "Do you believe in ghosts ?"
25. He said to the conductor, "When will the bus start ?"

EXERCISE 43

Change the following sentences into indirect speech (Imperative) :

1. I said to him, "Please give me your book."
2. The commander said to the soldiers, "Do not move forward."
3. The teacher said to the students, "Be quiet and listen to me."
4. The accused said to the judge, "Please pardon me, sir."
5. He said to the servant, "Leave this room."
6. The teacher said to the student, "Show me your note-book."
7. The teacher said to the students, "Listen to me attentively".
8. "Stand up, boys" the teacher said.
9. Mother said to the son, "Work hard if you want to succeed."
10. I said to him, "Wait till I return."
11. He said to the driver, "Do not park your car here."
12. The principal said to the peon, "Remove all the files from my table."
13. The doctor said to the patient, "Go for a walk every day."
14. The engineer said to the worker, "Switch off the plant."
15. The gardener said to the children, "Don't pluck flowers."
16. He said to his father, "Please give me some extra pocket money."
17. The Headmaster said to the teachers, "Please see to it that all students do well."
18. The employer said to him, "Make it a habit to reach office in time."

EXERCISE 44

Change the following sentences into Indirect speech : (Exclamatory and Optative) :

1. The boys said, "Hurrah ! We have taken all the wickets."
2. They said, "What a beautiful weather !"
3. "Alas ! she died such a tragic death", he said.
4. "What a trouble you have brought to the family !" he angrily said.
5. They said, "What a horrible sight !"
6. He said, "How cruel of the king !"
7. They said, "What a bad luck !"
8. He said to me, "May you live long !"
9. I said, "What a rare sight !"
10. We said, "What a terrible storm !"

EXERCISE 45

Change the following sentences into Direct Speech :

1. The commander ordered the soldiers to shoot.
2. He exclaimed that he was ruined.

3. I asked him if he had finished his work.
4. My mother asked me why I was up so early that day.
5. He inquired where the cinema hall was.
6. The teacher asked me what my name was.
7. My friend told me that he was writing a book.
8. The teacher said that she had been teaching that class for six months.
9. My aunt asked me who taught me English in the school.
10. She asked a passerby how far the Taj Mahal Hotel was.
11. I told my friend that I might not be in the town that week.
12. He informed me that he would visit my home soon.
13. She asked her mother if she might go out with her friends.
14. The magistrate told the accused that he could do nothing to save him.
15. I told him that he had put the best efforts to accomplish the work assigned to him.
16. I told her that I had seen her in the party a few days before.
17. She asked her mother if the food was ready.
18. I told my servant that I might come late that day.
19. My parents told me that I had not come up to their expectations.
20. I asked my teacher when the next examinations were likely to be held.
21. The chairman asked the members if they were satisfied with the decision taken in the meeting.
22. She asked me where I lived.
23. My father asked me if I was taking proper interest in my studies.
24. The students asked the teacher whether they had to answer all the questions.
25. He asked the manager what the working hours of the office were.
26. I asked my friend when he would come back from his home town.
27. My servant asked me respectfully if he might go to his house then.
28. She asked me if I would take part in the annual school function of my school.
29. The customer asked the shopkeeper what the cost of sugar was.
30. She asked me how long it would take to reach the air port.
31. He ordered his servant to leave the room.
32. The employer asked him to be punctual.
33. He exclaimed joyfully that it was a very fine weather.
34. The boys shouted joyfully that they had won the match.
35. I requested him to give me a glass of water.
36. He asked me to switch off the lights.
37. The notice cautioned to beware of pick-pockets.
38. She exclaimed that it was pity that her only son was dead.
39. The boy exclaimed happily that his kite had soared very high in the sky.

MISCELLANEOUS EXERCISE 46

Change the following sentences into Indirect Speech :

1. A passerby said, “Can you tell me the way to the nearest inn ?” “yes” said she “Do you want one in which you can spend the night ?” “no” replied the passerby “I only want a meal”.
2. “My hour has come”, said the soldier, “I must accept death boldly”
3. He said to his daughter ? “I am going out. Do you want to accompany me ?”
4. The teacher said to the students, “I have been teaching you for a long time. You do not seem to improve.” “We shall certainly show improvement”, the students replied. “when” ? the teacher asked.
5. He said to the servant, “Go to the market and bring the items given in the list. Have you understood ?” “yes, sir” the servant replied.
6. “Cheer up boy” ? he said, “Don’t get disheartened”, “I have failed” the boy replied “nothing is lost if you have failed in the examination. There are many opportunities in life. Do you follow me ?” “yes, sir”, replied the boy.
7. “Do you think our lives are happier than those of our ancestors” ? he said to me “I think we have got all but we have lost our peace of mind” I replied. “I also think so”, he said.
8. The mother said to the child, “Do not desire to have the moon as it is thousands of miles away and it is not a play-thing for children and no child ever got it, I can get you anything else which you wish to have.”
9. The teacher said angrily, “What are you thinking ? Why are you not paying attention ? If you do not concentrate in your lessons, I shall send you to the principal who is sure to punish you. Pay attention and stop everything else.”
10. “Are you angry with me ?“ The son said to the father, “yes” the father said. “But why ?” “You were very late to come back home”. “I am sorry. I will never come late again”, the son said.

16

Finite and Non-Finite Verbs

When a verb is limited by a person and number, it is called a **Finite Verb**; as,

She goes to school.

She goes to school to study.

In the first sentence, the verb 'goes' has its own subject 'she' and is thus a **Finite verb**.

In the second sentence, 'to study' is not limited by the subject 'she' and it merely names the action denoted by the verb 'goes'. It is therefore called **Non Finite Verb**.

Non Finite Verbs are :

(i) Infinitive

(ii) Participle

(iii) Gerund

The verb infinitive. The verb infinitive is a kind of noun but it also has the feature of the verb. We may therefore call it a verbial noun.

The word 'to' is used with the Infinitive but with certain verbs such as hear, see, dare, need, make, let, bid, 'to' is left out; as,

1. I made her do the work.
2. You need not come to office.
3. I bade her go.
4. I shall let her know.
5. He dare not disobey me.

USES OF INFINITIVE

1. As the subject of a verb; as,

   To err is human.

   To solve the sum is not easy.

2. As the object of a transitive verb; as,

   I want to learn French.

   She meant to harm

3. As the object of a preposition; as,

   The function was about to start.

   I had no choice except to surrender.

4. As the complement for a verb; as,

   Your duty is to obey.

   His aim is to succeed.

5. As an objective complement; as,

   I saw him play.

In the above sentences, the infinitive is used like a noun, called the simple infinitive.

The infinitive can also be used :

1. To qualify a verb :
   (i) She came to study.
   (ii) I exercise to improve my body.
2. To qualify an adjective :
   (i) Orange is sweet to taste.
   (ii) I am excited to meet him.
3. To qualify a Noun :
   (i) He is the boy to be appreciated.
   (ii) This is not the time to talk
4. To qualify a sentence :
   (i) To conclude the matter, we must work hard.

Pattern A

No.	*Subject + Verb*	*(Not) + to-infinitive*
1.	Did you remember	to give the message ?
2.	She has come	to study
3.	He has promised	to help me
4.	I forgot	to telephone him
5.	He has agreed	to attend the function

EXERCISE 47

Complete each of these sentences with a to-infinitive :

1. Does he want .... ?
2. She always forgets ....
3. Did you remember .... ?
4. She has failed ....
5. Please try ....
6. Would you like .... ?

Pattern B

In this pattern, the verb is followed by a Noun or Pronoun and by (not) to and infinitive :

No.	*Subject + Verb*	*Noun or pronoun*	*(Not) + to-infinitive*
1.	She wants	me	to help her
2.	He asked	her	to switch off the lights
3.	I asked	him	not to pluck flowers
4.	The principal allowed	me	to speak to the children

EXERCISE 48

Complete the following sentences with a suitable to-infinitive :

1. I requested him ....
2. I can not allow you ....
3. She wanted me ....
4. Do you want me .... ?
5. The principal wanted the students ....

Pattern C

No.	*Subject + Verb*	*Conjunctive/pronoun*	*to-infinitive*
1.	I did not know	how	to speak good English
2.	She knows	how	to solve this sum
3.	I am learning	how	to drive
4.	Do you know	when	to start ?
5.	We did not know	what	to do

Infinitive after something, anything, nothing, somebody, nobody etc.

No.	*Subject + Verb*	*Indefinite pronoun*	*to-infinitive*
1.	She has	nothing	to say
2.	The orphan has	nobody	to look after him
3.	The accused has	something	to say
4.	Do you have	nowhere	to go ?
5.	He has	nothing	to wear

EXERCISE 49

Complete each sentence with a suitable to-infinitive :

1. He did not know how ....
2. Did you know when ....?
3. You have nothing ....
4. I want something ....
5. We have a long way ....
6. The orphan has no where ....

The use of Infinitive after too :

No.	Subject + Verb	too	adjective/adverb	to-infinitive
1.	It is	too	hot	to go out
2.	I am	too	tired	to walk
3.	The wall is	too	high	to climb
4.	She is	too	proud	to beg

EXERCISE 50

Complete the following sentences with to-infinitive :

1. This news is too good ....
2. I am too tired ....
3. She was too old ....
4. It is too cold ....
5. The sum is too difficult ....

Infinitive after an Anticipatory 'It'

No.	*It + to be*	*Subjective complement*	*to-infinitive*
1.	It is	easy	to blame others
2.	It is	difficult	to solve the sum
3.	It was	wrong	to abuse
4.	It is	easy	to climb
5.	It will be	wrong	to say so

EXERCISE 51

Rewrite the following sentences after using the Introductory word "It" :

1. To solve this sum is not easy.
2. To swindle your friend is unethical.
3. To live without water is impossible.
4. To climb this hill is not easy.
5. To fiddle with this equipment is not wise.
6. To borrow money is not a good habit.
7. To insult the weak is immoral.

Use of infinitive after some adjectives :

No.	*Subject + verb*	*Adjective*	*to-infinitive*
1.	This box is	heavy	to carry
2.	Your story is	interesting	to hear
3.	His lecture was	easy	to understand
4.	These shoes are	difficult	to mend
5.	This sum is	hard	to solve

Use of infinitive after enough :

No.	*Subject + verb*	*Adjective/ or adverb*	*enough*	*to-infinitive*
1.	She was	generous	enough	to help me
2.	You are	wise	enough	to guide me
3.	He is	rich	enough	to purchase a house
4.	We are	strong	enough	to retaliate
5.	I spoke	loud	enough	to be heard

EXERCISE 52

Complete the following sentences by using infinitive phrases :

1. It is a pleasure ....
2. He is strong enough ....
3. You are wise enough ....
4. The teacher spoke loud enough ....
5. It is a blunder ....
6. You are tough enough ....
7. She is clever enough ....
8. It is a shame ....

17

The Participle

A **Participle** is a word which is partly a verb and partly an adjective. There are three participles :

1. Present participle
2. Past participle
3. Perfect participle

Present participle ends in 'ing' and represents an action as going on; as,

1. I was him *climbing* the hill.
2. Slowly *speaking*, they entered the examination hall.

Past Participle represents completed action; as,

1. *Surrounded* by the Indian Army, the enemy forces surrendered.
2. *Deceived* by his friends, he lost all hope.
3. There were many trees *laden* with apples.

Perfect Participle represents an action as completed at some time; as,

Having completed his studies, he went abroad.

When a **participle** is used as a Simple qualifying adjective in form of a noun, it is called participial adjective; as,

1. There is *shining* object in the sky.
2. They fought a *losing* battle.
3. He is a *learned* man.

We may recapitulate the use of participles :

A participle is a verbial adjective.

A participle may govern a noun or pronoun; as,

Seeing the lion, they ran away.

Here the noun 'lion' is governed by the participle 'seeing'.

Like a verb, a Participle may be modified by an adverb; as,

Loudly weeping, she went away.

Here the participle 'weeping' is modified by the adverb 'loudly'

Like an adjective, a participle may qualify a noun or pronoun; as

Having done his work, he rested.

Like an adjective, a participle may be compared; as

He is the most troubling boy.

Here the participle 'troubling' is compared by prefixing most.

The forms of different participles are given below :

	Active	Passive
Present :	Caring	being cared
Perfect :	Having cared	having been cared
Past :		cared

The **continuous** tenses (Active Voice) are formed from the present participle with the tense of the verb 'be'; as,

You are helping — You were helping — You will be helping

The **Perfect** Tenses (Active Voice) are formed from the past participle with the tense of the verb 'have'; as,

You have helped — You had helped — You will have helped

The Passive Voice is formed from the Past Participle with the tense of the verb 'be'; as,

You are helped — You were helped — You will be helped

EXERCISE 53

Complete the following sentences with suitable participles :

1. I saw a house ....to ashes.
2. All the trees are .... with fruit.
3. I saw him .... the money.
4. .... the loud cries, we woke up.
5. We saw the thief ....
6. The principal caught many students ....
7. I smell something ....
8. He kept me ....
9. We noticed some one ....
10. .... by the forces, the guard surrendered.
11. I found her .... mentally.
12. We saw a .... body in the water.
13. .... completed his work, he left for home.
14. I saw him .... the baskets.
15. We saw them .... the stones.

18

Gerund

A **gerund** as that form of the verb which ends in 'ing' and is partly verb and partly noun (It is a verbail noun).

Both the **gerund** and the **infinitive** have the force of a noun and a verb and their uses are also similar.

Study the following sentence :

Swimming is a good exercise.

The word 'swimming' is formed from the verb 'swim' by adding 'ing'. It also does the work of a noun as it is used as a Subject of a verb. It is therefore a verb-noun and is called **'Gerund'**.

A gerund may be used as :

1. Subject of a verb; as,
   (i) Smoking is injurious to health.
   (ii) Swimming is a good exercise.
2. Object of a transitive verb; as,
   (i) Stop talking.
   (ii) Boys love playing.
3. Object of a preposition; as,
   (i) I am tired of writing.
   (ii) He is fond of hunting.
4. Complement of a verb; as,
   (i) Seeing is believing.
   (ii) What I most dislikes is lying.

Absolutely; as,

Rising early being his routine, we got up early.

EXERCISE 54

Provide suitable Gerunds/Gerundial phrases in the following sentences :

1. Birds love ....
2. .... is easier than obeying.
3. I dislike ....
4. She is tired of ....
5. She taught me ....
6. I thanked him for ....
7. .... is his hobby.
8. He likes ....
9. .... is a bad habit.
10. .... leads to problems.
11. Children love ....
12. .... gives me joy.
13. .... is better than receiving.
14. We enjoyed ....
15. I hate ....
16. .... is not allowed in this office.
17. She is fond of ....
18. I always disapprove of ....
19. She dislikes .... in a queue.
20. I enjoy .... in the sun on a cold a day.

19

Phrases

Phrase. A Phrase is a group of words which does not have its own **Subject** and **Predicate**. Such a group of words makes some sense but not complete sense; as,

(i) in the corner
(ii) on the hill
(iii) about my success
(iv) in the east
(v) on my success

A phrase can be turned into a meaningful sentence; as,

1. He sat in the corner.
2. We climbed on the hill.
3. My parents were happy about my success.
4. The sun rises in the east.
5. He congratulated me on my success.

Kinds of Phrases

There are three kinds of Phrases :

1. Adjective Phrase
2. Adverb Phrase
3. Noun Phrase

Adjective Phrase. When a group of words without having **Subject** and **Predicate**, does the work of an **Adjective**, it is called **Adjective** Phrase; as,

(i) of great honesty
(ii) with a kindly nature
(iii) in white dress
(iv) with short hair

The above **Adjective Phrases** can be turned into meaningful sentences :

1. He is man of great honesty.
2. She is a woman with kindly nature.

3. The woman in white dress is my aunt.
4. Most men do not like girls with short hair.

EXERCISE 55

Pick out the Adjective Phrases in the following sentences :

1. The girl with blue eyes is my cousin.
2. A friend in need is a friend indeed.
3. The king wore a crown made of gold.
4. I presented her a shawl of green colour.
5. The poacher shot the tiger with a grey skin.
6. She is the girl with blue eyes.
7. She is the woman of great popularity.
8. These are the paintings of great value.
9. She told tales of great valour.
10. I met a man of great worth.
11. A man always in need is disliked.
12. He narrated his experiences of trials and tribulations.

EXERCISE 56

In each of the following Sentences, replace the Adjective given in italics by an Adjective Phrase :

1. A *dark* cloud appeared in the sky.
2. A *tall* boy rushed forward.
3. You will be criticized for the *cowardly* act.
4. It was a *horrible* sight.
5. The *Indian* tricolour was hoisted in the Asian games.
6. I gave her a *golden* watch.
7. It was a *brave* act.
8. Any *terrorist* act is hated by the people.
9. I passed through a *noisy* street.
10. She gave me a *witty* reply.

EXERCISE 57

Replace each of the following Adjective Phrases in italics with an Adjective of same meaning :

1. He is a *man of worth.*
2. The king presented a jug *made of gold.*
3. This equipment is *of no use* to *me.*
4. He has done a *deed of shame.*
5. She is a woman *with bad temper.*

6. He is a man *without a blame*.
7. The doctor was *full of hope* of his recovery.
8. He is a man *of boastful nature*.
9. You are a man *without any luck*.
10. This child likes pictures *without colour*.

Note. All Adjective Phrases can not be replaced by Adjectives.

EXERCISE 58

Fill in the blanks suitable Adjective Phrases :

1. She is a woman ....
2. Birds .... flock together.
3. I want to lead a life ....
4. He reads stories ....
5. She drew a picture ....
6. The house .... is very beautiful.
7. He gave me a reply ....
8. She took a decision ....
9. It is a life ....
10. He brought a jug ....
11. He encaged a bird ....
12. She purchased a house ....
13. I know the man ....

ADVERB PHRASE

An **Adverb Phrase** is a group of words, without having its **Subject** and **Predicate** and which does the work of an adverb; as,

1. He runs quickly (adverb)
   He runs with great speed (adverb phrase)
2. I spoke softly (adverb)
   I spoke in soft manner (adverb phrase)
3. He will come now (adverb)
   He will come at this moment (adverb phrase)
4. She went there (adverb)
   She went to that place (adverb phrase)
5. I am working now (adverb)
   I am working at this moment (adverb phrase)

In each of the above pairs of sentences, first there is a single word (adverb) which modifies a verb and then a group of words modifying a verb in the same way.

For example 'with great speed' tells us how she runs and modifies the verb 'runs', as adverb 'quickly' does. Thus it does the work of an adverb and is called adverb phrase.

Note. An Adverb Phrase like an Adverb may also modify an Adjective or another Adverb; as,

This book is good *for competitive examinations.*

EXERCISE 59

Pick out the Adverb Phrases in the following sentences :

1. I met her in the evening.
2. The warriors fought in a brave manner.
3. In former times, he was in Indian Air Force.
4. I shall meet my old friend at an early date.
5. He hit the ball in a beautiful manner.
6. She left the meeting in a hurry.
7. He went to a foreign country for higher studies.
8. He had shifted to another place.
9. The prince lived on top of the hill.
10. You are invited into the drawing room.
11. She kept her purse in the almirah.
12. You spoke in a rude manner.
13. The children go to school early in the morning.
14. I shall meet you in the party.
15. Peace should be maintained in the Parliament.
16. He swindled his friend in a clever manner.

EXERCISE 60

In each of the following sentences, replace he adverb in italics by an Adverb Phrase of the same meaning :

1. She received the guests *cheerfully.*
2. He did not behave *rudely.*
3. The President spoke *eloquently.*
4. He treated us *nicely.*
5. You left the place *hurriedly.*
6. The gun went off *suddenly.*

7. The warriors fought *fiercely*.
8. Let us rest *here*.
9. We shall hear of a good news *soon*.
10. He *never* tells a lie.
11. She spoke *angrily*.
12. We shall arrive *there*.
13. We should treat animals *kindly*.
14. She hugged her son *passionately*.
15. You should revise your lessons *thoroughly*.

EXERCISE 61

Replace each of the following Adverb Phrases in italics by an adverb of the same meaning :

1. You should lift the box *with great care*.
2. He behaved *in a rude manner*.
3. The storm struck *with great violence*.
4. I thanked him *with all my heart*.
5. She was not supposed to talk *in an impudent manner*.
6. You did your work *in a careless manner*.
7. The soldiers fought *with great courage*.
8. He vowed *in a sincere manner* that he was not to blame.
9. I have dome the work *to the satisfaction*.
10. You must answer *at this very moment*.
11. The terrorists beat them *in a terrible manner*.
12. He will meet me *some time afterwards*.
13. I got success *in the long run*.

Note. All Adverb Phrases can not be replaced by adverbs.

EXERCISE 62

Fill in the blanks with suitable Adverb Phrases :

1. The team played ....
2. The brave soldiers fought ....
3. He acted ....
4. The boy behaved ....
5. You must do the work ....
6. The judge gave his judgement ....
7. You can meet me ....
8. The boy kicked the ball ....
9. She knows me ....

10. The holy man sat ....
11. The students left the class ....
12. The teacher spoke ....
13. You have acted ....
14. She will solve the sum ....
15. The examiner will speak ....
16. The girls were dancing ....
17. The ferocious lion attacked ....
18. The birds fly ....
19. She met me ....
20. My aunt lives ....

Note. The same phrase may be an Adjective Phrase in one sentence and an Adverb phrase in another sentence. Thus, we can not say what kind of phrase a given phrase is until we see the work done by it in a sentence; as,

1. The umbrellas in the corner are for sale.
2. The umbrellas were kept in the corner.

In sentence 1, the phrase in the corner, tells us which umbrellas are for sale, that is, it qualifies the noun umbrellas. It is therefore an adjective phrase. In sentence 2, the phrase in the corner tells us where the umbrellas were kept, that is, it modifies the verb 'kept'. It is therefore an adverb phrase.

NOUN PHRASE

A **Noun Phrase** is a group of words that does the work of a Noun; as,

(i) to win the game
(ii) playing cricket
(iii) to learn driving
(iv) reading novels

The above **Noun Phrases** can be turned into sentences :

1. He wants to win the game.
2. All boys love playing cricket.
3. She wants to learn driving.
4. Reading novels is his hobby.

Note. In order to understand a Noun Phrase more clearly, question 'what' should be asked after the verb and what follows is either a noun, a noun phrase or a noun clause; as,

He wants 'what' .... to win the game.

Therefore 'to win the game' is a noun phrase.

EXERCISE 63

Pick out the Noun Phrases in the following sentences :

1. Early to bed is a good habit.
2. I have a strong desire to win the game.
3. Reading books gives us pleasure and knowledge.
4. He promised to help me in future.
5. We love to sit in the open air.
6. Swimming in the hot sun is a pleasure.
7. Getting up early can keep you fit and energetic.
8. I wish to meet the principal.
9. Did the director ask you to be on time ?
10. I know the way to the restaurant.
11. She speaks ill of others.
12. Did you intend to harm him ?
13. Taking regular exercise keeps the body and mind healthy.
14. She wanted to go on leave.

EXERCISE 64

Supply a Noun Phrase in the following blanks :

1. I wish ....
2. She wanted ....
3. You had promised ....
4. We hope ....
5. He dislikes ....
6. .... gives us a great joy.
7. It is a pleasure ....
8. He always expects ....
9. You intended ....
10. We all hoped ....
11. .... was not an easy task.
12. .... can keep you healthy.
13. Do you know .... ?
14. Have you promised .... ?

EXERCISE 65

Pick out the phrases in the following sentences and say whether they are Adjective Phrases, Adverb Phrases or Noun Phrases :

1. He keeps his money in the bank.
2. The waiter spoke in a rude manner.

3. I want to learn driving.
4. He passed the Civil Services Examination.
5. We climbed to the top of the hill.
6. No one knows the ways of God.
7. Rising early will prove beneficial for you.
8. A man in a great problem came to me.
9. The tiger jumped off the cage.
10. Computers were not known in the medieval period.
11. Sita knows her work.
12. The birds in small cages present a pathetic view.
13. King Ashoka was a man of great virtues.
14. I went there in the evening.
15. She will try to know the secret.
16. The items were scattered all over the place.
17. Why do you keep company of such persons ?
18. To qualify the IAS examination was his only ambition.
19. Those were the men of great patience.
20. Much water has flowed under the Ganges since then.
21. He ekes out his livelihood by selling newspapers.
22. You left the party in haste.
23. She treated the guests in a polite manner.
24. The examinees rushed into the examination hall.
25. A cloud of black colour spread over the horizon.
26. The storm blew with great violence.
27. She is a woman of great internal strength.
28. He wants to meet his uncle.
29. The bullet fell at this spot.
30. She has behaved in a foolish manner.
31. A man of courage is liked by all.

20

Clauses

The Principal clause or the Main clause has its own **Subject** and **Predicate**. It can stand independently in relation to a Subordinate Clause; as,

(i) You should help him if he helps you.

In the above sentence, the Clause 'you should help him'.

has its own Subject and Predicate and it can stand independently and is therefore called the Principal Clause or Main Clause.

Subordinate Clause. A Subordinate Clause is a part of a sentence which does not make complete sense on its own but has to depend on the Principal Clause or other Subordinate Clause for its action; as,

(i) If you work hard you will pass.

In the above sentence, 'If you work hard' is a Subordinate Clause because though it has its own Subject and Predicate, it can not stand independently, and depends on the Main Clause 'you will pass' for its action.

Coordinate Clause. A Coordinate Clause is of equal standing to the other clause or clauses. Coordinate clauses can be joined together with coordinating conjunctions to make a Compound Sentence; as,

(i) I went to the market and I purchased an umbrella.

In the above sentence, two clauses — 'I went to the market' and 'I purchased an umbrella' are joined together with Conjunction 'and'. They are called **Coordinate Clauses.**

Kinds of Clauses

There are three kinds of Clauses :

1. Adverb Clause
2. Adjective Clause
3. Noun Clause

Adverb Clause. An Adverb Clause is a group of words which contains a subject and a Predicate of its own and it does the work of an Adverb; as,

(i) She can meet me wherever she likes.
(ii) She can meet me if she likes.

In the above sentences 'wherever she likes' and 'if she likes' are adverb clauses.

Note. An adverb, an adverb phrase or and adverb clause qualifies a verb, an adjective or another adverb and thus they answer the questions — how, when, where and why.

An adverb clause may be classified as

Adverb clause of

1. Time
2. Place
3. Purpose
4. Cause or reason
5. Condition
6. Result
7. Comparison
8. Supposition or Concession

1. **Adverb Clause of Time.** They are introduced by Subordinating Conjunctions — when, wherever, while, before, after, since, as etc.

(i) The students can meet the principal *when the class is over.*
(ii) Don't disturb me *while I am doing my work.*
(iii) *As the Principal entered the classroom*, the students rose to their feet.
(iv) You should show me the work *before you go home.*

All the above Clauses in italics are the adverb clauses of time.

2. **Adverb Clause of Place.** Adverb Clauses of Place are introduced by subordinating conjunctions — when, wherever, whence etc.

(i) The captain led the soldiers *where he was ordered.*
(ii) I met her *wherever I liked.*
(iii) She can go back *whence she came.*
(iv) We stayed *where we liked.*

3. **Adverb Clause of Purpose.** Adverb clauses of Purpose are introduced by subordinating conjunctions — that, lest, so that, in order that.

(i) I studied hard *in order that I could good marks.*
(ii) She closed all the doors *so that the rain water might not come in.*

(iii) *That he might be well brought up*, his parents suffered.

(iv) Walk slowly *lest you should fall.*

(v) Come here *that I may bless you.*

4. **Adverb Clause of Cause or Reason.** Adverb clauses of cause or reason are introduced by subordinating conjunctions — because, since, that etc.

(i) *Because you studied hard*, you got good marks.

(ii) *Since you are not well* you can go home.

(iii) She is very happy *that her son has come back.*

(iv) *As the chairman was on leave*, we spoke to the director.

5. **Adverb Clause of Condition.** Adverb clauses of condition are introduced by the subordinating conjunctions — if, unless, whether.

(i) *If it does not rain*, we shall go out.

(ii) *If you work hard*, you will pass.

(iii) We must do our duty *whether we like it or not.*

(iv) *Unless you work hard*, you can not pass.

(v) She can meet me *if she likes.*

(vi) *Unless you improve your behaviour*, no one will like you.

Note. Sometimes, the subordinating conjunction is omitted in the past conditionals; as,

(i) Had you worked hard, you would not have regretted.

(ii) Were I the Head of the Organisation I would improve the administration.

6. **Adverb Clause of Result or Consequence.** Adverb clauses of Result or Consequence are introduced by the subordinating conjunctions — that, so, or, such.

Note. 'so' or 'such' are used before 'that' in the principal clause; as,

(i) I studied *so* hard *that I got distinction in all subjects.*

(ii) *Such* was her behaviour *that every one disliked her.*

(iii) *So* good were your deeds *that everyone appreciated you.*

(iv) I worked *so* hard *that I spoiled my health.*

7. **Adverb Clause of Comparison.** Adverb clauses of Comparison are of two kinds :

(i) Adverb clauses of comparison of degree.

(ii) Adverb clauses of comparison of manner.

Adverb clauses of comparison of degree are introduced by the subordinating conjunction 'that' or Relative Adverb; as,

(i) This building is higher *than that* (building is)

(ii) I like singing better *than you* (like).

(iii) He runs faster *than you* (run).

(iv) She is not as honest *as you think* (she is).

(v) He is as stupid *as he is dishonest.*

(vi) His handwriting is better *than that of yours* (handwriting is).

Note. The verbs of Adverb Clauses of comparison of degree are generally understood and are not expressed as those in brackets above.

8. **Adverb Clauses of comparison** of manner are introduced by the Relative adverb 'as'.

(i) I do everything *as I like.*

(ii) The meeting ended *as we had expected.*

(iii) He hit the ball *as he liked.*

9. **Adverb Clause of supposition or concession.** Adverb clauses of supposition or concession are introduced by the subordinating conjunctions — though, although, even if.

(i) *Even if he failed* he did not lose heart.

(ii) *Although he is rich* he is greedy.

(iii) *Although you failed* you had worked hard.

(iv) You should continue working *even though you are tired.*

(v) *Even if he is weak,* he does a lot of work.

EXERCISE 66

Pick pout the Adverb Clauses in the following sentences and tell the kind of each clause :

1. You should wait till I return.
2. The guests can sit wherever they like.
3. Had you come to me in time, I would have helped you.
4. The thief fled that no one could catch him.
5. Don't disturb me because I am studying.
6. Although you worked hard, you could not succeed.
7. Since he is an honest person I helped him.
8. He is studying hard so that he can get good marks.
9. He flew so high that he fell down.
10. It is so hot that one can not go out.

11. You can meet me wherever you like.
12. When you are free you can join us.
13. Even if you improve your behaviour she will not pardon you.
14. Though we walked fast we could not board the train.
15. The students were punished because they were very late.
16. If you overeat you will fall sick.
17. This area is more beautiful than that.
18. Since I am ill I can not attend the office.
19. As the manager was not in the office, his secretary received my application.
20. She has not yet finished though she had started early.
21. You should wait until he comes back.
22. When they came to us, we all honoured them.
23. Our Army won the battle even if it suffered many casualties.
24. The boys did the work as they were told.
25. It was so hot that nothing moved.
26. Wherever I go I hear the same noise.
27. As the Principal entered the class room, all rose to their feet.
28. Let her go wherever she likes.
29. He writes better English than he speaks.
30. I lost more than I had earned.
31. It has been a long time since we met.
32. He ran so fast that I could not catch him.
33. The robbers struck when the house was locked.
34. You should walk slowly lest you should slip.
35. A glutton lives that he may eat.
36. Although he did not study much he got good marks.
37. If I were you I would not do it.
38. We sow that we may reap.

EXERCISE 67

Supply suitable Adverb Clauses in the following sentences :

1. He is not so intelligent ....
2. She worked so hard ....
3. All love him ....
4. You will succeed ....
5. Her mother died ....
6. You will miss the train ....
7. I shall visit him ....
8. I can not help him ....

9. .... he is greedy.
10. This room is more tidy ....
11. I did ....
12. He is walking slowly ....
13. You speak so low ....
14. His handwriting is so bad ....
15. Water is heavier ....
16. He always does his work ....
17. He will come in time ....
18. You can meet me ....
19. He spoke so well ....

EXERCISE 68

In each of the following sentences replace each Adverb Phrase by an adverb Clause :

1. I am very grateful to you for your kindness.
2. He did to the best of his ability.
3. It is too hot to go out.
4. His heart was too full for words.
5. This news is too good to be true.
6. I met my uncle on his arrival.
7. In spite of poor health she worked well.
8. It being very cold we can not go out.
9. Because of his good manners every one likes him.
10. In spite of adversity he did not lose heart.
11. All stood up on seeing the principal.
12. In the event of King's death, the prince will succeed.
13. With a view to supplement his income he took up a part-time job.
14. He wants rest after such a hard work.
15. This wall is too high to climb.

EXERCISE 69

In each of the following sentences replace each adverb clause by an adverb or an adverb phrase :

1. The mayor has called me that he may help me.
2. Although he is poor yet he is contented.
3. When the principal entered the classroom, he saw a noisy scene.
4. The commando crawled as a snake does.
5. We are glad that the patient has recovered.
6. He worked so hard that he got very good marks.

7. She employed me because you had recommended me.
8. He is kind to you because you are kind to him.
9. The soldiers fought as heroes do.
10. You have been unwell since you returned from London.
11. When it is dark the birds go to their nests.
12. When he comes I shall inform him.
13. The Indian soldiers gave their lives in war that the countrymen could live.
14. He speaks low because he is weak.
15. We were astonished when we heard your strange voice.

Adjective Clause

An **Adjective clause** is a group of words which has a subject and a Predicate of its own and does the work of an adjective.

An Adjectives clause is introduced by relative pronouns — who, which, that, but and relative adverbs — where when, why.

1. This is the book *which he gave me.*
2. She is the woman *whom we respect.*
3. The reason *why he did it* is not clear.
4. The time *when the train will arrive* is not known.
5. The house *where you stayed* is not far off.
6. The man *who invited you to diner* is my friend.
7. There is no one *but loves Sonu* (There is no one who does not love Sonu).

Note. Relative adverbs — why, when, where — used in the sentences above are also used in the adverb clauses but in the above sentences they are used to make Adjective clauses. In the above sentences they answer which reason ? which time ? and which house ?

Note. Sometimes a Relative Pronoun may introduce a coordinate clause but it may appear as adjective clause; as,

She met Sohan who gave her a gift.

'Who gave her a gift' may appear to be an adjective clause but this sentence in no way is describing the noun 'Sohan'. This sentence should actually mean She met Sohan and he gave her a gift.

EXERCISE 70

Pick out the adjective clauses in the following sentences and say what noun or pronoun they qualify :

1. This is the watch which he presented me.
2. Students who work hard are liked by the teachers.

3. Uneasy lies the head that wears the crown.
4. She has typed the letter which you gave her.
5. She lives in the house where she was born.
6. Please complete the work which I gave you.
7. The time when he will come is not known.
8. The reason why he did this is not clear.
9. This is the book which you wanted to purchase.
10. God helps those who help themselves.
11. He never does anything which is praiseworthy.
12. You are telling a tale which is very interesting.
13. He that climbs too high is sure to fall.
14. The time which is lost will never come back.
15. I have received the letter which he had posted.
16. Men who are honest and sincere are trusted.
17. Those who take regular exercise have no need of a physician.
18. Those who boast do little.
19. He who is righteous need not fear anyone.
20. You should do the work which your teacher gave you.
21. The idea which he proposed was liked by all.
22. I love all creatures which are made by God.
23. This is the path which will lead to your ruins.
24. He is the person who will harm none.
25. Persons who lead simple life experience bliss.

EXERCISE 71

Supply suitable Adjective Clauses in the following sentences :

1. I know the way ....
2. She is the girl ....
3. This is the book ....
4. Students .... will be punished.
5. I have lost the book ....
6. We shall purchase the house ....
7. People ....do not suffer.
8. I read a story ....
9. We saw a movie ....
10. She knows the person ....
11. She sold the house ....
12. The books .... were liked by every one.

EXERCISE 72

In each of the following sentences, replace each adjective phrase by an adjective clause :

1. A town with industries has many workers.
2. The time of her arrival is uncertain.
3. A man of courage is admired by all.
4. He told us the time of the meeting.
5. The snow on the higher reaches of the mountains will not melt.
6. The time of Prime Minister's arrival is near.
7. Do you know the way leading to the cave ?
8. This is the temple built by Birlas.
9. You purchased everything of your choice.
10. The people in the remote areas do not have access to many facilities.

EXERCISE 73

In the following sentences, replace adjective clauses by adjectives or adjective phrases :

1. The house which is purchased by him is very beautiful.
2. The labourers who are working in these fields hail from Bihar.
3. This is the city which has many industries.
4. She knows the way which leads to the old fort.
5. The boy who is standing in the front row, is my cousin.
6. The employees who were on strike were suspended.
7. The book which has green jacket is a classic.
8. The driver who was drunk has been arrested.
9. The dacoits who robbed the bank have been arrested.
10. Men who are honest, sincere and hardworking are trusted.

Noun Clause

A **Noun Clause** is a group of words which contains a **Subject** and **Predicate** of its own and it does the work of a noun. A noun clause answers the question — 'what' ? as,

We hope *that we shall win the match.*

The group of words 'that we will win the match' contains a Subject and Predicate of its own and answers the question — hope what ? It is therefore a Noun Clause.

A Noun Clause can be —

1. The subject of a verb.
2. The object of a transitive verb.

3. The object of a preposition.

4. In apposition to a Noun or Pronoun.

5. The complement of a verb of incomplete predication.

1. Noun Clause as a Subject of a Verb :

   (i) *That he will pass* is not certain.

   (ii) *Why she visits this place* is a mystery.

   (iii) *What he says* is not true.

   (iv) *Whether he will come* seems uncertain.

2. Noun Clause as an object to a Transitive verb :

   (i) He said *that he would come in time.*

   (ii) I can not say *when he will come.*

   (iii) She asked me *what I wanted.*

   (iv) He said *that he would attend the office.*

3. Noun Clause as an object to a preposition :

   (i) We should listen to *what they say.*

   (ii) There was no meaning in *what he said.*

   (iii) The students should pay attention to *what the principal says.*

4. Noun Clause in apposition to a noun or pronoun :

   (i) His belief *that there is no God* is not true.

   (ii) The Captain's idea *that we must sail* was appreciated.

   (iii) The fear *that the storm would strike* was baseless.

5. Noun Clause as the complement of a verb of incomplete predication.

   (i) His fear was *that you would not come in* time.

   (ii) This is *how he solves the sums.*

   (iii) This was *how he behaved.*

EXERCISE 74

Point out the Noun Clauses in the following sentences :

1. She does not know what I want.
2. He says that he will pass.
3. The boys said that they would not go out.
4. I wish to see what you have purchased.
5. I know that you will work hard.
6. Do you know what he said ?
7. I thought that you would invite him to the party.

8. He spends what he earns.
9. We paid full attention to what the teacher said.
10. That he should say such words is very strange.
11. He knows that you are teaching in this school.
12. What I like most in him is his courage.
13. That she left her husband is known to us.
14. I don't understand how long he wants to remain unmarried.
15. We should have confidence in what we say.
16. His fear is that he will lose his job.
17. The question is whether I should attend the function or not.
18. My belief is that discipline and hardwork bring success.
19. Do you have any idea about where he has gone ?
20. There is no point in what you say.

EXERCISE 75

Complete the following blanks by adding suitable Noun Clauses :

1. He said ....
2. This is ....
3. I wonder ....
4. You don't know ....
5. Did you hear .... ?
6. .... is not known.
7. We listened to ....
8. .... is an open secret.
9. I can't understand ....
10. John Keats said ....
11. I am not sure ....
12. He told me ....
13. .... is a mystery.
14. We are aware ....
15. She must know ....

EXERCISE 76

In each of the following sentences replace the words in italics by suitable Noun Clauses :

1. He knows *of my success.*
2. The weather office predicted *a change of weather.*
3. We had completely forgotten *about your arrival.*
4. *The reason of his failure* is known to all of us.
5. The judge found *the prisoner guilty.*
6. The accused *admitted his guilt.*
7. We always hope *for his prosperity.*
8. I know *your love for me.*
9. The doctors expect *an improvement in his health.*
10. *Your arrival* was least expected.

EXERCISE 77

In each of the following sentences replace each Noun Clause by a Noun or a Noun Phrase :

1. I hope *that he will pass the test.*
2. He believes in *what I say.*
3. The doctor is hopeful *that you will recover.*
4. I don't know *where he lives.*
5. It is very unfortunate *that she died so young.*
6. He had predicted *that you would succeed.*
7. He said *that he was preoccupied.*
8. They knew *that I would reach in time.*
9. *That she will obey every one* is known to me.
10. He admitted *that he was guilty.*

21

Structural Classification of Sentences

Sentences can be divided into four classes from **structural** point of view as,

1. Simple Sentence
2. Compound Sentence
3. Complex Sentence
4. Compound-Complex (or Double Sentences)

1. **Simple Sentence.** A simple Sentence has only **one Subject** and **one Predicate**. It has only **one Finite Verb**; as,

(i) She went to market.
(ii) I shall attend the function.
(iii) The students have done their homework.
(iv) The sun sets in the west.
(v) Man is a social animal.
(vi) Brevity is the soul of wit.

2. **Compound Sentence.** A compound sentence consists of **two or more Co-ordinate clauses**; as,

(i) I was tired and I rested.
(ii) I went to market and purchased a television.
(iii) You tried hard but could not succeed.
(iv) We went to Delhi and visited Qutab Minar.

Note. All the clauses of a compound sentence are of the equal rank.

Sometimes the subject is omitted in the second coordinate clause as in sentences (ii) (iii) and (iv) above.

3. **Complex sentence.** A complex sentence consists of **one Main clause** and **one or more Subordinate clause**; as,

(i) I don't know where he lives.

(ii) She went abroad after she had completed her graduation.

(iii) If you work hard you will pass.

(iv) He rested when he was tired.

Subordinate Clauses

The Subordinate clauses have already been discussed. They are :

(i) Adverbial clause

(ii) Adjective clause

(iii) Noun clause

Note. A complex sentence may have any or all the subordinate clauses, besides having one Principal or Main clause.

EXERCISE 78

State which of the following sentences are Simple, Compound and Complex. In the case of a compound sentence, separate the Coordinating clauses and the Conjunction(s). If a sentence is Complex, separate the Main clause and the Subordinate clause or clauses :

1. She asked me where I was going.
2. The children are paying.
3. She goes to temple to worship.
4. He went to market and purchased books.
5. She said that she would come.
6. She knew that I would help her.
7. The answer which you wrote was not correct.
8. Some people live to eat but some eat to live.
9. The boy who is standing in the corner is my cousin.
10. Although he worked hard, he did not pass.
11. That he would cheat us was not expected.
12. Pay attention and note down the points.
13. A guest is not liked if he stays for a long time.
14. Sonu passed but Monu failed.
15. He went abroad to do higher studies.

22

Analysis of Simple Sentence

We have already examined that a sentence is a **group of words** which gives **complete meaning** and a sentence contains a **Subject** and **Predicate**.

The Subject in a sentence may consist of **one word** or **several words**. The chief word in the subject is called the **Subject word** or **Simple subject**.

Subject word or Simple subject. A noun, a word or a group of words that does the work of a noun is called the Subject word.

1. Words used as subjects.
   (i) Noun : *Men* are mortal.
   (ii) Pronoun : *She* will attend the function.
   (iii) An Adjective used as a Noun : *The old* have no where to go.
   (iv) To-infinitive : *To err* is human.
   (v) Gerund : *Swimming* is a good exercise.
   (vi) Phrase : *A friend in need* is a friend indeed.

The Subject word must be qualified by an Adjective or an equivalent word and we call it an attribute or enlargement.

Many words can be used as an attribute or enlargement.

Enlargement or Attribute

A word or a group of words which does the work of an Adjective or an Adjective equivalent is known as an Enlargement or Attribute.

1. Words used as attributes
   (i) *Article*
   A boy is flying kites.
   (ii) *Adjective*
   Honest persons are trusted.
   (iii) A noun in Possessive case or Possessive Adjective.
   Your book is here.
   Sonu's shirt is here.

(iv) A noun or phrase in apposition.
Suneeta, a *social worker* lives here.

(v) An Emphatic pronoun.
I *myself* gave you money.

(vi) A Participle used as an Adjective.
Barking does seldom bite.

(vii) A prepositional phrase.
Birds *of the same feather* flock together.

(viii) To infinitive
Your willingness *to help the poor* is good.

(ix) An Adjectival phrase.
The principal, *considerate as ever*, pardoned me.

Predicate

The essential word in the Predicate is a verb and it is often modified by an Adverb or an Adverb equivalent which is called the **Adverbial Qualification**.

Words used as Adverbial Qualification.

(i) *Adverb*
She spoke *politely*.

(ii) *Adverbial phrase*
She ate her food *in a hurry*.

(iii) *Present and Past participles used as Adverbs.*
(a) He went away *crying*.
(b) She looked *disturbed*.

(iv) *'To' infinitive*
They started *to climb*.

(v) *An Adverbial object.*
She came *home*.

(vi) *An absolute phrase*
The show, *having ended*, we came back.

Object

When a verb in the Predicate is a Transitive verb, it must have an object to give complete meaning.

Words used an object.

(i) *Noun*
She brought *mangoes.*

(ii) *Pronoun*
All love *her.*

(iii) An Adjective used as Noun.
We must help *the needy.*

(iv) *'To' infinitive*
She wanted *to write.*

(v) *Gerund*
She loves *reading.*

(vi) A phrase
She requested me *to solve the sum.*

Kinds of object. There are two kinds of objects.

(i) Direct object
(ii) Indirect object

Direct object : She brought *mangoes.*
Indirect object : She taught *us* English.

Complement. When the predicate contains verb of Incomplete Predication, it requires a word to complete the meaning. The word which completes the meaning of the verb is called Complement.

The main verbs of incomplete predication are be, seem, appear, look, become, grow, feel.

Complement. A word that is required to complete the meaning of an intransitive verb is called a complement.

Words used as complement.

(i) *Noun*
She is a *lawyer.*

(ii) *Adjective*
He looks *handsome.*

(iii) *Pronoun*
The solution is *this.*

(iv) *Present Participle*
This poem appears *boring.*

(v) *'To' infinitive*
The movie is *to begin.*

(v) *Adverb*

Problems are *everywhere.*

(vi) *Phrase*

My brother is *in the field.*

Kinds of complements. There are two types of complements :

(i) Subject Complement

(ii) Object complement

(a) **Subject complement.** A complement which describes the subject is called subject complements; as,

She looks *worried.*

(b) **Object complement.** A complement which describes the object is called an object complement; as,

(i) They elected him *captain.*

(ii) I consider you *a dishonest person.*

First stage. Note the Analysis of the following simple sentences :

1. The girls are dancing.
2. The sun sets in the west.
3. The parents named him Chirag.
4. She gave me a present.
5. I am learning grammar.

S.No.	Subject	Predicate
1.	The girls	are dancing
2.	The sun	sets in the west
3.	The parents	named him Chirag
4.	She	gave me a present
5.	I	am learning grammar

Second stage. Note the analysis of the following simple sentences.

1. She taught us English.
2. I gave him a present.
3. Father wrote me a letter.
4. I leant him money.
5. She showed me the album.

S. No.	Subject	Verb	Indirect object	Direct object
1.	She	taught	us	English
2.	I	gave	him	a present
3.	Father	wrote	me	a letter
4.	I	lent	him	money
5.	She	showed	me	the album

Third stage. Note the analysis of the following Simple sentences :

1. The weather became fine.
2. Sunita is a doctor.
3. You look worried.
4. Your parents are here.
5. My wife is to arrive.

S. No.	Subject		Predicate	
	Attribute	Subject word	Verb	Subject complement
1.	The	weather	became	fine
2.		Sunita	is	a teacher
3.		You	look	worried
4.	Your	parents	are	here
5.	My	wife	is	to arrive

Fourth stage. Note the analysis of the following simple sentences :

1. She kept me waiting.
2. The judge found him guilty.
3. I found Ramu dishonest.
4. His misconduct put him in a fix.
5. My mother compelled me to stay.

S. No.	Subject		Predicate		
	Attribute	Subject	Verb	Object	Complement
1.		She	kept	me	waiting
2.	The	judge	found	him	guilty
3.		I	found	Ramu	dishonest
4.	His	misconduct	put	him	in a fix
5.	My	mother	compelled	me	to stay

Fifth stage. Note the analysis of the following simple sentences :

1. He looked exhausted after the race.
2. My father's cousin helped me in many ways.
3. The physician examined the sick patients carefully.
4. She has been teaching Sonu grammar.
5. All the sailors appointed him their Captain.

S.No.	Subject		Predicate					
	Attribute	Subject word	Verb	Indirect object	Direct object	Subject Comple-ment	Object Comple-ment	Adverbial Qualific-ation
1.		He	looked			exhaused		after the race
2.	My father's	cousin	helped	me				in many ways
3.	The	physician	examined	the sick patients				carefully
4.		she	has been teaching	Sonu	grammar			
5.	All the	sailors	appointed	him			their captain	

EXERCISE 79

Analyse the following Simple sentences :

1. The boys are flying kites.
2. She wants to learn French.
3. They found him guilty.
4. She bought the girl a doll.
5. His father is a teacher.
6. A stitch in time saves nine.
7. His attitude is quite clear.
8. Shakespeare, the playwright wrote Othello.
9. They elected him captain.
10. The guests have arrived.
11. The students, anxious to pass, worked hard.
12. Birds of same feathers flock together.
13. The fire spread in all directions.
14. Bad habits die hard.
15. She called me again.

16. The village life improved his health.
17. They spoke in soft manner.
18. The old man is dead.
19. She teaches us English.
20. He seems worried.
21. Nothing will make him happy.
22. The weather became clear.
23. We saw the splinters falling.
24. All the members appointed him the secretary.
25. The teacher evaluated the answer sheets carefully.

23

Analysis of Compound (Double and Multiple) Sentence

A **compound sentence** is made up of two or more main clauses or Independent sentences which are joined together by coordinating conjunctions; as,

He climbed high and he fell down

The above sentence consists of two independent clauses.

Each Main clause of a compound sentence is either A Simple sentence or A Complex sentence.

A sentence is called 'Double' which is made of two main clauses and 'Multiple' if it is made of more than two Main clauses.

While analyzing a compound sentence we should analyse each of the Main clause separately and point out the conjunctions by which they are connected. If there is a 'contracted sentence', the 'omitted words' should be supplied before analyzing the sentence.

Study the following sentences :

(i) The soldiers were tired and they went to the rest room.

(ii) The night was dark and we were far from home.

(iii) The sky was clear, the winds had gone down and the hot sun was shining brightly in the north.

We may analyse the above sentences and put them in the 'tabular form' as under.

Clauses	Coonective	Subject			Predicate	
		Simple Subject	Attribute of Subject	Verb	Complement	Adverbial Qualification
A. The soldiers were tired		Solidier	The	were	tired	
B. They went to the rest room (Coordinate with A)	and	They	went			to the rest room

Clauses	Connective	Subject			Predicate	
		Simple Subject	Attribute of Subject	Verb	Complement	Adverbial Qualification
A. The night was dark		night	The	was	dark	
B. We were far from home (Coordinate with A)	and	we		were	far from home	
A. The sky was clear		sky	The	was	clear	
B. The winds had gone down		winds	The	had gone		down
C. The hot sun was shining brightly in north.		sun	(i) The (ii) hot	was shining		(i) brightly (ii) in the north

The Principal was sad and the students stood.

As if they were changed into blocks of stone.

Note. This sentence is made up of two co-ordinate clauses, one of which is a Simple sentence and the other a Complex sentence. Hence it is a Compound or 'Double' sentence.

Sentence or clause	Kind of sentence or clause	Connective	Subject		Predicate		
			Simple Subject	Attribute of Subject	Verb	Complement	Adverbial Qualification
A. The Principal was sad	Simple sentence		Principal	The	was	sad	
B. The students stood as if they were changed into blocks of stone	Complex sentence (Co-ordinate with A)	and	students	The	stood		as if they were changed into blocks of stone
C. As if they were changed into blocks of stone	Adverb clause Modifying 'stood' in B	as if	they		were changed		into blocks of stone

They asked him how he received money but he refused to answer.

In the above sentence, the first clause is a Complex Sentence and the second clause is a Simple Sentence. Its analysis is given below :

Sentence or clause	Kind of sentence or clause	Connective	Subject	Predicate		
			Simple subject	Verb	Object	Complement
They asked him how he received money	Complex sentence Noun clause Object to verb asked	 how	they he	asked received	him money	
He refused to answer	Simple sentence	but	he	refused		to answer

EXERCISE 80

Analyse the following compound sentences : (Double, Multiple)

1. The chief guest was happy and he gave us presents.
2. He is a hard worker and he succeeds in his efforts.
3. He was sure that he would succeed but he failed.
4. He entered the house and greeted everyone but he did not speak.
5. He was a gentleman and all loved him.
6. The workers felt tired and they went to their rest room.
7. I know that he will not help you but you believe otherwise.
8. The students worked hard, they took the test and they passed.

24 Analysis of Complex Sentence

While analyzing a Complex sentence, the first step is to find out the 'Principal clause'. The next step is to find out the 'Subordinate clause' or 'clauses', showing the relation which each clause has to the 'Principal clause'.

Study the analysis of the following Complex sentence carefully :

When he was tired, the wounded soldier, who was walking limpingly said that he wanted rest.

1. The wounded soldier said → 'Principal clause'.
2. when he was tired → Adverb clause of time modifying the verb said in No. 1.
3. who was walking limpingly → Adjective clause modifying the Noun soldier in No. 1.
4. That he wanted rest → Noun clause object to the verb 'said in No. 1.

Following is the detailed analysis of each clause in Tabular Form :

No.	Connective	Subject		Predicate			
		Subject	Attribute	Verb	Object	Complement	Adverbial Qualification
1.	soldier		(i) the (ii) wounded	said			
2.	When	he		was		tired	
3.		who		was walking			limpingly
4.	That	he		wanted		rest.	

Study the analysis of the following complex sentence.

I know that she has typed the letter which you sent here.

1. I know → principal clause.
2. That she has typed the letter → Noun clause object of the verb 'know' in No. 1.

3. Which you sent here → Adjective clause qualifying the Noun letter in No. 2.

Following is the detailed analysis of each clause in the Tabular Form.

No.	Connective	Subject	Predicate		
			Verb	Object	Adverbial Qualification
1.		I	Know		
2.	That	she	has typed	the letter	
3.	Which	you	sent		here

Study the Analysis of the following Complex sentence :

We know the men who said that they would attend the meeting.

1. We know the men — Principal clause.
2. Who said — Adjective clause modifying the Noun 'men' in No. 1.
3. That they would attend the meeting — Noun clause object to the verb 'said' in No. 2.

Following is the detailed analysis of each clause in the Tabular Form :

No.	Connective	Subject	Predicate	
			Verb	Object
1.		we	know	the men
2.		who	said	
3.	that	they	would attend	the meeting

EXERCISE 81

Analyse the following sentences :

1. We who are lucky enough to live in this enlightened century hardly realize how our forefathers suffered from their belief in the existence of mysterious and malevolent forces.
2. We tried to listen to what he said.
3. The boys who are sitting in the front rows shall be given awards.
4. If you work hard you are sure to pass.
5. Every one who knows him is sure that he is a good person.
6. We hope that we can convince him that he is wrong.
7. The book that he gave me was lost when I was travelling.
8. I knew that those boisterous people would disturb all who were present in the meeting.

9. I know that hard work, sincerity and honesty are the virtues of the righteous man who never treads a wrong path.
10. If you had studied sincerely, you would not have failed.
11. History says that Mirabai, when she was given a glass of poison continued to talk to her nurse who was standing near her, as she drank it.
12. The man who does not think that the goodness of every living creature is his goodness, is a fool.
13. They had been only a few weeks in the organization when it was declared that the trainees had to leave.
14. One who is sincere and disciplined faces the least problems in life as these are very important traits of one's character.
15. Men fear death as children fear to go in dark.
16. The robbers who broke into the bank have been arrested.
17. I don't know how I should solve this sum which is very difficult.
18. As his elder daughter was a genius, he sent her to city so that she could pursue higher studies.
19. No one helps the person who is a swindler for, this would lead to many problems.
20. The house where you lived is up for sale.
21. You should listen carefully to what I say.
22. Can you tell who wrote Hamlet ?
23. They set a strong guard lest any one should escape when it was dark.
24. I think that she has typed all the letters which you gave her when she was here.
25. The children feel very happy when they see a rainbow as it presents a very beautiful sight.
26. Whenever he was angry, he spoke against the system which, according to him was corrupt, inefficient and bureaucratic.
27. Man who has lived life beyond fifty is sure to believe that life is not a bed of roses.

25

Articles

The Articles are 'a', 'an' and 'the'

'A' and 'An' are called Indefinite Articles.

They are so called because they don't refer to any particular person or thing; as

(i) *A girl* (any girl)

(ii) *A boy* (any boy)

(iii) *A movie* (any movie)

'The' is called Definite Article as it points out some particular person or thing; as,

(i) *I met the girl.* Meaning that some particular girl.

(ii) *We saw the movie.* Meaning that some particular movie.

Article A

Article 'a' is used before 'Singular Countable Nouns' beginning with 'Consonants'; as,

A boy, a table, a girl, a pen

Article 'an' is used before Singular Countable Nouns beginning with vowels; as, an umbrella, an ox, an egg, an almirah.

Note. The choice between 'a' and 'an' is determined by sound. Thus, we say 'an hour', 'a union', a university, a 'European', 'a useful thing', 'a one-rupee note', 'a one-eyed man'.

We say 'an hour' because though 'h' is a consonant, it is not pronounced. Similarly, we say 'a European', because the pronunciation of the word 'European' is 'Yuropean' and as 'Y' is a consonant, article 'a' is used.

Article 'the'

The definite Article 'the' is used :

1. When a **particular person or thing is spoken of**, or which has already been referred to; as,

(i) I know *the way.*

(ii) Did you give him *the* message ?

(iii) *The* present you gave him is very beautiful.

2. When a *'Singular Noun'* is meant to represent a whole class; as,

(i) *The* dog is a faithful animal.

(ii) *The* tiger is a fearless animal.

Note. The nouns 'man' and 'woman', when representing the whole class don't have either article; as,

(i) Man is born to experience joys and sorrows.

(ii) Woman is man's better half.

3. With names of rivers, seas, oceans, gulfs, group of islands and mountain ranges; as,

The Ganges
The Yamuna
The Beas
The Red Sea
The Indian Ocean
The Alps

4. Before the names of scriptures; as,

The Gita
The Mahabharata
The Ramayana
The Quran

5. Before Common Nouns which are names of things unique of their kinds; as,

The sun, the moon, the earth, the sky

6. Before a Proper Noun only when it is qualified by Adjective.

The great Hamlet
The immortal Charles Dickens

7. Before the superlative Degree of Adjective; as,

(i) He is *the best* player of our school.

(ii) You have given *the best* answer.

(iii) She is *the most* beautiful girl of our class.

8. Before ordinals; as,

(i) *The third* page of this book is torn.

(ii) 'She is *the first* Indian woman to win a silver medal in the Asian Games.

9. Before musical instruments; as,

I can play *the guitar.*

10. Before an Adjective when the noun is understood; as,

The rich are not always happy.

11. Before an Adverb with Comparative; as,

(i) *The more* you get, the more you want.

(ii) *The higher* you go, *the cooler* it is.

Omission of 'the' Article

'The article is not used.

1. Before a Common Noun used in its 'widest sense'; as,

(i) Man is mortal.

(ii) What kind of man are you ?

2. Before Names of Materials; as,

Diamond is a precious stone.

3. Before Proper Nouns; as,

Delhi is the Capital of India.

Note. When 'the' article is used before proper Nouns, they become 'common nouns'; as,

Kalidas is *the Shakespeare* of India.

4. Before Abstract Nouns used in a general sense; as,

(i) Wisdom should be dear to all.

(ii) Honesty is the best policy.

Note. When an Abstract Noun is qualified by an Adjective or Adjective phrase, it may have 'the' article; as,

The wisdom of Shakespeare is well known.

5. Before languages; as,

She is learning French.

6. Before 'college', 'school', 'church', 'bed', 'hospital', 'market', 'prison', when these places are visited or used for their primary purposes; as,

(i) She has been admitted in hospital.

(ii) He goes to church on Sunday.

(iii) One should not stay in bed after sunrise.

Note. 'the' article is used with these words when they are referred as 'Definite'; as,

(i) He came to see me in *the hospital.*

(ii) *The school* will remain closed tomorrow.

7. Before names of relations; as,

   Father, mother, aunt, uncle

8. Before 'Predicative Noun' denoting a position held at one time by one person; as,

   He was elected *Secretary* of the Group Housing Society.

9. In certain 'Phrases' consisting of 'Transitive verb' followed by its 'object'; as,

   To give ear, to set sail, to lose heart, to leave office, to catch fire.

10. In certain phrases consisting of 'Prepositions' 'followed by' their objects; as,

    At break, at lunch, at sunset, by air, on foot, under ground, on ground.

EXERCISE 82

Fill in 'a' or 'an' or 'the' according to requirement in the following sentences :

1. Haridwar is .... holy city.
2. We discussed .... matter seriously.
3. She is .... honour to her family.
4. Sonu got .... best prize.
5. French is .... difficult language.
6. While there is life, there is .... hope.
7. She has come without .... umbrella.
8. I bought .... horse .... ox and .... cow.
9. You are .... untidy boy.
10. Sanskrit is not .... easy language.
11. .... Ganges is .... holy river.
12. This is .... longest bridge.
13. We sailed to .... south.
14. French is .... language of .... people of France.
15. .... umbrella which you have brought is useless in such .... storm.
16. I know .... way to .... nearest restaurant.
17. .... Himalayas are .... highest mountains in .... world.
18. Gold is .... very useful metal.
19. She waited for me for .... hour.

20. She has lost .... purse I gave her.
21. We met .... one-eyed man in the fair.
22. I met .... European in the party.
23. She is .... university lecturer.
24. How beautiful .... sky looks !
25. The saint has .... wonderful lamp.
26. .... lotus is .... beautiful flower.
27. You returned after .... hour.
28. He is .... fool to utter these words.
29. Which is .... longest river in India ?
30. The child found .... egg in the nest.
31. .... lion is .... king of beasts.
32. .... sun shone brightly and we got .... glimpse of its beauty.
33. Honest persons speak .... truth.

EXERCISE 83

Insert 'Articles' where necessary :

1. Sun sets in west.
2. Do not look gift horse in mouth.
3. Sun melts snow.
4. She is poor woman.
5. He is intelligent boy.
6. Have you never seen camel ?
7. Draw map of Delhi.
8. What beautiful scene this is !
9. The river was spanned by iron bridge.
10. Sun did not rise till ten.
11. Like true sportsman you should give enemy fair play.
12. There is nothing like staying at this place for comfort.
13. I do not use this sort of medicine.
14. Time makes worst enemies friends.
15. I have not seen her since she was infant.
16. They started late in afternoon.
17. Has she been told about accident ?
18. He who dies in great cause becomes immortal.
19. She has not seen me since I was child.
20. May I have pleasure of your company ?
21. This is one of best books written by Kalidas.

22. They went to church to attend mass.
23. Do you know answers to questions ?
24. Get K.G. of ghee from nearest store.
25. I have seen movie when I was boy.
26. Where did you buy present ?
27. Who wishes to walk with me ?
28. I have solved all sums.
29. Carry on work in my absence.
30. Cylon is island.
31. The teacher gave me easy sum to solve.
32. London is on Thames.
33. You have scored best marks.
34. This is easiest sum which all students of class can solve without least problem.
35. Qutab Minar is famous historical monument.
36. He seems to be hollow from inside.

26

Agreement of the Verb with the Subject

The 'verb' should agree with the **'Subject'** in **'Number'** and **'Person'**.

1. Two or more singular subjects joined by 'and' take a verb in the Plural; as,

(i) Sohan and his brother *have* come.

(ii) Books and pens *are* on the table.

(iii) Ram and Sham *are* colleagues.

(iv) Sohan and I *take* exercise regularly.

2. When two singular Nouns 'refer to the same person' or thing, the verb has to be, 'singular'; as,

(i) My friend and guide *has* arrived.

(ii) The Captain and doctor *is* examining the patient.

3. When different persons are referred to, 'the' article is used before each noun and the verb is 'plural'; as,

(i) The poet and the teacher *have* passed away.

(ii) The head girl and the prefect *have* arrived.

4. If two objects together 'express one idea', the verb may be 'singular' as,

(i) Slow and steady *wins* the race.

(ii) Bread and butter *is* his only food.

When 'each' and 'every' are used before the singular subjects, the verb is 'singular'; as,

(i) Each day and each night *brings* joy.

(ii) Every man, woman and child *was* present in the festival.

5. Two or more Singular Subjects, connected by 'or', 'nor', 'either', or 'neither' 'nor' take a 'singular verb'; as,

(i) No man or woman *was* left unattended.

(ii) Neither Sunita nor *her* friend *was* given an award.

(iii) Either you or your daughter *has* collected the report card.

6. When the subjects joined by 'or', 'nor' are of different number, the 'verb' *must be plural* and the plural subject must be placed 'before the verb'; as,

(i) Ramu or his friends *have* done this work.

(ii) Neither the secretary nor the members were present in the meeting.

7. When the subjects joined by 'or', 'nor' are of different persons, the verb should agree in person with the one nearest to it'; as,

(i) Either you or I *am* to blame.

(ii) Neither she nor you *are* to blame.

8. When subjects differing in number or person or both are connected by 'and', the verb must be 'in the plural'; as,

(i) He and I *have* come.

(ii) My mother and I *have* worked hard.

(iii) You and he *are* always present.

(iv) You and I *have* completed our work.

9. A collective noun takes a 'Singular verb' when the collection is thought of 'as a whole'; a plural verb', when the individuals of which it is composed are *considered*; as,

(i) Parliament *is* in session.

(ii) The mob *has* set this building on fine.

(iii) The committee *has* elected its secretary.

(iv) The crew *was* large.

(v) The crew *were* asked to report on time.

10. 'Nouns' which are 'Plural in form', but 'singular in meaning' take 'Singular verb'; as,

(i) No news *is* good news.

(ii) Politics *is* the last refuge of a scoundrel.

(iii) Mathematics *is* an easy subject.

11. Nouns which are singular in 'form' but plural 'in meaning' take a Plural verb; as,

Two dozen of eggs *cost* forty rupees.

12. When a plural Noun comes between a singular subject and its verb, care should be taken to ensure that the verb is 'not made to agree with the nearest plural noun but the 'real subject'; as,

(i) Each of the girls *was* given a present.

(ii) Neither of the members *was* present in the conference.

(iii) The quality of the mangoes *is* not good.

(iv) One of my best friends *has* arrived.

(v) If the delivery of clothes *is* not taken in time, we shall not compensate the loss.

(vi) Each of the sisters *was* present in the hall.

13. Words connected to a singular subject by 'as well as', 'together with', 'in addition to' etc. do not affect the 'number of the verb'; as these words are parenthetical; as,

(i) Ram along with his sisters *was* present.

(ii) She, together with her parents *has* arrived.

(iii) The commander, with all his soldiers, has marched. forward.

(iv) Reena as well as Sita and Savitri *likes* oranges.

14. If the subject of the verb is a 'Relative Pronoun', the verb should agree in number and person with the 'Antecedent of the Relative'; as,

(i) We who *are* here should help her.

(ii) I who *am* tired, will take rest.

(iii) She who *is* my friend is doing her MBA.

EXERCISE 84

Supply a verb in agreement with its subject in the following sentences :

1. The Arabian Nights .... a great work of fiction.
2. The author and teacher .... given a prize.
3. One of my best friends .... arrived.
4. Two and two .... four.
5. The difficulty of crossing the river .... great.
6. Each of the guests .... present in the function.
7. Neither you nor I .... mistaken.
8. She and you .... the birds of the same feathers.
9. Neither his father nor his mother .... alive.
10. Milk as well as bread and butter .... found in this shop.
11. Twenty steps .... not a great distance.
12. Sita as well as her cousin .... come.
13. The criminal and the terrorist .... been absconding.
14. It is I who .... behind your success.
15. Hundred rupees .... an excessive price for this book.

16. Each of the criminals .... absconding.
17. Neither of the students .... good at mathematics.
18. Which of the pens .... yours ?
19. Shakespeare is one of the greatest dramatists who .... ever lived.
20. Parsimony as well as extravagance .... to be avoided.
21. Formation of paragraphs .... important in letter writing.
22. To borrow and then not to return .... dishonest.
23. None of the athletes .... able to qualify for the Olympic Games.
24. Neither of the examinees .... able to solve this sum.
25. She, in addition to her colleagues .... on leave.
26. The long and short of the matter .... this.
27. One's joy or sorrow .... in one's hands.
28. Good thought as well as good deed .... to be appreciated.
29. The commander along with his soldiers .... able to climb the rock.
30. It is he who .... done this work.
31. Early to bed and early to rise .... a man healthy wealthy and wise.
32. Neither Sheela nor her parents .... present in the parents-teacher meeting.
33. Either the girl or her friends .... done this work.
34. The Colonel and Officer Commanding .... involved in the victory.
35. Each of the minerals .... found in India.
36. The quality of these mangoes .... good.
37. The Lt. Governor, with his secretary .... arrived.
38. The wages of sin .... death.
39. This news .... not true.
40. Politics .... not liked much by science students.

27 Determiners

A Determiner is a word that, comes 'before a Noun and limits its meaning'. Apart from Articles (a, an, the), the other most Common Determiners are : any, much, several, few, little, each, every, all, both, either, neither; no, half, my, our, your, his, her, its, their, this that, these, those, one, third etc.

Thus, we can say that **Determiners** include

(i) Articles → (a, an, the)

(ii) Demonstrative Adjectives → (This, that, these, those)

(iii) Possessive Adjectives → (My, our, your her, his, its, their)

(iv) Adjectives of Quantity and Number → (few, the few, a few, little, some, any, much, many, all, both, each, every, either, neither, one, two, three, first, second third, fewer, a lot of, a large number of, a great deal of, a good deal of etc.)

Some, any → 'Some' is used in the Affirmative sentences and **'Any'** in Negative sentences to express quantity; as,

(i) I bought *some* dresses but did not blue *any* sheets.

(ii) She had *some* sugar but did not have *any* milk.

1. Some is used in interrogative sentences when making polite requests.

   (i) Will you give me some oil ?

   (ii) Will you have some more rice ?

2. In conditional sentences; as,

   (i) If there are *any* mangoes in the market, please buy *some.*

3. Use of 'any' in Interrogative or Negative Sentences :

   (i) Did you buy *any* oranges ?

   (ii) Do you have any articles for publishing ?

   (iii) I do not have *any* articles on the latest events.

Each; very; either; neither — 'Each' means one of two things or one of any number exceeding two. Every is used in speaking of some number exceeding two; as,

(i) Each of them was given an award.
(ii) Each of you can solve this sum.
(iii) Every man wants to be happy.

'Either' has two meanings :

(i) One of two or
(ii) each of two that is both.

'Neither' is the Negative of either and means neither the one nor the other.

You can go by *either* way (by one way or the other).
There is sand on *either* side of the bank (both sides).
I looked at *neither* side of the river (neither this side nor the other).

Much; Many : 'Much' denotes *quantity* and 'many' stands for number; as,

(i) Is there *much tea* left in the pot ?
(ii) Were there *many* spectators watching the match ?
(iii) I have not got *much* money.
(iv) They have got *many* counsellors.

Note. Expressions which are given below, may be used instead of 'many'.

Plenty of, a lot of, lots of, a great many, a great number of, a good many, a great many.

Expressions given below can be used instead of much :

A lot of, plenty of, a great deal of, a good deal of, a large quantity of.

Little, a little, the little

'Little is used to denote a negative meaning, which means hardly any, or not much; as,

(i) There is *little* hope of his survival.
(ii) The doctor did *little* to save the patient.

A little : A little has positive meaning and means 'some at least :

(i) There is a little oil left in the pot.
(ii) A little knowledge is a dangerous thing.

The little : the little means some. It can be used both positively and negatively.

The little help which he got was not enough to pass the test. (Negative)
The little money I have is enough to survive (Positive)

Few, a few, the few : Few has a Negative meaning :

(1) No decision was taken in the meeting because *few members* attended it. (hardly any : Negative meaning).

(ii) **The Few** : the few means 'not many'. It has both Positive and Negative meaning.

The few members who came to attend the meeting left soon.

"A few' : A few means some at least : It has a positive meaning.

A few members were present in the meeting.

Less, fewer : *Less* is used with reference to 'quantity' and *fewer* with reference to number; as,

(i) I cannot accept *less* than forty rupees for this item.

(ii) No *fewer* than five thousand persons were present in the rally.

EXERCISE 85

(A) Fill in the blanks with 'Some' or 'Any' :

1. I can accompany you .... time you want.
2. There were .... interesting people in the meeting.
3. They said that they did not have .... fun without us.
4. Did you buy .... new items ? No, I didn't buy ....

(B) ***Fill in the blanks with 'Much' or 'many' :***

1. How .... times have you seen this movie ?
2. How .... money do you need ?
3. There was not .... rain this year.
4. One has to face .... problems in one's life.

(C) ***Fill in the blanks with 'few', 'a few', 'little', 'a little' :***

1. The patient has made .... recovery.
2. I don't expect to pass as I got .... help from tutors.
3. .... money I had was spent in buying medicine.
4. There were .... customers in the shop; for the shopkeeper was relaxing.
5. I am happy because I have made .... progress in my work.
6. .... tourists visited this place this year as there were heavy and incessant rains.
7. .... days holiday will make your mind and body relaxed.

(D) ***Fill in the blanks with 'Each', 'every', 'either', 'neither' :***

1. .... of the examinees was disqualified.
2. You can enter from .... side.
3. .... person was searched thoroughly.
4. .... book will do.
5. .... boy was hopeful.

(E) ***Fill in the blanks with 'less' or 'fewer' :***

1. No .... than ten persons were absent in the office.
2. His income is not .... than ten thousand per month.
3. This gold chain weighs .... than twenty grams.

28

The Sequence of Tenses

The **Sequence of Tenses** is the principle according to which the **Tense of the verb in a Subordinate Clause is used**. The principle applies chiefly to **Adverb Clauses of Purpose and all the Noun Clauses**. If the Principal Clause is in the **Past Tense**, the **Subordinate Clause** is also supposed to be in the **Past Tense**.

Examples

1. He said that he was tired.
2. The jury found that the accused was guilty.
3. She declared that she would resign her job.
4. I knew that you would succeed.
5. The Director hinted that I would get the job.
6. He studied hard so that he could get good marks.
7. They ran fast that they could reach in time.

Exception

There are two exceptions to this rule

(1) If the Subordinate Clause expresses a universal truth, a Past Tense in the Principal Clause, may be followed by a Present Tense; as

1. Our teacher said that honesty is the best policy.
2. Our geography teacher taught us that the earth revolves round the sun.
3. Euclid proved that the three angles of a triangle are equal to two right angles.

(2) When **Than** is used to introduce a Subordinate Clause, it may be followed by any tense, even if the Principal Clause is put in the Past Tense; as,

1. You helped his children more than you help my children.
2. He walked more than he usually walks.
3. He visited this place more than he usually does.
4. The Principal listened to you more attentively than she listens to me.

(3) When the Principal Clause is in the Present or Future Tense, the Subordinate Clause may be put in any tense required by the sense; as,

1. He will say that we were present in the party.
2. You think that I am not the man of my word.
3. He thinks that I shall be present.
4. You think that I disobeyed my parents.

However, if the Subordinate Clause denotes purpose, the verb in the Subordinate Clause is Present or Future; as,

1. We eat so that we may live.
2. He helped the poor that God may bless him

EXERCISE 86

Insert the correct tense of verb in the following sentences :

1. She walks as though she .... a queen. (To be)
2. He waited for me until I .... (To come)
3. You ran as quickly as you .... (Can or Could)
4. The terrorists fled where the police .... not follow. (Can or Could)
5. As the Chairman .... not there, we talked to the Managing Director. (To be)
6. The soldiers advanced as far as they .... (To dare)
7. I stayed at home because I .... not well. (To be)
8. He studied hard so that he .... succeed. (may or might)
9. I told her that I .... come. (will or would)
10. I drove so fast that he .... not overtake me. (can, could)
11. He makes such a noise that I .... not study. (can or could)
12. I lost more than I .... afford. (can or could)
13. He studied hard in order that he .... get success. (may or might)
14. She went abroad so that she .... meet her uncle. (can, could)
15. Wherever the saint .... large crowds gather to listen. (To preach)
16. You did not know it until I .... (To tell)
17. So long as the storm .... we did not go out. (To continue).
18. He does not come here because he .... afraid. (to be)
19. They told us that they .... come. (will or would)
20. The teacher told the students that they ....collect their answer sheets. (can or could)

EXERCISE 87

Fill in the blanks with an appropriate Auxiliary :

1. He said that he .... resign his job.
2. He asked me what my father ....
3. I studied hard that I .... pass the examination.
4. You .... enter only if you have a pass.
5. On the understanding that you return my money soon, you .... get it.
6. He said that he .... admit me.
7. The children made such a noise that we .... not learn our lessons.
8. I asked my mother whether supper .... be ready soon.
9. I wished that I ....scored higher mark.
10. She carried away whatever she .... find in the house.
11. We started early that we ....reach in time.
12. I am so tired that I .... hardly work.
13. She came to me so that she .... meet me.
14. In order that he .... improve his grammar, he engaged a tutor.
15. The soldiers died that the countrymen .... live.

EXERCISE 88

Supply verbs in correct concord in the following complex sentences :

1. When the rain started we .... home.
2. I sold my car because it .... very old.
3. The teacher told the student that he .... wrong.
4. We shall nurse him so that he .... live.
5. Newton discovered that the force of gravitation .... apples fall.
6. Euclid proved that the three angles of a triangle .... equal to two right angles.
7. The judge told the accused that he .... be punished.
8. The teacher said that the next day .... be a holiday.

29

Same Word Used as Different Parts of Speech

It is the function or use that determines to which **Part of Speech** a word belongs in a given sentence.

Following are some of the most important words which may belong to different **'Parts of Speech'** according to the way in which they are used :

About

Adverb	: The child wandered *about* in shorts.
Preposition	: She knows all *about* my family.

Above

Adverb	: Look above.
Preposition	: No one is *above* the law.
Adjective	: Analyse the *above* sentence.
Noun	: Our joys and sorrows come from *above.*

After

Adverb	: I left the class soon *after.*
Preposition	: You take *after* your father.
Adjective	: *After* effects of this medicine are bad.
Conjunction	: I reached the place *after* the meeting was over.

All

Adjective	: *All* persons are present.
Adverb	: Why are you *all* alone?
Pronoun	: *All* praised her achievement.
Noun	: He lost his *all* in gambling.

Any

Adjective	: Are there *any* examinees ?
Pronoun	: Have *any* of you brought the grammar book ?
Adverb	: Was that *any* better ?

As

Adverb	: We ran *as* fast as we could.
Conjunction	: *As* he was not well, he could not teach the class.
Relative Pronoun	: You like the same book *as* I do.

Better

Adjective	: He has got *better* marks.
Adverb	: She knew *better.*
Noun	: Leave this job for your *better.*
Verb	: Try to *better* your performance.

Both

Adjective	: *Both* banks have sand.
Pronoun	: *Both* of you can go.
Conjunction	: *Both* the coach and the player are here.

But

Adverb	: It is *but* (= only) right to apologise.
Preposition	: None *but* (except) Sonu was present.
Conjunction	: He studied hard, *but* could not pass.
Relative Pronoun	: There is no one *but* likes her (= who does not like her)

Down

Adverb	: He went down.
Preposition	: They went *down* the hill.
Adjective	: The *down* train is late by four hours.
Noun	: I have seen many ups and *downs* in my life.
Verb	: The shopkeepers will *down* the shutters.

Either

Adjective	: *Either* book will do.
Pronoun	: *Either* of the book can be reprinted.
Conjunction	: You must *either* work or go.

Else

Conjunction	: Work hard, *else* you will fail.
Adverb	: You can look anywhere *else.*
Adjective	: She has something *else* for me.

Enough

Adverb	: She knew well *enough* what I wanted.
Adjective	: There is time *enough* and to spare.
Noun	: She has had *enough* of that.

Even

Adjective	: The opportunities are *even.*
Verb	: We shall *even* the score.
Adverb	: Do you *even* smoke ?

Except

Verb	: We, if I *except* you, are sincere.
Preposition	: All have come *except* Chirag.
Conjunction	: He did not let me come *except* (= unless) I promised to help him.

For

Preposition	: You can see *for* yourself.
Conjunction	: It may rain, *for* there are dark clouds.

Less

Adjective	: You have done *less* work today.
Adverb	: This place is *less* hot.
Noun	: You must give me five hundred rupees. I shall not be happy with *less.*

Like

Adjective	: You are boys of *like* body and mind.
Preposition	: You should not behave *like* that.
Noun	: We saw your *like* in the park.
Verb	: Children *like* animals.

Little

Adjective	: There is *little* work left to be done.
Noun	: I want but *little* on the earth.
Adverb	: You eat quite *little.*

More

Adjective	: She wants *more* books.
Pronoun	: *More* of you will get work.
Adverb	: You should study *more.*

Much

Adjective	: There is *much* work left to be done.
Pronoun	: *Much* of it is unbelievable.
Adverb	: You need not brag too *much.*

Near

Adverb	: She went *near* and stood.
Preposition	: My house is *near* the market.
Adjective	: You are my *near* relation.
Verb	: The time *nears* and adds to his joy.

Need

Noun	: Our *needs* should be controlled.
Verb	: You *need* not hurry.
Adverb	: You *need* must come.

Neither

Conjunction	: I want *neither* this book nor that.
Adjective	: *Neither* book is good.
Pronoun	: I have invited both but *neither* is expected.

Next

Adjective	: You can call us on *next* Tuesday.
Adverb	: What *next* ?
Preposition	: She was sitting *next* me.
Noun	: You shall hear more in your *next.*

No

Noun	: She will not hear a *no.*
Adverb	: Ram is *no* more.
Adjective	: It is *no* fun.

Once

Adverb	: All old men were young *once.*
Conjunction	: *Once* he enters the hall, we shall be on our feet.
Noun	: I wish that some one would help me for *once.*

Only

Adjective	: It is your *only* chance.
Adverb	: She was *only* hungry.
Conjunction	: Say what you want to say, *only* (= but) allow me to go.

One

Adjective : *One* day all will glide to the grave.
Pronoun : The young *ones* are not allowed to come here.

Over

Noun : Only one *over* is left to be bowled.
Preposition : At forty five a change comes *over* all of us.
Adverb : I read it *over* again.

Right

Verb : You have to *right* your behavior.
Adjective : He is the *right* person for this work
Noun : We must protect our *right*.
Adverb : She stood *right* in my way.

Round

Adjective : Make a *round* hole.
Noun : The trip was a *round* of joys.
Adverb : You must come *round* to my views.
Preposition : The earth revolves *round* the sun.
Verb : They will *round* the whole country.

Since

Preposition : He has been studying *since* morning.
Conjunction : *Since* you are not well, you can go home.
Adverb : She has not met me *since*.

So

Adverb : He is *so* happy.
Conjunction : He was tired, *so* he wanted rest.

Some

Adjective : We have to chalk out *some* plan.
Pronoun : *Some* were provided seats but others were not.
Adverb : *Some* fifty students were present.

Still

Verb : Mothers *still* their children by some fairy tales.
Adjective : *Still* waters run deep.
Noun : I heard a strange sound in the *still* of the night.
Adverb : He is *still* in his office.

Such

Adjective : *Such* customs are not practised here.

Pronoun : *Such* is not my way of working.

That

Demonst. Adjective : I like *that* house.

Demonst. Pronou : *That* was the answer liked by all.

Adverb : I did *that* much.

Relative Pronoun : The work *that* you did will be remembered in all ages.

Conjunction : Some eat *that* they may live.

The

Def. Article : *The* message has been delivered.

Adverb : *The* higher you go, the cooler it is.

Till

Preposition : Don't put off the work *till* tomorrow.

Conjunction : You should wait *till* I come back.

Up

Adverb : Move *up*.

Preposition : He went *up* the hill.

Adjective : The *up* train is late.

Noun : Every one experiences *ups* and downs of life.

Well

Adjective : We hope you are now *well*.

Adverb : *Well* begun is half done.

Interjection : *Well*, who would have thought it ?

What

Inter. Adjective : *What* proof do you have ?

Interjection : *What* ! She has failed ?

Inter. Pronoun : *What* do you want ?

Relative Pronoun : *What* will happen, God only knows.

While

Noun : Come back and rest a *while*.

Verb : We *while* away our time with games and books.

Conjunction : *While* a great author, he is a great teacher.

Why

Inter. Adverb	: *Why* do you go there ?
Relative Adverb	: She knows the reason *why* I did it.
Interjection	: *Why,* it is certainly Chirag ?
Noun	: I don't have time to go into the *why* and the wherefore of the matter.

Yet

Adverb	: There is more proof *yet* to be offered.
Conjunction	: He is very poor, *yet* happy.

EXERCISE 89

Write the Parts of Speech of each word given in italics :

1. He works *hard.*
2. The answer is *hard* to give.
3. He is *little* remembered.
4. *Little* knowledge is a dangerous thing.
5. I like this *best.*
6. She is my *best* friend.
7. *But* for her help I would have been ruined.
8. Fear nothing *but* sin.
9. You are *like* your mother.
10. She will *like* the gift.
11. We have not seen the *like* of it.
12. Do not talk *like* that.
13. She gave me a beautiful *watch.*
14. Children *watch* too much television.
15. It is a beautiful *watch* tower.
16. It was my *only* chance.
17. She is *only* foolish.
18. Do what you want, *only* let me go.
19. She is the *right* person for this job.
20. The constitution protects our fundamental *right.*
21. The cat sat *right* in the way.
22. A great change came *over* him.
23. The captain took one wicket in one *over.*
24. She must read it *over* carefully.

25. It is a *round* table.
26. They came *round* to the point.
27. It is a *round* of problems.
28. The earth revolves *round* the sun.
29. *All* persons must glide to grave.
30. He is *all* alone.
31. *All* spoke on the same point.
32. He lost his *all* in the gamble.
33. The stars are *above.*
34. Our joys and sorrows come from *above.*
35. You can analyse the *above* sentence.
36. The moral duty is *above* the civic duty.
37. I reached *after* he had left.
38. He takes *after* his father.
39. He arrived soon *after.*
40. *After* generations will sing his praise.
41. Did he have *any* answer ?
42. Is this *any* better ?

30

Modal Auxiliaries

Auxiliary is a **helping verb** which is used to make the form of another verb.

Apart from 'be' 'have' and 'do' the other Auxiliaries are — **can, could, may, might, shall, should, will, would, must, ought, used, need** and **dare.** They are called **Modal Auxiliaries** or Modals because they perform special functions.

Can, Could, May, Might

'Can' is used to express ability or capability; as

1. I **can** solve this sum.
2. He **can** lift 350 kgs.
3. **Can** you climb this hill ?

'May' is used;

1. To seek permission; as
   (i) **May** I come in ?
   (ii) **May** I use your pen ?
2. To Give Permission; as
   (i) You **may** go now.
   (ii) You **may** take these books.
3. To express Possibility in Affirmative Sentences; as
   (i) My father **may** come back today.
   (ii) It **may** rain today.
4. To express a wish; as
   (i) **May** you live long!
   (ii) **May** God bless her with a son!

In spoken English **Can** is often used in place of **May** to express permission; as

(i) You **can** go now.
(ii) **Can** I use your telephone ?

Could and **Might** are used as a Past Equivalent of **Can** and **May**; as

(i) She asked me if she might come in. (Permission)

(ii) I could climb this hill when I was young. (Capability)

(iii) I thought it might rain that day. (Possibility)

(iv) He prayed to God that she might live long. (Wish)

Could and **Might** can also be used in the Present time context; as

(i) Could I speak to Mrs. Sharma ?

(ii) Could I use your pen ?

This is different way of saying May or Can.

Could is used in the Present Context to express polite request; as

(i) Could you pass me the dish ?

(ii) Could you move a little ?

Might is used in the present time context to convey less possibility than **'may'**; as

It might rain today. (Less positive than may)

Shall, Should, Will, Would

Shall is used in the first person Singular Number (I) and Plural Number (We) and **Will** in the second and third persons to express Simple Futurity; as

(i) I *shall* be fifty five next birthday.

(ii) Tomorrow *will* be Monday.

(iii) When *shall* I see you again?

'Shall' is used in the **'Second'** and **'Third person'** to express a **'command'** **'a promise'**, **'a revenge'** or **threat**; as

(i) He **shall** have a precious present on this birthday. (Promise)

(ii) You **shall** not sit here. (Command)

(iii) You **shall** be punished for your negligence. (Threat)

Shall is used in the 'Second' and 'Third Persons' to ask after the **will of the person addressed**; as

(i) Shall I show you the sample (Do you wish me to show it ?)

(ii) Which present shall I buy (What is your suggestion ?)

(iii) Shall the host serve food ?

Will is used;

1. To express the **exercise of the will**; as

   (i) I **will** take these books. (Willing to)

   (ii) I **will** show better performance. (Promise)

   (iii) I **will** get distinction in all subjects. (Determination)

2. **Characteristic Habit**; as

   She **will** discuss nothing but movies.

3. **Probability**; as

   This **will** be the shirt, you want, I think.

'Will you' denotes an Invitation or a Request; as

(i) Will you have tea?

(ii) Will you lend me your pen?

Note. In Modern English there is a tendency to use will with all persons.

'Should' and **'Would'** are used as the Past Equivalents of **shall** and **will**; as,

(i) I **would** visit her house every week when I was in Mumbai. (Past habit)

(ii) I hoped that you **would** come in time.

Should is used with all persons to express **'Obligation'** or **'duty'**; as,

(i) We **should** obey our teachers and parents.

(ii) You **should** keep your word.

(iii) He **should** report in time.

'Should' and **'would'** are also used as in the examples below

(i) I **would** like her to accompany me.

(ii) I **should** like her to obey her parents.

(They are examples of **polite wants**)

Would you lend me your dictionary ? — Here **would** is more polite than **'will'**.

(i) She **should** have helped me. (It indicates past obligation which was not fulfilled).

(ii) He **should** be in Delhi now. (probability)

(iii) I **wish** you **would** come personally. (*Would* after wish expresses a strong desire.)

MUST, OUGHT

1. **'Must'** expresses necessity or obligation; as,

   (i) You **must** obey the traffic rules.

   (ii) We **must** work or starve.

2. Determination; as,

   I **must** get this book.

Ought (to) expresses moral obligation or desirability; as,

(i) We **ought** to respect elders.

(ii) We **ought** not to kill animals.

(iii) You **ought** to help the needy.

Used (to) Need, Dare

Used to expresses a Past habit (which is discontinued)

(i) I **used to** swim every day when I was young.

(ii) She **used to** help me when I was in difficulty.

Need expresses **obligation** or **necessity** and can be conjugated **with do** or **without do**. When conjugated without do, it has no-s-ed forms and is used with Infinitive without **to** only in Negative and Interrogative sentences that contain **hardly** or **scarcely**; as,

(i) She **need** not come here.

(ii) **Need** I inform him ?

(iii) I **need** hardly take your money.

When conjugated with **do** need has the usual forms — needs, needed and is used with a to + infinitive. It is used with **Negative** and **Interrogative** and sometimes in **Affirmative Sentences;** as,

(i) Does she **need** to help you ?

(ii) I do not **need** to go there.

(iii) He **needs** to be cautious.

The Auxiliary **Dare**, which means **be brave enough to**, does not take -s in the Third Person Singular Number in Present Tense. When conjugated without do, it is followed by an infinitive without to, when conjugated with do, it takes an infinitive with or without to; as,

(i) She **dare** not enter my house.

(ii) He does not **dare** come here.

(iii) How **dare** he speak against me?

(iv) You **dared** not speak in his presence.

Note. The ordinary verb **dare** which means to **challenge**, does not fall in the category of modal **Auxiliary**.

EXERCISE 90

Fill in the correct Modals in the following sentences :

1. .... you like to come with me for walk ?
2. We .... save some money for rainy days.
3. The manager said that I .... leave the office whenever I wanted.
4. .... I use your mobile phone ?
5. You were not in the office. I thought you .... be with your boss.
6. .... God make you prosperous !
7. There is no .... for you to come to office tomorrow.
8. He .... work seriously or he will lose his job.
9. You .... type all the letters today, only three will do.
10. One .... be punctual in one's duty.
11. I wish you .... invite me in time.
12. He .... not enter my office.
13. .... you please pass over the salt ?
14. When she was young, she .... play a lot of tennis.
15. .... the waiter serve coffee ?
16. I .... avenge all the wrongs done to me.
17. You .... get up early to maintain your health.
18. He .... watch many movies in his youth.
19. It .... rain today.
20. He .... be at home by now.
21. She said that I .... stay with her.
22. One .... to do one's duty.
23. We .... respect the laws of the country.
24. I .... lift this heavy box.
25. No one .... pump the ocean dry.
26. You .... reach office in time, or your services .... be terminated.

27. I don't think I .... be able to help him.
28. How .... he disobey you ?
29. He .... not speak to me.
30. You .... not light a match, the room is full of gas.
31. She .... talk about nothing but literature.
32. He said that he .... carry my bag.
33. She .... sit for hours listening to music.
34. Children .... obey their parents and teachers.

31

Punctuation

The word **Punctuation** means correct use of putting in **'stops in writing'**. The following are the main stops :

Full Stop (.)	Comma (,)
Semicolon (;)	Colon (:)
Sign of Interrogation (?)	Sign of Exclamation (!)
Dash (—)	Hyphen (-)
Parentheses ( )	Inverted Commas (" ")
Apostrophe (')	Capital Letters

The **Full Stop** is used :

1. To mark the end of a **Declarative or an Imperative** sentence; as,
   (i) She goes to college every day.
   (ii) The sun sets in the west.
   (iii) Switch off the lights.
2. To mark Abbreviations and Initials; as,
   M. A., B. A., M. B. A., D. S. Ahuja

The **Comma** represents the **'shortest pause'**. It is used :

1. To separate a series of words in the same construction; as,
   (i) She was deserted by friends, relations, parents and spouse.
   (ii) The path was tiresome, circuitous and dull.
   (iii) Sonu, Monu, Sheenu and their parents have arrived.
2. To separate each pair of words connected by **and**; as,
   One should be sincere and honest, punctual and dutiful.
3. After a **Nominative, Absolute**; as,
   (i) The weather being fine, we decided to sail.
   (ii) It being very hot, I decided to stay in.

4. To mark off a **Noun** or **Phrase in Apposition**.

(i) Ramu, the son of Sheela, has stolen your wallet.

(ii) Ram, the king of Ayodhya was sent on exile.

(iii) Shakespeare, the great English dramatist, lived in seventeenth century.

5. To mark off the **Nominative** of Address or **Vocative**; as,

(i) Help me in my work, Sonu.

(ii) India, the country of many cultures, I love you.

6. To mark off **two or more Adverbs** or **Adverbial Phrases** coming together; as

Slowly, at last, we won the match.

7. **Before and after a Participle Phrase**; as,

Rakesh, having completed his graduation, went abroad.

8. **Before and after words, phrases or clauses**, let into the body of Sentence; as,

(i) She could not, however, complete the work in time.

(ii) Your story, in many ways, is flawed.

(iii) He should not, I repeat, have any quarrel with me.

(iv) The people of rural India, when they are their best, manifest the best human qualities.

(v) It is the strong will-power, after all, that leads one to success.

9. **To indicate the Omission of a word**, especially a verb; as,

(i) I received a television, he, a record player.

(ii) He is an atheist, you, a believer.

10. **To separate short Coordinating Clauses** of a compound sentence; as,

(i) The destination was far, and we were fully exhausted.

(ii) I waited, I watched, I surveyed, I left.

(iii) He came, he rested, he left.

11. To mark off a **Direct quotation** from the rest of the sentence; as,

(i) He said to me, "Please bring a glass of water".

(ii) "We have", he said, "won the victory at last".

12. Before certain **Coordinating Conjunctions**; as,

To do such deeds is not righteousness, but sin.

13. To separate from the verb **a long Subject opening a sentence**; as,

All that you did to win the game, was in vain.

14. **To separate a Noun Clause** — whether subject or object — preceding the verb; as,

(i) Why he failed in the examinations, is a mystery.

(ii) That he would not pass, was not expected.

15. **To separate a clause that is not restrictive in meaning**, but is coordinate with the principal clause; as,

(i) Students, who waste their time, generally don't do well in the examination.

16. When the **Adjective clause is restrictive in meaning**, the comma should not be used; as,

(i) This is the book which she gave me.

(ii) The proposal was appreciated by all who came to attend the meeting.

17. To separate an **Adverbial clause from its main clause;** as,

(i) If you work hard, you will pass.

(ii) When she met me, she was smiling.

18. When the Adverbial clause follows the **Principal clause**, the Comma is generally omitted; as,

(i) She can meet me if she wants.

(ii) I cannot accompany you as I am not well.

The Semi Colon. Semi Colon represents a pause of greater importance than that shown by the comma. It is used :

1. To separate the clauses of Compound Sentence, when they contain a Comma; as,

(i) She is brave, bold and wise; and we all admire her.

2. To separate a series of 'loosely related clauses; as,

What we were in the past; we are not today; what we are today; we will not be tomorrow.

The Colon. The colon marks a **still more complete pause** than that expressed by the **semi colon**. It is used with a **Dash after it**.

1. To introduce a quotation; as,

Elias Canetti says : **"All the things one has forgotten scream for the help in dreams"**.

2. Before **enumerations**, Examples etc; as,

The main Tenses in English are : — The **Present Tense**, the **Past Tense** and the **Future Tense**.

Sign of Interrogation

This mark is used, instead of the Full Stop after the Direct Questions; as,

(i) Have you completed your work ?

(ii) How do you go to your office ?

(iii) Why did you go there ?

Note. Sign of interrogation is not used in **Indirect Speech**; as,

She asked me what I wanted.

Sign of exclamation

This mark is used after **'interjections'** and **'after phrases'**, and sentences expressing sudden feelings of **joy**, **sorrow**, **surprise** or **wish**; as,

(i) Hurrah ! We have won the match.

(ii) What a beautiful weather !

(iii) What a rash deed you have done !

(iv) May you live long !

Inverted commas

Inverted commas are used to enclose the exact words of a speaker or a quotation; as,

"I have solved all the sums", he said to the teacher, "which you gave me to solve".

Note. If a quotation comes within a quotation, it is marked by **Single Inverted Commas**.

The **'dash'** is used :

1. To indicate a **sudden stop** or change of thought; as,

If I had reached in time — but why blame the luck.

2. To resume a scattered subject; as,

Joys, sorrows, sufferings — all are there in human life.

Hyphen

Hyphen is a shorter line than dash which is used :

1. To connect the parts of a Compound word; as,

(i) The early-bird catches the worm.

(ii) We have state-of-the-art equipment.

2. To connect parts of a word divided at the end of a line.

Parentheses or **Double Dashes** are used to separate from the main part of the sentence, a phrase or clause which does not grammatically belong to it; as,

(i) She came in time (it was my desire) to help me.

(ii) At last, the ordeal — the hijacking of aeroplane, one person was killed, the commandos stormed the plane — came to an end.

The Apostrophe is used

1. To show the omission of a letter or letters; as,
   don't didn't, wasn't, I'd, He's
2. To form the **Plural of letters** and figures; as,
   (i) Dot your **n's** and circle your **m's**.
   (ii) Add two 5's and three 6's.
3. In the Genitive Case of Nouns; as,
   (i) It is Sheela's skirt.
4. These are father's shoes.

Capital Letters. Capital Letters are used;

1. To begin a Sentence.
2. To begin each fresh line of poetry.
3. To begin the Proper Nouns and Adjectives derived from them; as,
   India, Calcutta, Bombay, Indian, Kalkatan, Shkespearean, Delhi, Delhites
4. For all Nouns and Pronouns which indicate the Deity; as,
   Parvati, Ganesha, Shiva, Krishna
5. To write the Pronoun I and the Interjection O

EXERCISE 91

Insert Commas, where necessary in the following sentences :

1. The list is unending and we have to bring books pencils erasers notebooks compasses maps and many other items.
2. Sir I would like to have one day leave.
3. Even a fool when he remains silent is considered wise.
4. At the stroke of the midnight hour when the world sleeps India will awake to life and freedom.
5. He is sincere diligent polite helpful and conscientious.
6. If you work hard you will pass.
7. At dawn however he goes out for a walk.
8. Shakespeare the great English Playwright lived in seventeenth century.

9. Sheela the owner of this building knows how the neighbours disturb everyday.
10. By hard work honesty and dedication he rose to great heights.
11. India Pakistan New Zealand and Australia will play the triangular series.
12. He lost money friends reputation and property.
13. It was dull long wearisome journey.
14. One should be polite and humble honest and sincere.
15. Titanic the great English ship perished in 1912.
16. Rich and poor wise and foolish high and low are all mortal.
17. Come into the parlour dear.
18. One should write quickly neatly and accurately.
19. Indian soldiers having defeated the enemy returned to their camp.
20. Your behaviour to say the least is uncouth
21. He could not however succeed in his goal.
22. It rained very heavily and there was a terrible flood.
23. The journey was long and the wind was heavy.
24. That he will pass is certain.
25. People who are superstitious say that it is unlucky to part with money on Thursday.
26. He said "Please give me some food".
27. When I was young I often went on long treks.
28. India with all your beauties I love you.
29. Jealously anger pride uncharity cruelty self-righteousness touchiness doggedness and sullenness are the ingredients of ill-temper.
30. No form of vice not worldliness not greed of gold not drunkenness itself does more to unchristianise society than evil temper.
31. Many people unfortunately seem to think that Government can always pay out money quite easily and in any quantity and they forget or else they do not know that the Government can only pay out money that it has received in taxes.

EXERCISE 92

Punctuate the following sentences :

1. The mother finding her child missing exclaimed what shall I do now.
2. Perhaps said he I may be wrong as you say.
3. Bring me a glass of water he said to his servant.
4. You have all done very badly remarked the teacher.
5. They had played together in childhood they had worked together when young they were now tottering about and gossiping away in the evening of life and in a short time they will probably be buried together in the neighbouring churchyard.
6. King Francis was a great lover of all kinds of sport and one day he and his courtiers noble men and ladies sat watching wild savage lions fighting each other in the enclosure below.

Among the courtiers sat count de lorge beside a beautiful and lovely lady of noble birth whom he loved and hoped to marry the lions roared and bit and tore each other with savage fury until the king said to his courtiers gentlemen we are better up here than down there.

7. (Continued) The lady hearing him thought she would show the king and his court how devoted her lover was to her so she dropped her glove down among the fighting lions and then looked at count de lorge and smiled at him. He bowed to her and leaped down among the savage lions without hesitation recovered the glove and climbed back to his place. Then he threw the glove right in the lady's face. King Francis cried out well and bravely done but it was not love that made you lady set you such a dangerous thing to do but her vanity.

8. The lady was angry with her servant and said why have you again disturbed me in my sleep. I am sorry madam excuse me again this time I shall not repeat the mistake the servant said.

9. The principal said to the students where do you want to go for picnic either to Nehru Park or to Buddha Jayanti Park said the students.

10. Mr. Boggis clapped one hand over his heart staggered to the nearest chair and collapsed into it breathing heavily what's the matter with you Claud asked. Its nothing he gasped It'll be all right in a minute please — a glass of water. Its my heart. Best fetched him the water handed it to him and stayed close beside him staring down at him with a fatuous leer on his face.

11. So when will you come back to work feld asked him. To his surprise sobel burst out never. Jumping up he strode over to the window that looked out upon the miserable street why should I come back he cried I will raise your wages. The shoe-maker knowing he didn't care what else to say. What do you want from me sobel nothing. I always treated you like you were my son. Sobel vehemently denied it.

12. Listen he said to me you know the old Imam, don't you. I saw you talking to him once yes I said I talked to him once my wife's ill, Khamees said. I want the Imam to come to my house to give her an injection he won't come if I ask him he doesn't like me you go and ask he doesn't like me either I said never mind Khamees insisted he'll come if you ask him — he knows you are a foreigner he will listen to you.

32 Transformation of Sentences

Transformation of Sentences is very useful exercise as it teaches how **one thing** can be expressed **in many different ways.**

1. **Removing Adverb 'too'**

Study the following sentences

1. It is too hot to go out.
2. This wall is too high to climb.
3. This news is too good to be true.

1. It is so hot that we/one cannot go out.
2. This wall is so high that one cannot climb it.
3. This news is so good that it cannot be true.

The **adverb 'too'** used in the first three sentences has been **removed** in the subsequent three sentences and expression so .... that has been used instead.

2. **Interchange of the Degree of Comparison.** It is also possible to change the Degree Comparison of an Adjective or Adverb in a sentence without changing the meaning of the sentence.

Positive : This sword is not as sharp as that one.
Comparative : That sword is sharper than this one.
Positive : Ram is as strong as Sohan.
Comparative : Sohan is not stronger than Ram.
Positive : Few boys are as intelligent as Rakesh.
Comparative : Rakesh is more intelligent than many boys.
Positive : No other boy is as strong as Dara Singh.
Comparative : Dara Singh is stronger than any other boy.
Superlative : Dara Singh is the strongest of all boys.
Superlative : Delhi is the largest city in India.

Comparative : Delhi is larger than any other city in India.
Positive : No other city in India is as large as Delhi.
Superlative : Mumbai is one of the richest cities in India.
Comparative : Mumbai is richer than most other cities in India.
Superlative : Sohil is not one of the cleverest boys in the school.
Comparative : Some boys of the school are cleverer than Sohil.
Positive : Sohil is less clever than some other boys of the school.
Positive : Sohil is not so clever as some other boys of the school.

Interchange of Active and Passive Voice

We can change a sentence in the **Active form** into the **Passive form** and vice versa.

Active : He betrayed his friend.
Passive : His friend was betrayed by him.
Active : Who teaches you English ?
Passive : By whom are you taught English.
Or
By whom is English taught to you ?
Active : The people will laugh at you.
Passive : You be laughed at by the people.
Active : Obey the rules.
Passive : Let the rules be obeyed.
Active : The cop arrested him.
Passive : He was arrested by the cop.
Active : It is time to close the office.
Passive : It is time for the office to be closed.
Active : The chief guest was giving away the prizes.
Passive : The prizes were being given away by the chief guest.
Active : People speak English all over the world.
Passive : English is spoken all over the world.

Note. It is unnecessary to mention the agent (i.e. the doer of the action) in the passive form whenever it is evident who the agent is. Thus in the last example, the agent is not mentioned in the passive form, because it is understood that English is spoken all over the world by people.

Passive : My salary has been paid.
Active : The cashier has paid my salary.

Passive : The road is being repaired.
Active : The labourers are repairing the road.
Passive : The answer-sheets were being evaluated.
Active : The teacher was evaluating the answer-sheets.

Note. The Active Voice is used when the agent or the doer of the action is to be made prominent and the Passive Voice is used, when the thing acted upon is to be made prominent.

Interchange of Affirmative and Negative Sentences

A sentence in the **Affirmative** form can be made **Negative** and **Vice versa without changing the meaning.**

1. Mother loves the child.
   Mother is not without love for her child.
2. You are stronger than he.
   He is not so strong as you (are).
3. Kiran is the best girl of our school.
   No other girl of our school is as good as Kiran.
4. I am doubtful whether he will succeed.
   I am not sure whether he will succeed.

Interchange of Interrogative and Assertive Sentences

1. What though the field is lost ?
   It does not much matter if the field is lost.
2. Were you not given your salary in time ?
   You were given your salary in time.
3. Didn't I tell you to be punctual ?
   I told you to be punctual.
4. Who can know the ways of God ?
   No one can know the ways of God.
5. Why waste time in trivia ?
   We should not waste time in trivia.

Interchange of Exclamatory and Assertive Sentences

1. How beautiful the sky looks ?
   The sky looks very beautiful.
2. O that I were a millionaire !
   I wish that I were a millionaire.

3. Alas that her only son should pass away !
   It is very sad to think that her only son should pass away.
4. How stupid of you !
   It is very stupid of you.

Interchange of one Part of Speech to another

1. My parents will not *consent* (verb) to our marriage.
   My parents will not give their *consent* (Noun) to our marriage.
2. The soldiers fought *bravely* (adverb).
   The soldiers put up a *brave* (adjective) fight.
3. This room is *beautiful* (Adjective).
   This room has *beauty* (Noun).
4. Gandhiji showed *generosity* (Noun) even to his enemies.
   Gandhiji was *generous* (Adjective) even to his enemies.
5. The captain hit the ball *strongly* (Adverb).
   The captain hit the ball in a *strong* (Adjective) manner.
6. The two figures are *slightly* (Adverb) different.
   There is a *slight* (Adjective) difference between the two figures.
7. The servant replied *curtly* (Adverb).
   The servant gave a *curt* (adjective) reply.
8. He *hopes* (verb) to succeed.
   He has *hope* (Noun) of his success.
9. How *frequently* (adverb) do you visit your friend ?
   How *frequent* (Adjective) is your visit to your friend ?
10. He has *disgraced* (verb) his family.
    He has brought *disgrace* (Noun) to his family.

Conversion of Simple Sentences to Compound Sentence

1. Simple : Unluckily, he met with an accident.
   Compound : He was unlucky and therefore he met with an accident.
2. Simple : Your late arrival will delay us.
   Compound : You arrive late and we shall be delayed.
3. Simple : He was punished for being late.
   Compound : He was late and therefore he was punished.

4. Simple : Besides having a house he owns a shop.
   Compound : He not only owns a house but owns a shop also.
5. Simple : Being occupied with work, he could not call me back.
   Compound : He was occupied with work and therefore could not call me back.
6. Simple : In addition to financial help he gave blankets to the poor.
   Compound : He gave not only financial help but also gave blankets to the poor.
7. Simple : Notwithstanding your hard labour you could not succeed.
   Compound : You laboured hard but you could not succeed.
8. Simple : It being very cold, no one wanted to go out.
   Compound : It was very cold and no one wanted to go out.

Conversion of Compound Sentences to Simple Sentences

1. Compound : He completed his graduation and went abroad.
   Simple : Having completed his graduation, he went abroad.
2. Compound : You must work hard or you cannot continue here.
   Simple : You must work hard to continue here.
3. Compound : He is poor and faces great problems.
   Simple : Being poor he faces great problems.
4. Compound : Everyone attended the function but Sohan did not.
   Simple : Everyone except Sohan attended the function.
5. Compound : He came late and was admonished.
   Simple : Having come late he was admonished.
6. Compound : You were very tired and you wanted rest.
   Simple : Being very tired you wanted rest.
7. Compound : You must not be late, or you will miss the flight.
   Simple : In the event of being late, you will miss the flight.
8. Compound : The boy completed his home work and went to sleep.
   Simple : Having completed his home work the boy went to sleep.
9. Compound : The weather was very fine and we went on a picnic.
   Simple : The weather being very fine we went on a picnic.
10. Compound : You must either improve your behaviour or resign the job.
    Simple : Failing improvement in your behaviour you must resign the job.

Conversion of Simple Sentences to Complex Sentences

1. Simple : We saw a wounded soldier.
   Complex : We saw a soldier who was wounded.
2. Simple : Sohan purchased Geeta's house.
   Complex : Sohan purchased the house which belonged to Geeta.
3. Simple : The accused confessed his crime.
   Complex : The accused confessed that he was guilty.
4. Simple : He is trying his best to succeed.
   Complex : He is trying his best so that he can succeed.
5. Simple : You always write according to instructions.
   Complex : You always write as you are instructed.
6. Simple : On the arrival of the chief guest, the function will start.
   Complex : The function will start as soon as the chief guest arrives.
7. Simple : He went to London to meet his uncle.
   Complex : He went to London so that he could meet his uncle.
8. Simple : Being honest, he does not cheat anyone.
   Complex : As he is honest he does not cheat anyone.
9. Simple : Sunita owes her success to God.
   Complex : It is owing to God that Sunita has succeeded.
10. Simple : He is sure of his success.
    Complex : He is sure that he will succeed.

Conversion of Complex Sentences to Simple Sentences (Noun clause)

1. Complex : That you will succeed is certain.
   Simple : Your success is certain.
2. Complex : He does not know when he will return.
   Simple : He does not know the timing of his return.
3. Complex : You said that you were ignorant.
   Simple : You declared your ignorance.
4. Complex : Tell me what you want.
   Simple : Tell me your requirement.
5. Complex : That he will fail was not expected.
   Simple : His failure was not expected.

6. Complex : He ordered his servant that he should close the door.
   Simple : He ordered his servant to close the door.
7. Complex : I don't know where he lives.
   Simple : I don't know his address.
8. Complex : She said that she would arrive in time.
   Simple : She said of her timely arrival.
9. Complex : That he is drunk proves his guilt.
   Simple : His drunkenness proves his guilt.
10. Complex : The doctor declared that the case was hopeless.
    Simple : The doctor declared the case to be hopeless.

Adjective Clause

1. Complex : I have nothing which I can offer you.
   Simple : I have nothing to offer you.
2. Complex : He has seen the flat which belongs to you.
   Simple : He has seen your flat.
3. Complex : The time which is lost is lost for ever.
   Simples : The lost time is lost forever.
4. Complex : We saw a palace where a king lived.
   Simple : We saw a king' s palace.
5. Complex : I have no money which I can give you.
   Simple : I have no money to give you.
6. Complex : Those who are honest need not fear anyone except God.
   Simple : Honest persons need not fear anyone except God.
7. Complex : This is the watch which my friend gifted me.
   Simple : This is the watch gifted by my friend to me.
8. Complex : The manager who was the feather of Director's cap is no more.
   Simple : The manager, the feather of Director's cap is no more.
9. Complex : The boy who is standing in the last row is very intelligent.
   Simple : The boy standing in the last row is very intelligent.
10. Complex : Those who help themselves are helped by God.
    Simple : Persons helping themselves are helped by God.

Adverb Clause

1. Complex : This wall is so high that I cannot climb it.
   Simple : This wall is too high for me to climb.
2. Complex : When the teacher is absent the students will make a noise.
   Simple : In the absence of the teacher, the students will make a noise.
3. Complex : Although he is rich yet he is greedy.
   Simple : In spite of being rich, he is greedy.
4. Complex : The principal was annoyed that the teacher had not carried out his orders.
   Simple : The principal was annoyed at the teacher having not carried out his order.
5. Complex : Your daughter has succeeded better than she hoped.
   Simple : Your daughter has succeeded beyond her hopes.
6. Complex : A good soldier will always do as he is commanded by his officer.
   Simple : A good soldier will always carry out the commands of his officer.
7. Complex : I am searching my lost son wherever I can.
   Simple : I am searching my lost son at all possible places.
8. Complex : Do you know the consequences if you fail ?
   Simple : Do you know the consequences of your failure ?
9. Complex : If you make a promise you should keep it.
   Simple : You should make a promise only to keep it.
10. Complex : You must buy this book, cost what it may.
    Simple : You must buy his book at any cost.

Conversion of Compound Sentences to Complex Sentences

1. Compound : Work hard and you will succeed.
   Complex : If you work hard you will succeed.
2. Compound : The Principal entered the classroom and the students stood up.
   Complex : When the principal entered the class room, the students stood up.
3. Compound : The soldier was wounded but not killed.
   Complex : Although the soldier was wounded he was not killed.

4. Compound : Honesty is the best policy, and this is a fact.
   Complex : This is a fact that honesty is the best policy.
5. Compound : Cross the boundary and you will be imprisoned.
   Complex : If you cross the boundary you will be imprisoned.
6. Compound : The Defence Minister reached Kargil and there the soldiers were overjoyed.
   Complex : When the Defence Minister reached Kargil, the soldiers over there were overjoyed.
7. Compound : He called at my house but my mother was out.
   Complex : When he called at my house, my mother was out.
8. Compound : The boy saw the tiger and he ran away.
   Complex : The boy ran away when he saw the tiger.
9. Compound : Keep quiet or face the consequences.
   Complex : If you don't keep quiet, you will face the consequences.
10. Compound : He is poor but he is honest.
    Complex : Although he is poor he is honest.

Conversion of Complex Sentences to Compound Sentences

1. Complex : Although he could not come, he sent his Assistant.
   Compound : He could not come but he sent his Assistant.
2. Complex : We are happy that you have succeeded.
   Compound : You have succeeded and we are happy of it.
3. Complex : Unless you work hard you cannot succeed.
   Compound : You must work hard or you will not succeed.
4. Complex : I have found the pen winch I had lost.
   Compound : I had lost a pen but I have found it.
5. Complex : We hope that good sense will prevail on him.
   Compound : Good sense will prevail on him and we are hopeful of it.
6. Complex : As soon as he received the message, he left for his home town.
   Compound : He received the message and immediately he left for his home town.
7. Complex : The teacher said that you are quite intelligent.
   Compound : You are quite intelligent and the teacher said so.

8. Complex : The child will run away if you open the door.
   Compound : Open the door and the child will run away.
9. Complex : We should not go out because it is very hot.
   Compound : It is very hot, and so we should not go out.
10. Complex : Unless you do your home work regularly the teacher will be angry with you.
    Compound : You must do your home work regularly or the teacher will be angry with you.

Miscellaneous

1. As soon as he saw the tiger he ran away.
   Begin with no sooner.
   No sooner did he see the tiger than he ran away.
2. It is possible that she will return.
   (make it a simple sentence and replace 'possible' and 'return' by Nouns.)
   There is possibility of her returning.
3. He believes that all the people on this earth are bad as he has seen good in none.
   Reduce to one Principal and one Subordinate clause.
   Having seen good in no one he believes that all the people on this earth are bad.
4. You did not reply me for one month.
   Rewrite using Noun form of 'Reply'.
   You sent no reply to me for one month.
5. As soon as the speaker entered the Parliament, all stood on their feet.
   Begin with — Hardly
   Hardly had the speaker entered the Parliament when all stood on their feet.
6. Sohan is the best student of our class and Sita is the prettiest girl of our school.
   Rewrite using Positive Degree, for 'best' and Comparative Degree for 'prettiest'.
   No other student of our class is as good as Sohan and Sita is prettier than any other girl of our school.
7. The hurdle was removed when the Principal suggested a new idea.
   Rewrite using 'Noun' form of suggested.

The hurdle was removed with the suggestion of a new idea by the Principal.

8. The boy was applauded, praised at the end of the show and the Secretary gave him the best prize.

   Use the Active Voice throughout.

   They applauded the boy, praised him at the end of the show and the Secretary gave him the best prize.

9. The wall was so high that no one could climb it.

   Rewrite the sentence using 'too' for 'so'.

   The wall was too high for anyone to climb.

10. The management will terminate this services if he does not improve his behaviour.

    Begin the sentence with **His services** and use the **'Noun form** of Improve'.

    His services will be terminated if he does not show improvement in his behaviour.

11. He worked sincerely and succeeded in his planning.

    Rewrite the sentence using **'Noun'** form of sincerely, **'Noun'** form of succeeded and **'verb'** form of planning.

    He worked with sincerity and got success in whatever he had planned.

12. There is hardly a youth present here who does not desire to take the autograph of the cricketer.

    Rewrite the sentence after **removing Negatives.**

    All the youth present here desire to take the autograph of the cricketer.

13. I am compelled by circumstances to leave Delhi and go to my home town where I can get my peace back.

    Change to **simple sentence, Active Voice**.

    Circumstances compel me to leave Delhi in order to go to my home town to get my peace back.

14. You should take regular exercise so that you can maintain your body throughout your life.

    Rewrite using the **'adverb'** form of regular and making it a simple sentence.

    You should exercise regularly to maintain your body throughout your life.

15. As he was very hungry, he had a strong desire to have something immediately.
Rewrite as a Simple Sentence, using **Adverb form of 'Strong'**.
Being very hungry he desired strongly to have something immediately.

EXERCISE 93

Rewrite the following sentences after removing the Adverb 'too' :

1. He is too stupid to understand your advice.
2. Her heart was too full for words.
3. Our teacher taught too fast to be understood.
4. This watermelon is too cheap to be good.
5. He is too clever not to see through your trick.
6. She is too proud to beg.
7. The boy is too small to be beaten.
8. She is too grieved to make a statement.
9. We were too late to see the whole movie.
10. Your words are too good to require any testimony.

EXERCISE 94

Change the Degree of Comparison without changing the meaning :

1. The Himalayas are the highest mountains in the world.
2. Robin is as strong as his friend.
3. He is the best boy of our class.
4. Very few cities in India are as crowded as Kolkata.
5. Ashoka was one of the greatest Indian emperors.
6. No other boy in our class is as intelligent as Rakesh.
7. No other island in the world is as large as Australia.
8. The U.S.A. is one of the richest countries in the world.
9. Punjab is not as cool as Himachal Pradesh.
10. Some cities in India are at least as beautiful as Bangalore.
11. Paris is more beautiful than any other city in the world.
12. Rahul is as strong as Ankur.
13. Sunil is the best sportsman of our school.
14. Sunita is one of the most beautiful girls of our school.
15. He is the best athlete.

EXERCISE 95

Change the following sentences into Passive Voice : (You can omit the agent where possible)

1. Every one admires the brave.
2. Children enjoy bathing.

3. One must endure what one cannot cure.
4. He gave me a beautiful present.
5. Will you accompany me to the market ?
6. No one knows the ways of God.
7. We appointed him captain of the school cricket team.
8. She will blame us.
9. Have you typed all the letters ?
10. Who bought the furniture ?
11. I can not climb this hill.
12. She saw me off at the airport.
13. Pay this bill now.
14. He disturbed all of us.
15. Did you draft the letter according to the instruction he gave you ?
16. All desire happiness.
17. The shop-keepers have downed the shutters.
18. Had the Minister answered all the questions when you entered the Parliament House ?
19. Close the door.
20. Don't make a noise.
21. Were the boys playing cricket ?
22. Has he solved all the sums ?

EXERCISE 96

Change the following sentences into Active Voice :

1. He was dismissed from the service.
2. I was seen off by my friend.
3. The late-comers were punished.
4. By whom was the speech delivered ?
5. The children will be gladdened by the rainbow ?
6. The children were praised by the Principal.
7. Has he been given his salary ?
8. The letters are being typed by the receptionist.
9. Were you being admonished ?
10. We are forbidden by the law.
11. Was he appointed secretary by the Managing Committee ?
12. Let the light be switched off.
13. The award was collected by the widow.
14. The sword of honour was being presented to the best cadet.
15. The message will be delivered in time.

EXERCISE 97

Change the meaning of the following sentences in a Negative form :

1. As soon as the President entered the hall, all stood up.
2. As soon as the rain stopped, we went out.
3. All will agree that he is an honest person.
4. You have performed better than him.
5. He is stronger than Sohil.
6. You are as disciplined as he.
7. I care very little what others say about me.
8. Only a maniac can do such a deed.
9. She is the best student of our class.
10. These books are all the wealth he owns.

EXERCISE 98

Convert the following Negatives into Affirmative :

1. No one will deny that you are an honest person.
2. I shall not forget the wrongs done to me.
3. There is no body but believes in your sincerity.
4. He is never in time.
5. Not many persons would doubt his honesty.
6. There is no one present who is not crying.
7. She did not live many years in London.
8. Not many would disagree with me.

EXERCISE 99

Change the following sentences into Assertive Sentences :

1. Can you gather grapes from thistles ?
2. Who does not know our Prime Minister ?
3. Shall I ever forget these unhappy days ?
4. Why waste time in useless talk ?
5. Who can know the ways of God ?

EXERCISE 100

Change the following sentences into questions :

1. No one can pump the ocean dry.
2. It is useless to offer advice to a person who is fool.
3. This is not the custom we follow here.
4. There is nothing better than complete peace.
5. He is not the person who will listen to you.

EXERCISE 101

Transform the following Exclamatory sentences into Assertions :

1. What a beautiful rainbow !
2. Shame on you to slap your father !
3. What a sweet joy this place gives !
4. How weak you are !
5. O that we were young again !
6. Ah, what a bloody deed !
7. O for a draught of fresh air !
8. How well fitted you are for this work !
9. What a wonderful bird a peacock is !
10. Oh ! For a little solace !

EXERCISE 102

Change the following into Exclamatory Sentences :

1. It was a horrible journey.
2. He has done a rash deed.
3. It is a very beautiful scene.
4. You lead a very unhappy life.
5. She has done a great job.

EXERCISE 103

In the following sentences replace the Nouns in italics by verbs :

1. He has achieved a great *success.*
2. His *intention* is to prolong his stay.
3. He has made an *endeavour* to improve the working of this office.
4. He made one *attempt* to pass the Civil Service examination.
5. I have *inclination* for success.
6. We accepted all his *proposals.*
7. He cannot get *admission* in this situation.

EXERCISE 104

Rewrite the following sentences so as to replace the Adverbs in italics by verbs :

1. He did the work *successfully.*
2. Gandhiji was *admittedly* the greatest advocate of non-violence.

EXERCISE 105

Rewrite the following sentences so as to replace the verbs and Adjectives in italics by corresponding Nouns :

1. The accused *regretted* that his deed was *hateful.*
2. *She is as intelligent* as a great scholar.

3. He is *admired* by all because he is *honest.*
4. He *clarified* that he was *guilty.*

EXERCISE 106

Rewrite the following sentences replacing Nouns in italics by Adjectives of similar meaning :

1. The boy gave me a great deal *of joy.*
2. In all *probability* it will rain today.
3. The boy has achieved great *success* and is admired by his schoolmates.

EXERCISE 107

Rewrite the following sentences replacing Adjectives in italics by Adverbs of similar meaning :

1. Your dress is *shabby* and *careless.*
2. The punishment given to you by your teacher is not *wrong.*

EXERCISE 108

Rewrite the following Simple Sentences as Compound (Double) Ones :

1. On the hill sat the saint meditating.
2. Being unhappy, he tendered his resignation.
3. To my great surprise, he failed in the examination.
4. Besides owning a Rolce Royce, he owns a Mercedez Benz.
5. Being preoccupied he could not come to receive us at the railway station.
6. The weather being fine, we decided to resume our journey.
7. In spite of his poor health, he walked a long distance.
8. Owing to heavy rains, there is water-logging everywhere.
9. Seeing the tiger coming, the boys climbed up a tree.
10. With all his knowledge, he cannot be called an educated person.
11. By his pleasant behaviour, he achieved a great success.
12. Notwithstanding his hard work he could not succeed.
13. Taking pity on the poor, he helped him in every manner.
14. Taking oft his clothes, he jumped into the river.
15. You had not reached there by evening.

EXERCISE 109

Change the following simple sentences to compound sentences :

1. His uncle being now in London, he will go there to meet him.
2. The soldier's fire-arms having been snatched, he felt helpless.
3. Hearing the stranger's footsteps, he came out.
4. People dislike him on account of his arrogance and stubbornness.

5. In your ignorance, you are following the wrong path.
6. In the event of his coming late, we shall cancel the meeting.
7. The flood having caused a havoc, many people became homeless.
8. In spite of his best efforts he could not win a medal.
9. His best friend having cheated him, he became hopeless.
10. To avoid being seen he hid behind the cupboard.

EXERCISE 110

Rewrite the following Compound (Double) Sentences as Simple one :

1. He was very poor, but he never complained.
2. His friend died and he became depressed.
3. We ran fast but we could not board the train.
4. He was very poor, and often had to go without food.
5. He killed his partner and became the owner of the property.
6. I was shocked for I found that my son was missing from home.
7. He went abroad for he wanted to see his mother there.
8. We accepted the proposal but they rejected it.
9. Work hard or you will fail.
10. All went to meet the film star, but I did not.
11. He must have started in time, for he is a very disciplined person.
12. Madhu Bala was rich, but she was not happy.
13. He did his M.A. and went abroad for higher studies. .
14. The students saw the teacher and they greeted her.
15. I wrote him a letter but he did not reply it.
16. He is very rich but he is not contented.

EXERCISE 111

Convert the following Compound (Double) Sentences to Simple Sentence :

1. The rain stopped and we resumed our play.
2. The train had departed and we could not board it.
3. I have an unpleasant work but I must do it.
4. He performed his duty well and he left the place.
5. The accused evaded arrest many times but was finally put behind bars.
6. The Principal entered the classroom and everyone rose from his seat.
7. He worked exceedingly well for he was a hard worker and sincere.
8. Do this and every one will go against you.
9. He was taught for a long time but he did not show any progress.
10. The Commander ordered him to fire but he did not care.
11. The movie began and the lights were switched off.

12. He practised every day and so rose to great heights.
13. He met his old friend after a long time and was delighted.
14. The doctor had examined him and was hopeful of his recovery.
15. He is very weak and he must rest.

EXERCISE 112

Convert the following Simple Sentences to Complex Sentences, each containing a Noun Clause :

1. He hoped to pass the examinations.
2. I always think of God's presence everywhere.
3. They expected to meet me in the party.
4. The accused confessed his guilt.
5. You are pleading ignorance of traffic rules.
6. Your mother is not likely to question you.
7. They overheard our conversation.
8. We shall be glad of your presence in the function.
9. You should reveal the truth.
10. I order you to obey him.
11. Your father will be happy to hear of your success.
12. The Commander asked the soldiers to prepare for war.
13. He is said to be a smuggler.
14. You should listen to me.
15. He is said to be a man of his word.

EXERCISE 113

Chang the following Simple Sentences to Complex Sentences, each containing, an Adverb Clause :

1. He did this in my presence.
2. In spite of poor health, he continued his journey.
3. Being quite late for duty, he decided not to go.
4. It is too hot to go out.
5. You should wait till his arrival.
6. I have come to meet my old friends.
7. Being unwell, I can't teach you today.
8. I saw him jumping the wall.
9. On being questioned, he admitted his fault.
10. Being quite happy, he prolonged his stay.
11. Being unhappy with the new boss, he resigned his job.
12. You are liked for your straightforwardness.

13. This sum is too difficult to be solved.
14. With my father's consent I can accompany you.
15. The boy would be happy with more pocket money.
16. I spoke to the best of my ability.
17. He went abroad to meet his mother.
18. We overstayed with a view to meet the Director.
19. The rain having stopped, we decided to go out.
20. The soldiers moved very slowly to avoid being seen by the enemy.
21. Don't come here before 9 o'clock.
22. She was annoyed at being criticized.

EXERCISE 114

Rewrite the following Simple Sentences as Complex Sentences :

1. After paying obeisance, we departed.
2. Do you know the time of her arrival ?
3. We expect every employee to work sincerely and honestly.
4. My mother having slept, I switched on the T.V.
5. I found my lost pen.
6. The exact date of the birth of Lord Rama is not known.
7. We can meet at any place convenient for you.
8. Taking into consideration your problems, we can excuse you.
9. The Prime Minister having been deposed, the Army General became the Head.
10. The day of her arrival is not known.
11. Work hard to prevent reappear in the test.
12. I convinced him of the importance of English Grammar.
13. A noble person is not expected to do ignoble deeds.
14. The duration of the conference is uncertain.
15. There is little hope of his arrival.
16. Very few know the author of Othello.
17. You can prove your ignorance.
18. Late-comers were punished.
19. Finding the car missing, he went to the police station.

EXERCISE 115

Convert the following Complex Sentences to Simple Sentences (Noun Clause) :

1. The magistrate ordered the police that they should arrest the trouble-makers.
2. The son did not know when his mother would return.
3. I hope that good sense will prevail on you.
4. The result of your negligence was that you failed.

5. The news that he has departed is not true.
6. I asked him why he failed.
7. The judge declared that he was innocent.
8. The principal ordered that the late-comers should be punished.
9. It has been reported that the Prime Minister has left for Washington.
10. Everyone believes that you have blundered.
11. Tell us what you mean by your statement.

EXERCISE 116

Convert each of the following Complex Sentences to a Simple Sentence :

1. A man who is industrious is sure to meet success.
2. He has no money that he can lend me.
3. This is the place where I worship.
4. I have no money which I can spend.
5. This is the boy who stood first in the Board examination.
6. This is the box which belongs to her.
7. I told her the time when I was expected to return.
8. People who live in this area are boisterous.
9. A man who has risen by his own efforts is sure to succeed.
10. She has found the purse which she lost.
11. I saw a man who had one eye.
12. Do you remember him who was formerly your principal ?
13. The answer which you have given is irrelevant.
14. Have you nothing which you can offer to the deity ?
15. I regained my lost ground by the help I got from my friends.
16. A person who is learned needs no riches.
17. The smoke which is coming from the burnt houses is suffocating.
18. This is the house which belongs to him.
19. I have no time that I can waste on useless discussion.
20. The help I have rendered to my relations should not be underestimated.

EXERCISE 117

Change the following Complex Sentences into Simple Sentences (Adverb Clause) :

1. As I am sick I am unable to work.
2. I am annoyed that you have not obeyed your teacher.
3. You can eat as much you like.
4. He will not improve unless he is compelled.
5. I have achieved better than I hoped.

6. When the teacher is away, the students will shout.
7. I am so tired that I cannot work more.
8. He became depressed when he heard the result.
9. Although he is rich he is not happy.
10. Because I am ill I don't wish to go out.
11. You can afford to spend because you are rich.
12. He will meet you when he hears from us.
13. Since he could not get a better job he accepted a lowly job.
14. The boys ran away when they saw a tiger.
15. No sooner did you see me than you hid behind the curtain.
16. He was so lazy that he could not succeed.
17. He is admired by all because he is sincere, honest and disciplined.
18. He is so old that he cannot walk.
19. I was surprised that you accompanied a dubious person.
20. While there is life there is hope.
21. You cannot come unless he consents.
22. I was very angry when I was refused admission.
23. Although he is poor he is contented.
24. I did the work as well as I could.
25. It was so dark that we could not see anything.

EXERCISE 118

Change each of the following Complex Sentences into a Simple Sentence :

1. No patient is admitted unless he is examined.
2. It is terrible that people should cheat their best friends.
3. It is doubtful whether he will arrive.
4. He asked me how old I was.
5. The sum is so difficult that I cannot solve it.
6. Those students who are successful will receive certificates.
7. It is certain that he will arrive.
8. We insist that we should get our salary today.
9. He has become so weak that he cannot walk.
10. The accused gave a graphic account of how he escaped.
11. The President awarded the soldiers after they were dead.
12. A child who has lost his parents is pitied by all.
13. I know this from the information which has been received by me.
14. This is the time when you should depart.
15. He went to a hill station so that he might recover his health.
16. Although the weather became inclement we continued our journey.

17. Although he was successful he could not get good marks.
18. If he makes a promise he keeps it.
19. The place where the saint was cremated has been discovered.
20. He has no advice which he can offer to anyone.
21. Except that I hurt my toe, I was lucky to escape.
22. How long he will stay is uncertain.
23. The fact that you are silent proves your guilt.
24. I owe my success to the one who is a Creator.
25. If you are not a member of the club you cannot be admitted.

EXERCISE 119

Change the following Compound Sentences into Complex Sentences :

1. We went to a hill station and there we enjoyed a lot.
2. He is my son and therefore I love him.
3. We called at your office yesterday but you were not available.
4. He studied hard and therefore he succeeded
5. Speak another word and you shall be taught a lesson.
6. Either he will come or he will inform.
7. He wishes to become great, therefore he is putting his best efforts.
8. We hurried to the airport but we missed the flight.
9. Do as you are told, or you will repent.
10. Sweep this area and you will find the ring.
11. The soldier was seriously wounded but he did not lose heart.
12. The children saw the danger and they ran away.
13. I aim at succeeding and therefore I am working hard.
14. I had to come, or be criticized.
15. He may not be rich but he is certainly contented.
16. You must improve or you will have to resign.
17. Life is not a bed of roses, still no one wants to die.
18. He was climbing the stairs and he fell down.
19. Take care of small things and big things will take care of themselves.
20. I received the message and I started at once.
21. You must reach office in time or you may lose your job.
22. You have lost all your wealth, consequently you will face problems.
23. Step out of the house and you will face serious problems.
24. The old man was tired, therefore he wanted to rest.
25. He was a traitor, therefore he was hanged.

EXERCISE 120

Change the following Compound Sentences into Complex Sentences :

1. You have insulted him but he will forgive you.
2. You have passed the examination but you have not got good marks.
3. Give me the documents and I will sign them.
4. I told him to improve his grammar but he did not care.
5. Take this medicine and you will be all right.
6. He is a coward but he always claims to be brave.
7. Avoid overeating and you will not fall sick.
8. The robber escaped or the cop would have killed him.
9. Send me the script and I will edit it.
10. I don't like this person and so I don't associate with him.
11. It is very hot, so we shall not go out.
12. You must pay cash, or else you can pay demand draft.

EXERCISE 121

Convert the following Complex Sentences to Compound Sentences :

1. If you do not study seriously you will fail.
2. Unless you improve you behaviour you cannot continue this job.
3. When the rain stopped, we went out.
4. Since you .say so, I must believe it.
5. He reached late because he had started late.
6. He ran away because he saw a tiger.
7. As he is brave, we admire him.
8. Although he is poor, he is happy.
9. Although the soldier fought valiantly he was defeated.
10. He knows what you told him.
11. As soon as he came, we started on our journey.
12. When you have written the letter, show it to me.
13. Though you work hard you seldom get success.
14. She was educated in a public school where she learnt French.
15. He studied so hard that he stood first in the school.
16. She has a cousin who speaks Latin fluently.
17. When the rain started we stopped playing.

EXERCISE 122

Convert the following Complex Sentences to Compound Sentences :

1. He came here as soon as he had finished his work.
2. You have never been sincere since you joined politics.

3. I don't think you will succeed.
4. As soon as you come we shall go.
5. She may go when she has typed all the letters.
6. If we offer good salary we expect good results.
7. She can come when she likes.
8. Although he is rich, he is not arrogant.
9. We have never heard from her since she left Delhi.
10. We may admire a poor man though we cannot admire a corrupt man.

EXERCISE 123

Change the following sentences as directed :

1. You sent me no reply for one week.

   (Rewrite using the verb form of *'reply')*.
2. He owns a Maruti as well as a Fiat.

   (Use the expression *'not only'* and *'but also'*).
3. As soon as the flight landed we proceeded towards the aeroplane.

   (Use *'No sooner'* for *'as soon as'*).
4. To the great surprise of us, we found half the staff absent.

   (Rewrite the sentence, using a **'verb'** for **'surprise'** and converting the predicate into phrase).
5. He was compelled by circumstances to sell a big house so that he could repay the loan.

   (Change to Simple Sentence Active Voice).
6. When a boy informed me that my son had passed the entrance test, I announced a great party.

   (Use the Passive Voice throughout).

33

Synthesis of Sentences

Synthesis means the **Combination of a number of Simple Sentences into one new sentence** which may be **Simple, Compound** or **Complex**. Synthesis is the **opposite** of **Analysis.**

The following are the chief ways of combining two or more simple sentences into one Simple Sentence :

1. By using a Participle

(i) The soldier entered the office. He saluted the officer.
Entering the office, the soldier saluted the officer.

(ii) The labourer was tired of work. He lay down.
The labourer being tired of work lay down.

(ii) He saw the mother. He ran away.
Seeing the mother, he ran away.

2. By using a Noun or a Phrase in Apposition

(i) He is my cousin. His name is Rakesh.
He is my cousin, Rakesh.

(ii) Delhi was once a beautiful city. It is now an overpopulated and polluted city.
Delhi, once a beautiful city is now an overpopulated and polluted city.

(iii) Sohan is one of the most intelligent boys in our class. Sohan is the son of a judge.
Sohan, the son of a judge, is one of the most intelligent boys in our class.

3. By using a Preposition with Noun or Gerund.

(i) The bell rang, my class work was not completed.
The bell rang before the completion of my class work.

(ii) The boy has attempted many times. He still wants to try.
In spite of many attempts, the boy wants to try.

(iii) His father arrived. He heard the news. He was overjoyed.
On hearing the news of his father's arrival he was overjoyed.

4. **By using the Nominative Absolute Construction.**

(i) The principal arrived. All stood up.
The principal having arrived, all stood up.

(ii) The Fort was protected by a strong guard. The foe was kept at bay.
The fort having been protected by strong guard, the foe was kept at bay.

5. **By using an Infinitive**

(i) This wall is very high. We cannot climb it.
This wall is too high for us to climb.

(ii) She went to London. She wanted to meet her uncle there.
She went to London to meet her uncle.

(iii) He has some urgent work. He must do it.
He has some urgent work to do.

(iv) It is very hot. I can't go out.
It is very hot for me to go out.

6. **By using an Adverb or an Adverbial Phrase.**

(i) It was 3 O'clock. The students had not solved the question paper.
The students had not solved the question paper by 3 O'clock.

(ii) You deserved punishment. You were punished.
You were punished deservedly.

Combination of two or more Simple Sentences into a Single Compound Sentence :

1. We walked a lot. We were tired.
We walked a lot and we were tired.

2. He was appreciated. He was given an award.
He was appreciated and given an award.
Or He was both appreciated and given an award.
Or He was not only appreciated but also given an award.
Or He was appreciated as well as given an award.

3. He ran. He became tired. He rested.

   He ran, became tired and he rested.

Note. The conjunction 'and' simply adds one statement to another.

The conjunction *'both ... and' 'not only ... but also', 'as well as'* are **emphatic forms** of 'and' and they do the same work.

Such conjunctions which merely 'add' one statement to another are called **Cumulative Conjunctions**.

(i) He is disturbed. He is sincere.

He is sincere but he is disturbed.

(ii) He failed. He was not disheartened.

He failed, yet (or still) he was not disheartened.

(iii) He did not approve of your behavior. He did not oppose you.

He did not approve of your behavior; he did not, however oppose you.

(iv) He is fine. He is weak.

He is fine, only he is weak.

(v) He was humiliated. He kept patience.

He was humiliated, nevertheless he kept patience.

The Conjunctions *but, still, yet, nevertheless, however,* express a contrast between one sentence and the other. Conjunctions still, yet, however, nevertheless are more **emphatic** than **but**. Conjunctions which express opposition or contrasts between two statement are called Adversative.

1. Move fast. You will miss the train.

   Move fast or you will miss the train.

2. Keep it here. Take it out.

   Keep it here or take it out.

3. Do not be a borrower. Do not be a lender.

   Do not be a borrower or a lender.

   Or

   Be neither a borrower nor a lender.

Conjunctions *...or, either ...or, neither ...nor,* express a choice between two alternatives. Such Conjunctions which express a choice between two alternatives are called **'Alternative'**.

1. It is very hot. I can't go out.

   It is very hot, so I cannot go out.

2. You were late. You were reprimanded.
   You were late; therefore you were reprimanded.
3. He cannot walk. He is very weak.
   He cannot walk, for he is very weak.

Conjunctions *so, therefore, for* etc. join sentences in which one statement is inferred from the other. Such conjunctions which express **'inference'** are called **'Illative'**.

Combination of two or more Simple Sentences into a single complex sentence.

In the following examples, the Subordinate Clause is a Noun Clause.

1. You may solve all the sums. I don't know.
   I don't know whether you can solve all the sums.
2. The accused was drunk. I am sure.
   I am sure that the accused was drunk.
3. His past record is good. That proves his innocence.
   That his past record is good proves his innocence.
4. You have been honest, sincere and devoted. We shall always remember.
   We shall always remember that you have been honest, sincere and devoted.
5. You would pass. That was our hope. Our hope was positive.
   Our hope that you would pass was positive.

Subordinate — Adjective Clause

In the following examples, the Subordinate Clause is an Adjective clause :

1. He is the boy. He has stood first in the class.
   He is the boy who has stood first in the class.
2. This is the watch. It was presented by my uncle
   This is the watch which was presented by my uncle.
3. A boy came here. The boy was very hungry.
   The boy who came here was very hungry.

Subordinate — Adverb Clause

In the following examples, the Subordinate Clause is an Adverb Clause :

1. The Director was not present. We met the manager.
   As the Director was not present, we met the manager.
2. You are very week. You can hardly walk.
   You are so weak that you can hardly walk.

3. Ram is brave... Sham is equally brave.
   Sham is as brave as Ram.
4. You started late. You reached first.
   Although you started late you reached first.
5. Walk slowly. You will fall.
   If you don't walk slowly you will fall.
6. We waited for the fight. We waited till it came.
   We waited for the flight until it came.
7. He is studying hard. He wants to get good marks.
   He is studying hard so that he can get good marks.
8. He is rich. He is greedy.
   Although he is rich, he is greedy.
9. The soldier fled somewhere. The Commander followed him.
   The soldier fled where the commander followed him.
10. He studied very hard. He spoiled his health.
    He studied so hard that he spoiled his health.

EXERCISE 124

Combine each set of the Simple Sentences into Complex sentence containing a noun clause.

1. I have seen you somewhere before. I don't remember the place.
2. You are innocent. I am sure of it.
3. You will waste your time. That is certain.
4. He has worked sincerely. No one can doubt this fact.
5. He has done a blunder. I think so.
6. Who wrote Hamlet ? Can anyone tell me that ?
7. You have cheated him. This is the truth.
8. He will not succeed. That is certain.
9. He distrusts his best friends. It is difficult to understand this.
10. The chief guest will arrive in time. We expect it.
11. Is it time for the aeroplane to land ? Ask some one.
12. You disturbed me. Do you deny this ?
13. The function will start at a certain time. Do you know the time ?
14. He is a great statesman. This fact cannot be denied.
15. What has he done ? Tell us.

EXERCISE 125

Combine each set of Simple Sentences into one Complex Sentence containing an Adjective Clause :

1. You are not working sincerely. Can you tell me the reason ?
2. This is the college. I studied here.
3. You were surmoned somewhere. Show me the place.
4. He is the boy. He has defied his parents.
5. The robbery was committed yesterday. The robbers have been arrested.
6. A man was proud of his strength. He disliked weak persons.
7. I have many plans. These plans will lead me to great heights.
8. I met a man. The man was a stranger in this city.
9. He has eaten food. The food was kept for me.
10. This man has become very weak. He used to take drugs.

EXERCISE 126

Combine each set of Simple Sentences into one Complex Sentence containing an Adverb Clause :

1. We had reached airport. The flight landed afterwards.
2. Her parents died. She has been very poor from that time.
3. This poem is very easy. Even a child can understand it.
4. I cannot teach you today. I am not well.
5. He will be hanged. He has committed a murder.
6. He is poor. He is happy.
7. The boy is being honoured. He has stood first in the examination.
8. She is very tired. She cannot work any more.
9. Sonu is a good boy. No other boy in our school is equally good.
10. He came late. He was admonished.
11. You must hurry. You will miss the flight otherwise.
12. I was returning from office. I was caught in a shower.
13. I went to your office. You were out.
14. We saw some strange footmarks on the ground. We were puzzled.
15. I was not well. I did not go out.
16. The principal arrived. The function started.
17. You entered the room. Just then the clock struck four.
18. He studied hard. He did so to get good marks.
19. You must be very tired. You had no sleep last night.
20. A tutor may call. Please ask him to wait.
21. He worked very hard. He soon rose to great heights.
22. I will dress up. Do not go till then.
23. You speak in a very low voice. No body can hear you.

24. The saint left the house. The house collapsed that very moment.
25. He studied hard. He could not get success.

EXERCISE 127

Combine each of the following sets of simple sentences into one complex sentence :

1. He was surrounded by bandits. He felt confused. Nothing can describe that confusion.
2. Milton did not educate his daughters in languages. He said that one tongue was enough for women.
3. He had read Shakespeare. He had read it when he was sixteen. He told me this.
4. I took the medicine. I then felt better. It cured my sickness.
5. You may like it. You may not like it. In either case I shall give you orders. It is my duty to do so.
6. You are sure to receive your money. It is due to you.
7. You will not participate in the debate. The decision is foolish. You are the best debater in our school.
8. I waited longer. I got very angry. I had asked you to be punctual.
9. This is the elephant. It had gone 'mast'. It killed two persons.
10. That is the man. He gave me a present. It was stolen.
11. You studied hard. You succeeded. It was expected.
12. That is the boy. He has topped the Civil Services examination. He is being interviewed by the reporters.
13. I have lost the pen. The pen was gifted to me by my father. It was a very costly pen.
14. Her behaviour is very strange. We are unable to understand it. We have been told about it
15. You stole a purse. It had the owner's name written on it. I was told this.
16. They despised their boss. He was very arrogant. He had an authoritarian temperament.
17. It was daybreak. They stood on a hill. The hill overlooked the moor.
18. It was 10 A.M. The chief guest entered the hall. He was received by the Principal. The Principal read the report.
19. You have passed. We are happy to know this. You deserved to pass.
20. You are a lethargic and careless boy. The report says so. I have received the report. I am very unhappy to receive it.
21. You will be given admission. Your working hard is a condition. The Principal has issued orders to that effect.
22. I am going to the U.S.A. I have got leave. My father is already there. He is a doctor.

EXERCISE 128

Combine each of the following groups of Sentences into one Compound or one Complex Sentence :

1. A group of robbers entered a village. The robbers were armed. They entered the village at wee hours. Some of the robbers had escaped from the prison. The robbers looted the villagers. The villagers dared not challenge the robbers.

2. His father died. He had to discontinue his studies. He had to look after his mother and two younger brothers. He searched a job. He got a job. The job did not give him complete satisfaction. He was compelled to continue his job.
3. We should spend only our earning. We should save a little. We should not look to anyone for financial help. It is a golden rule. Friends generally draw back their hand at the hour of need.
4. Most of us either live in the past or look forward to the future. The past may be glorious or otherwise. The future may have its glorious uncertainties. Our optimism makes the future a dream world. We breathe and exist in the present. We hope for something better and brighter to turn up.
5. Tagore's versatility is well known. He wrote poems, plays, novels and short stories. He was a great musical composer and director of stage production. In the last years of his life he took to painting also.
6. The school at Shantiniketan was started in 1901. Then Tagore was forty years old. For the next forty years Tagore gave to the school and Visvabharati, his life and love. In these institutions, Tagore strove to renew the ideals of a bygone age of forest hermitages, of simplicity of life, of clarity of spiritual vision, of purity of heart, of harmony with the universe.
7. He offered me help, I needed help. I persisted in refusing help. He left me to my fate.
8. The name of Buddha means the Awakened One. The Buddha attained spiritual realization. He gives us a way based on clear knowledge. Buddhism is a system of spiritual realization. In Buddhism personal realization is the starting point.
9. Man is a child of God. He can become immortal through union with God. Untill then he wanders in the darkness of the world. He is like a spark from the fire or a wave of the ocean. Man becomes perfect. Then he manifests God's will perfectly.
10. The spirit of science leads to the refinement of religion. Religion is not magic or witchcraft, quackery or superstition. It is not to be confused with outdated dogmas and incredible superstitions. These are hindrances and barriers. They spoil the simplicity of spiritual life.
11. All religions require us to look upon life as an opportunity for self-realization. They call upon us to strive incessantly. They call upon us to wrest the immortal from the mortal.
12. Religion reflects both God and man. Religion is a life to be lived. Religion is not a theory to be accepted. It is not a belief to be adhered to. Religion allows scope and validity to varied approaches to the Divine.
13. An author has written an interesting book. In it he tells the story of his life. Part of his life was spent in exile from his own country. In that country he is now absolute master.
14. She took the 'sadhu' to her home. She told him to remain there for the night. Then she found him hungry. She procured some fruits from outside. She then gave them to the 'sadhu' for supper.
15. He was man of very haughty and arrogant temper. He was treated very ungraciously by the king. He was supported whole-heatedly by the people. He would eagerly take the first opportunity of showing his power and satiating his anger. This might be expected.

34

Idioms and Phrases

Expressions which are peculiar to a language are called idioms. Idioms play an important part in all languages.

Many *verbs* when followed by various prepositions or adverbs acquire an idiomatic sense.

1. *Back up* — support — You should back up your friend in all circumstances.
2. *Blow over* — pass off — His difficulties soon blew over.
3. *Build one's hopes upon* — rely upon — He should not have built his hopes upon your promises.
4. *Clear up* — explain — Our doubts were cleared up by the teacher.
5. *Dispose of* — sell — You should dispose of your old car.
6. *Eat away* — corrode — Almirah has been corroded by rust.
7. *Grow upon* — have stronger and stronger hold — Drugs must be avoided because if tasted once, the habit will grow upon.
8. *Hear out* — hear to the end — The students heard the Principal out.
9. *Hit upon* — find — We have hit upon a good idea.
10. *Hang about* — loiter about — The soldiers were asked not to hang about the office of the Officer Commanding.
11. *Lead upto* — Culminate in — His bad deeds led upto his downfall.
12. *Light upon* — chance to discover — The Archaeological Survey of India lighted upon the remains of 4th century idols during excavations.
13. *Long for* — desire — She longed for her home when she was staying abroad.
14. *Prevail on* — persuade — The doctor prevailed on the patient to take medicine regularly.
15. *Shake off* — get rid of — We should shake off orthodox beliefs.

16. *Stave off* — avert — No one could stave off the U.S. attack on Iraq.
17. *Stick out for* — persist in demanding — He stuck out for better service conditions.
18. *Think over* — Consider — I shall think over the problem and suggest proper solution.
19. *Concoct* — fabricate — The boy was punished for concocting a story.
20. *Well off* — in comfortable circumstances — He is well off after his success in new business.
21. *Bear away* — win — Indian athletes bore away many prizes in the Asian Games.
22. *Bear out* — confirm — The statement given by you does not bear out the truth.
23. *Bear up* — not to despair — One should bear up even during the most difficult times.
24. *Bear with* — show patience — I hope you will bear with me for some time.
25. *Bear upon* — to be relevant — Your statement does not bear upon this discussion.
26. *Break down* — fail — His car broke down on the way.
27. *Break off* — stop — Suddenly the speaker broke off in the middle of his speech.
28. *Break into* — enter by force — The burglars broke into the house and decamped with cash and jewellery.
29. *Bring about* — cause — Your bad deeds will bring about your ruin.
30. *Bring forth* — cause/produce — His idle habits brought forth extreme poverty.
31. *Bring up* — rear — She brought up the adopted child.
32. *Bring in* — yield as rent — This flat brings in Rs. 18,000 a year.
33. *Bring out* — show — The teacher asked the students to bring out the meaning of the poem.
34. *Bring out* — publish — Career Publications have brought out English grammar with a Difference.
35. *Bring round* — convert — We faced difficulty in bringing him round to our proposal

36. *Call for* — demand — You will be called for an explanation for your behaviour.
37. *Call in* — send for — Call in the ambulance immediately.
38. *Call on* — pay a brief visit — We shall call you on next weak.
39. *Call up* — recollect — I can call up any past event.
40. *Carry out* — execute — The teachers agreed to carry out the order of the Principal.
41. *Carry away* — deprive of self-control — One should not be carried away by the emotional speeches of the leaders.
42. *Carry on* — manage/continue — The manager carried on the work in my absence.
43. *Carry off* — kill — AIDS will carry off many persons in the world.
44. *Cast away* — wrecked — The ship was cast away by the sea storm.
45. *Cast down* — depressed — He was cast down by severe losses in business.
46. *Come about* — happen — How did this come about ?
47. *Come by* — get — How did you come by my precious book ?
48. *Come off* — take place — When will the conference come off ?
49. *Come out* — transpire — The truth will come out before the judge.
50. *Come to* — amount — Teaching every day for one month will come to Rs. 5,000.
51. *Come up* — raise for discussion — The case will come up for hearing next Monday.
52. *Come round* — agree — We hope that you will come round to our proposal.
53. *Cry out against* — protest against — The innocent will always cry out against injustice.
54. *Cut off* — died — The youth was cut off in the prime of his life.
55. *Cut down* — reduce — You should cut down your consumption of alcohol.
56. *Cut out for* — specially fitted to be — She is cut out for a model.
57. *Cut one up* — depress — Her husband's death cut her up greatly.
58. *Done for* — ruined — She is done for.
59. *Done up* — exhausted — After overworking for quite some time, you are quite done up.

60. *Fall back* — yield, retreat — The Pakistani soldiers fell back in Kargil battle.
61. *Fall in with* — meet accidentally — I fell in with my old friend at the railway station.
62. *Fall through* — fail — The project fell through for want of funds.
63. *Fall out* — quarrel — The business partners have fallen out.
64. *Fall off* — deteriorate — At present times, the values have fallen off.
65. *Fall off* — diminish — The attendance in the Parliament fell off during Winter Session of Parliament.
66. *Get off* — escape — The accused got off with a small fine.
67. *Get on with* — agree or live sociably with — I cannot get on with my Personal Assistant.
68. *Get away* — escape — The intruder got away with cash and jewellery.
69. *Get out* — remove — The dry-cleaner could not get out with the stain on my shirt.
70. *Get under* — subdue — The 'mast' elephant was ultimately got under.
71. *Get through* — pass — My son has got through the competitive examination.
72. *Get out of* — escape from — The prisoner got out of the police van.
73. *Give up* — surrender — The accused gave himself up to the police.
74. *Give one up* — having no hope of recovery — The doctors have given the cancer patient up.
75. *Give off* — emit — The fire in the chemical factory gave off dense smoke.
76. *Give in* — yield — The stubborn children do not easily give in.
77. *Give out* — proclaim, declare — It was given out that the accused was a proclaimed offender.
78. *Give way* — break — The bridge gave way leading to many causalities.
79. *Give away* — distribute — The chief guest gave away the prizes after the function was over.
80. *Go by* — judge from — One cannot always go by appearances, as they may be deceptive.
81. *Go into* — examine — The Principal went into the problems of the students.
82. *Go over* — examine — The accountant went over the balance sheet.

83. *Go through* — suffer — It is the lot of every man to go through in life.
84. *Go through* — examine — You should go through the documents before signing them.
85. *Hold out* — offer resistance — The enemy forces held out for some days and then surrendered.
86. *Hold out* — give — We can hold out no promise of your career in this company.
87. *Hold up* — stop on the highway and rob — They were held up by the robbers.
88. *Hold over* — postpone — The matter was held over till next week.
89. *Keep in* — confine after school hours — Some students were kept in.
90. *Keep in* — confine to the house — She was kept in due to very high fever.
91. *Keep up* — carry on — The delegates kept up the discussion for a long time.
92. *Keep up* — maintain — People who are idle keep up the quarrels and trivial discussion.
93. *Keep up* — maintain — I am trying my best to keep up the honour of this family.
94. *Keep on* — continue — They kept on discussing the matter.
95. *Keep back* — conceal — You should keep back nothing from your doctor.
96. *Knock down* — sell in an auction — The whole furniture was knocked down for rupees one thousand.
97. *Knock up* — exhaust — They were knocked up after a long journey.
98. *Lay down* — surrender — The enemy forces laid down their arms.
99. *Lay out* — invest — He laid out a huge sum in property.
100. *Lay out* — spend — If you do not lay out your earning carefully, you will come to grief soon.
101. *Lay up* — confine to bed — He is laid up due to hypertension.
102. *Lay by* — save for future needs — We must lay by a part of our income.
103. *Let into* — make acquainted with — He was let into all my secrets.
104. *Let off* — punish leniently — You were let off with only a fine as it was your first offence.
105. *Look after* — take care of — She looks after an orphan.

106. *Look down upon* — despise — We should not look down upon the poor.
107. *Look up* — search for — She is looking up for her son.
108. *Look forward to* — (expect with pleasure) I am looking forward to meeting my friend after a long time.
109. *Look into* — investigate — The police is looking into the matter.
110. *Look on* — regard — She looks on me as her son.
111. *Look to* — rely on — You should not look to him for any help.
112. *Look to* — be careful about — You should look to your behaviour.
113. *Look up* — rise — The prices of essential commodities have looked up.
114. *Look up* — improve — His health is looking up.
115. *Look up to* — respect — His neighbours look up to him.
116. *Make for* — conduce — Good deeds make for happiness.
117. *Make out* — discover — No one can make out your handwriting.
118. *Make out* — prove — The accused failed to make out his case.
119. *Pass by* — overlook — You should not pass by the faults of your children.
120. *Pass through* — undergo — Every one has to pass through many ups and downs in life.
121. *Pass oneself off as* — pretend to be — He passed himself off as a police inspector.
122. *Pick out* — select — Very intelligent students were picked out for the competition.
123. *Pick up* — recover or regain health — He was seriously ill but is now picking up.
124. *Pull together* — cooperate — We must pull together or we shall not succeed in our mission.
125. *Pull through* — pass with difficulty — His daughter pulled through the English test.
126. *Pull through* — recover from sickness — Mother is happy because her son has pulled through.
127. *Pull down* — demolish — The Municipal Corporation pulled down many unauthorised structures.
128. *Pull up* — rebuke/scold — You will be pulled up for your negligence.
129. *Put on* — assume — There is no need for you to put on an air of superiority.

130. *Put out* — extinguish — It took one hour to put out the fire.
131. *Put out* — annoyed — He is put out with his mother for not getting enough money.
132. *Put one off* — evade — Don't try to put me off with false promises.
133. *Put in* — make — He has put in his best efforts.
134. *Put up with* — endure — You will have to put up with many problems when you grow up.
135. *Put one to* — give — She has put you to great problems.
136. *Put off* — postpone — The meeting was put off for one week.
137. *Put through* — pass — It is difficult to put through this legislation in the Parliament.
138. *Run down* — enfeeble — She is run down due to very high fever.
139. *Run out* — expire — The date for the renewal of your licence has run out.
140. *Run up to* — amount — The wedding expenditure ran up to a large sum.
141. *Run into* — incur — He has run into a huge sum of money as interest.
142. *Run against* — chance to meet — I ran against a very old friend at the airport.
143. *See through* — detect — I could see through your trick.
144. *See into* — discern — It is not difficult to see into your trick.
145. *See off* — witness departure — I went to the railway station to see my friend off.
146. *Set aside* — annul — The Supreme Court set aside the order of the High Court.
147. *Set about* — take steps towards — The new manager set about improving the administration of the office.
148. *Set off* — start — They set off on a long journey.
149. *Set apart* — reserve — No seats are set apart in this train.
150. *Set forth* — explain — The professor set forth his views very clearly.
151. *Set upon* — attack — The dacoits set upon the train passengers.
152. *Set in* — begin — This festival sets in January every year.
153. *Set one down* — snub — We should not set anyone down.
154. *Speak of* — worth mentioning — There is not a single amenity in this office, to speak of.

155. *Speak out* — express one's opinion freely — You should speak out without any fear.
156. *Stand up for* — maintain — We must stand up for the noble cause.
157. *Stand by* — support — I will stand by you for a good cause.
158. *Strike down with* — attack by — He has been struck down with paralysis.
159. *Strike off* — remove — His name was struck off from the Bar of Council.
160. *Take up* — occupy — The furniture has taken up too much room.
161. *Take up* — occupy — He took up a long time to complete his lecture.
162. *Take after* — resemble — She takes after her mother.
163. *Take in* — understand — It is difficult to take in the poetry of T. S. Eliot.
164. *Take to* — become addicted to — He has taken to drugs.
165. *Talk over* — discuss — Let us talk over the matter in detail.
166. *Tell against* — prove unfavourable to — Your speech will tell against you.
167. *Tell upon* — affect — Over work will tell upon your health.
168. *Throw out* — reject — The proposal was thrown out by the directors.
169. *Throw up* — resign — Being fed up, he threw up his job.
170. *Turn out* — produce — This mill turns out five lakh units every day.
171. *Turn off* — dismiss — He was turned off by the management.
172. *Turn out* — prove — He did not turn out to be a good person.
173. *Turn against* — become hostile — Even his best friends turned against him during his misfortune.
174. *Turn up* — happen — We did not know what would turn up.
175. *Turn up* — appear — We waited for him for long time, but he did not turn up.
176. *Work on* — influence — He was tempted with many promises but nothing would work on him.
177. *Work out* — solve — This problem is too difficult for me to work out.
178. *Work upon* — influence — He was able to work upon the illiterate people.
179. *To eat humble pie* — to apologise humbly — When all his schemes failed, he had to eat humble pie.
180. *To eat one's words* — to take back your words — If you blame him without reason, you will have to eat your words.
181. *Not worth one's salt* — quite worthless — If you don't help him now, you are not worth your salt.

182. *To meet trouble half-way* — to worry about before it comes — There is no need to meet trouble half way.

183. *To make both ends meet* — to live within one's income — He has become so poor that it is difficult for him to make both ends meet.

184. *Set one's face against* — oppose strongly — We should set our face against criminalisation of politics.

185. *Lose ground* — become less powerful — Commercial cinema is losing ground these days.

186. *Win laurels* — acquire glory — He has won many laurels in the field of medicine.

187. *With open arms* — with a warm welcome — Mother received her son with open arms.

188. *Play fast and loose* — saying one thing and doing another — No one trusts him because he plays fast and loose.

189. *Take to task* — rebuke — The principal took the naughty boy to task.

190. *Turn a deaf ear to* — disregard — She turned a deaf ear to her father's advice.

191. *Hold water* — stand scrutiny — His argument could not hold water for long.

192. *By hook or by crook* — by fair means or foul — He intends to pass the Board Examination by hook or by crook.

193. *Hang together* — to be consistent — The answers given by the accused did not hang together.

194. *Take exception to* — object to — The Members of Parliament took exception to Minister's remark.

195. *Gain around* — become more general — The belief in the existence of God is gaining ground.

196. *To pay off old scores* — to have one's revenge — Some people believe in paying off old scores.

197. *On and off* — at intervals — I worked on and off to write English books.

198. *Off and on* — occasionally — He visits this place off and on.

199. *Put a spoke in one's wheel* — thwart the execution of design — Some people are in the habit of putting a spoke in others' wheel.

200. *Make one's mark* — distinguish oneself — He made his mark as a great writer.

201. *Have at one's fingers' end* — know thoroughly — He has it at his fingers' ends.

202. *Fall flat* — meet with a cold reception — Subhash Ghai's new film has fallen flat.

203. *Put one's foot down* — take a firm stand — He puts his foot down where punctuality is concerned.

204. *Turn over a new leaf* — change for the better — My son has turned over a new leaf.

205. *Make up one's mind* — resolve/decide — I have made up my mind to wind up my business.

206. *No love lost* — not to be in good terms — There is no love lost between the brothers.

207. *From hand to mouth* — without any provision for the future — Many people in developing countries live from hand to mouth.

208. *In the long run* — eventually — Hard work, sincerity and honesty are rewarded in the long run.

209. *Call in question* — challenge — No one can call his honesty in question.

210. *In the nick of time* — just at the right moment — The cops arrested the kidnappers in the nick of time.

211. *Through thick and thin* — under all conditions — I will stand by you through thick and thin.

212. *Throw cold water on* — discourage — He threw cold water on all my proposals.

213. *Turn one's hand to* — adapt oneself to — Sultan could turn his hand to anything.

214. *With a high hand* — oppressively — Aurangzeb ruled the masses with a high hand.

215. *Hand and glove* — on very intimate terms — Both these boys are hand and glove with each other.

216. *Sit on the fence* — undecisive between two opinions — Politicians are generally accused of sitting on the fence.

217. *Bring to light* — disclose — Rampant corruption in the D.D.A. and M.C.D. was brought to light by the CBI.

218. *Burn one's fingers* — get oneself into trouble — You will burn your fingers if you interfere in his personal life.

219. *Strain every nerve* — make best efforts — He strained every nerve to top the CBSE examination.
220. *Beside oneself* — out of mind — When she heard of her husband's death she was beside herself with grief.
221. *At sixes and sevens* — in disorder — Everything is at sixes and sevens in your room.
222. *Give oneself airs* — behave arrogantly — Don't give yourself too much airs.
223. *The order of the day* — prevailing state of affairs — These days crime has become the order of the day in big cities.
224. *Out of date* — obsolete — All these textbooks are obsolete.
225. *Up to date* — modern — This publisher has published an up to date book in English literature.
226. *In hand* — under discussion — Your statements are not in accordance with the subject in hand.
227. *Speak volumes for* — serve as a strong testimony to — His success in the Civil Services examinations speaks volumes for his efforts.
228. *Hope against hope* — hope even when the circumstances are most unfavourable — He is hoping against hope to qualify the entrance examination.
229. *Into hot water* — into trouble — All know that you have got yourself into hot water.
230. *Get the better of* — overcome — Eventually you got the better of him.
231. *Get off easy* — get a light punishment — Though found guilty, he got off easy.
232. *Wash one's hands of* — refuse to have anything to do — He washed his hands of the whole issue.
233. *Out of hand* — beyond control — The police was called when the situation went out of hand.
234. *Hit the nail on the head* — say or do the right thing — He has hit the nail on the head.
235. *In high spirits* — joyful — You seem to be in high spirits today.
236. *Out of spirits* — sad — She is out of spirits after failing in the Board examination.
237. *An axe to grind* — personal interest — As values have deteriorated, many people have an axe to grind in many matters.

238. *Spread like wild fire* — spread rapidly — The news of Indira Gandhi's death spread like wild fire.

239. *Take to heart* — get affected deeply — He took his friend's death to heart.

240. *Take heart* — cheer oneself up — Failure in the examination broke him but he took heart and tried again.

241. *Has one's heart in the right place* — to be of a kindly and sympathetic disposition — You must have your heart in the right place in all matters.

242. *Throw out of gear* — disturb the working of — Life was thrown out of gear by the bandh.

243. *Go home to* — deeply appeal — The religious discourse of the saint went home to all the disciples.

244. *In the good books of* — In favour with — You are in the good books of your boss.

245. *In one's bad books* — out of favour with — You should know that you are in his bad books.

246. *Foot the bill* — pay for — After having his food in a restaurant, he refused to foot the bill.

247. *Tooth and nail* — with all power — The Indian soldiers fought the enemy tooth and nail.

248. *Take to one's heels* — run off — The boy took to his heels on seeing the tiger.

249. *Within a stone's throw of* — at a short distance from — My school is within a stone's throw of my home.

250. *Stand one's ground* — maintain one's position — We stood our ground against all odds.

251. *Keep in touch with* — has intimate knowledge of — You should keep in touch with the latest developments in technology.

252. *Where the shoe pinches* — where the trouble lies — Only the wearer knows where the shoe pinches.

253. *In the dark* — in ignorance — Don't keep me in the dark about anything.

254. *Turn one's head* — make one quite vain — Don't let success turn your head.

255. *Too many irons in the fire* — engage in many enterprises at the same time — Keeping too many irons in the fire will disturb your peace of mind.

256. *True to one's salt* — faithful to one's employers — His services were terminated for he was not true to his salt.

257. *One's wit's end* — quite puzzled — I was at my wit's end when I found an intruder in the house.
258. *Fall foul of* — quarrel with — Your falling foul of everybody will get you nothing but enemies.
259. *Go back on* — fail to keep — He is not expected to go back on his word.
260. *Put one's heads together* — consult one another — The directors of CBSE Board put their heads together about the change of syllabus.
261. *Give ear to* — listen to — you should give ear to what your teachers say.
262. *In the air* — prevalent — This fashion is in the air.
263. *Bad blood* — bitterness — Bad blood leads to hatred and violence.
264. *To read between the lines* — know the hidden meaning — You must read this news item between the lines.
265. *In cold blood* — not in the heat of passion — The murderer carried out the murder in the cold blood.
266. *In black and white* — in writing — You should give your statements in black and white.
267. *Smell a rat* — suspect something — I smell a rat in the whole planning.
268. *Nip in the bud* — make to fail before maturity — We should nip the evil in the bud.
269. *Out of the question* — not to be thought of — My attending the party is out of question.
270. *The long and short of it* — the simple fact — The long and short of it is that I am not interested in joining this club.
271. *Show teeth* — adopt a threatening attitude — Don't show me your teeth when your purpose is solved.
272. *Take stock of* — to survey — After entering my house, he took stock of the whole scene.
273. *In full swing* — very active — His business is in full swing.
274. *Born with a silver spoon in one's mouth* — born in wealth and luxury — Pt. Jawahar Lal Nehru was born with a silver spoon in his mouth.
275. *Stand one in good stead* — prove useful — My friends have stood me in good stead in my difficult times.
276. *Take the wind out of one's sails* — make one's words or actions ineffective — He took the wind out of your sails.

277. *Take one to task* — reprove — The teacher took all the late-comers to task.

278. *Take one's life in one's hands* — take great risks — The Indian soldiers took their life in their hands and attacked the enemy.

279. *End in smoke* — come to nothing — All his planning ended in a smoke.

280. *Leave no stone unturned* — use all available means — We left no stone unturned to search his lost son.

281. *To rest on one's laurels* — retire from active life — Sohan has decided to rest on his laurels.

282. *Harp on in the same string* — to dwell continuously on the same subject — We are sick of his harping on the same string.

283. *Blood running cold* — horrified — Our blood ran cold when we saw the terrorists killing innocent persons.

284. *Make good the loss* — compensate — He apologised and agreed to make good the loss.

285. *Kick up a row* — make great fuss — Don't kick up a row as it won't help you.

286. *Ill at ease* — uncomfortable — He was ill at ease while appearing for Civil Services interview.

287. *Hard of hearing* — somewhat deaf — Speak loud as I am hard of hearing.

288. *Neither head nor tail*- nothing — We could make neither head nor tail of what he said.

289. *Stir up a hornet's nest* — excite the hostility of a large number of people — Wise persons don't stir up a hornet's nest.

290. *Every inch* — completely — He is every inch a noble person.

291. *Rise to the occasion* — show oneself equal to dealing with the emergency — Everyone rose to the occasion while rescuing the trapped passengers.

292. *The ins and outs* — full details — The accountant knows the ins and outs of this company's affairs.

293. *Beyond all question* — without doubt — Beyond all question, he is a gentleman.

294. *Out of question* — impossible — My joining this company is out of question.

295. *Go out of one's way* — take special trouble — I went out of my way to help him in his difficulty.

296. *With one voice* — unanimously — The proposal was accepted with one voice.

297. *Hang in balance* — undecided — My fate still hangs in balance as I am not sure of my appointment.

298. *Carry off one's feet* — wild with excitement — I was carried off my feet when I came to know that I had topped the Board examinations.

299. *Make the most* of — use to the best advantage — We should make the most of any good opportunity.

300. *Fall short of one's expectations* — disappoint one — His result of the CBSE examination fell much short of his expectations.

301. *Like a fish out water* — in a strange situation — I feel like a fish out of water when someone discusses movies.

302. *By fits and starts* — irregularly — Students should not study by fits and starts.

303. *Take things easy* — not to work hard — You can take things easy after you have earned enough money.

304. *Cook the accounts* — prepare false accounts — The cashier was arrested as he had cooked the accounts.

305. *Take into account* — consider — Taking his honesty into account, he was given an award.

306. *To mean business* — to be earnest — When I say this, I mean business.

307. *To hold good* — to be valid — This offer will not hold good after one week.

308. *To be at one's beck and call*- under one's absolute control — This fellow is always at my beck and call.

309. *Burn the candles at both ends* — to overtax one's energies — We should not burn the candles at both ends.

310. *Bury the hatchet* — stop fighting — You should bury the hatchet and work together.

311. *Blow one's own trumpet* — praise oneself — He always blows his own trumpet.

312. *A far cry* — no easy change — It is a far cry from ignorance to knowledge.

313. *Make one's flesh creep* — horrify — The scene of massacre made my flesh creep.

314. *Pin one's faith to* — place full reliance upon — In modern world, one should pin one's faith to religious education.

315. *To let the grass grow under one's feet* — to remain idle — You are not the sort of person to let the grass grow under your feet.
316. *Split hairs* — dispute over petty matters — It is unwise of you to split hairs.
317. *Great a hand at* — expert at — You are great a hand at convincing people.
318. *Loaves and fishes* — material gains — Most men these days are after loaves and fishes.
319. *Leave one in the lurch* — desert in difficulties — My wife left me in the lurch.
320. *Man of Straw* — a man of no substance — It is difficult for a man of straw to get loan.
321. *Beside the mark* — irrelevant — The points put forward by you are beside the mark.
322. *Move heaven and earth* — make every possible effort — He moved heaven and earth to terminate his services.
323. *Stick to one's colours* — remain faithful to cause — The commander asked the soldiers to stick to their colours.
324. *Red — handed* — on the spot — The murderer was caught red-handed.
325. *Try one's hand* — make an attempt — As you have not succeeded in farming, you should try your hand in business.
326. *Give one the cold shoulder* — treat in a cold manner — Even his close relations gave him the cold shoulder during his bad times.
327. *On the cards* — probable — Another war was on the cards but was avoided by the efforts of great statesmen.
328. *Hang on one's lips* — listen eagerly to — Whenever he speaks, the listeners hang on their lips.
329. *Hang fire* — hesitate — The teacher asked the students to do the class work but some students hung fire.
330. *All ears* — deeply attentive — The students were all ears to the Principal's lecture.
331. *All eyes* — eagerly watching — The teacher was all eyes to see what the students would do.
332. *Keep a good table* — provide luxurious food — This restaurant keeps a good table.
333. *Keep one's hands above water* — to keep out of debt — It is difficult for him to keep his hands above water as he has a meagre income and many mouths to feed.

334. *Set the Thames on fire* — do some remarkable or surprising thing — As no miracles happen, you cannot set the Thames on fire.

335. *Come to grief* — fail — The scheme came to grief due to lack of funds.

336. *At arm's length* — at a distance — I keep selfish people at arm's length.

337. *Come of age* — reach the age of twenty one — When the prince came of age, he was coronated.

338. *Bag and baggage* — with all belongings, altogether — He has decided to leave Delhi bag and baggage.

339. *A bone of contention* — a matter of dispute — Kashmir is a bone of contention between India and Pakistan.

340. *Take away one's breath* — surprise greatly — She took away his breath when she proposed to him.

341. *Swollen* — headed — conceited — After becoming rich, he has become swollen — headed.

342. *Take up the cudgels for* — defend vigorously — The defense counsel took up the cudgels for the accused.

343. *Cut one's own throat* — ruin onself — If you associate with bad people you will cut your own throat.

344. *Cut one off with a shilling* — disinherit by bequeathing a small sum — The king cut the prince off with a shilling.

345. *Cut one short* — interrupt — Don't cut me short when I am speaking.

346. *A dead letter* — no longer in force — This custom is a dead letter.

347. *Draw the line* — fix the limit — I have to draw the line of your monthly expenditure.

348. *To see eye to eye* — to be in complete agreement with — The two brothers don't see eye to eye with each other.

349. *Put a good face on* — bear up courageously — We should put a good face on our defeats.

350. *Thrust one's nose into* — meddle officiously — You should not thrust your nose into his affairs.

351. *Under one's nose* — in one's presence — Don't be so oblivious that you are not aware of what passes under your nose.

352. *A hard nut to crack* — a difficult problem to solve — Brain drain from developing countries is a hard nut to crack.

353. *Rest on one's oars* — stop work and rest — After winning many laurels, he is resting on his oars.

354. *Come to a head* — reach a crises — The problem due to the strike of the mill workers has come to a head.

355. *Play with fire* — trifle ignorantly with matters which may cause suffering — Don't play with fire, or you may face the worst days of your life.

356. *Put one's hand in one's pocket* — give money in charity — Only generous people put their hands in their pocket.

357. *Right — hand man* — most efficient assistant — Girja Prasad Chaudhary is my right hand man.

358. *Speak volumes for* — serve as strong testimony to — His conduct towards his subordinates speaks volumes for his kindness.

359. *Up to the mark* — in excellent health — Today he is not looking up to the mark.

360. *Put two and two together* — draw a correct inference — The learned judge was always able to put two and two together.

361. *To have two strings to one's bow* — to have two sources of income — In these days of financial difficulties every one must have two strings to his bow.

362. *Under one's wings* — under one's protection — After his father's death the child is under his guardian's wings.

363. *A wild goose chase* — A foolish and fruitless search — You seem to be on a wild goose chase.

364. *Washing one's dirty linen in public* — discussing unpleasant matters before strangers — We should not wash our dirty linen in public.

365. *At daggers drawn* — having strained relations — Both these brothers are at daggers drawn.

366. *Yeoman's service* — excellent work — Gandhiji did yeoman's service to propagate the cause of non-violence.

367. *On the wrong side of sixty* — more than sixty years of age — Though on the wrong side of sixty, he is quite hale and hearty.

368. *A man of one's words* — A trustworthy person — You should not rely on him, for he is not a man of his words.

369. *Keep the wolf from the door* — keep off starvation — For some people it is difficult to keep the wolf from the door.

370. *Wolf in sheep's clothing* — a hypocrite — The man sitting beside you is wolf in sheep's clothing.

371. *Turn the corner* — pass the crises — The patient seems to have turned the corner.

372. *On tender hooks* — in a state of suspense and anxiety — I am on tender hooks unless my result is declared.

373. *At the top of the tree* — at the head of one's profession — Having joined this company five years ago, he is at the top of the tree.

374. *To have an old head on young shoulder* — to be wise beyond years — This boy seems to have an old head on young shoulder.

375. *Square meal* — full meal — Some people are compelled to eat one square meal a day.

376. *Rub shoulder* — come into close contact — This person has rubbed shoulders with persons of all walks of life.

377. *Shake in one's shoes* — tremble with fear — The child shook in his shoes when be saw a ferocious animal.

378. *Black sheep* — bad characters — One should not associate with black sheep.

379. *Make shift* — get along as best as one can — In the absence of the supervisor, the workers made shift.

380. *Show one up* — to disclose one's villainy — I will show you up if you don't amend your behaviour.

381. *Stand to one's guns* — maintain one's own position — He stood to his guns inspite of all the odds against him.

35

Answers

EXERCISE 1

1. Assertive	2. Assertive	3. Imperative	4. Interrogative	5. Imperative
6. Exclamatory	7. Optative	8. Imperative	9. Imperative	10. Exclamatory
11. Imperative	12. Imperative	13. Assertive	14. Exclamatory	15. Interrogative
16. Interrogative	17. Imperative	18. Imperative	19. Imperative	20. Assertive

EXERCISE 2

Subject	Predicate
1. They	have completed their home work.
2. She	knows me.
3. The boys	are playing.
4. The Himalayas	are the highest mountains in the world.
5. The uses of adversity	are sweet.
6. A thing of beauty	is a joy forever.
7. He	clad the naked everyday.
8. Nature	is the best physician.
9. Stone walls	do not a prison make.
10. Borrowed garments	never fit well.
11. No man	can serve two masters.
12. He	is a man of might.
13. The shepherd	heard a barking sound.
14. The sun	sets in the west.
15. Rising early	can keep your body and mind fit.
16. Your clothes	are here.
17. Boys	are flying kites.
18. The hunter	sat in the corner waiting for the prey.

EXERCISE 3

1.	won	Verb	3.	heard	Verb
	prize	Noun	4.	honest	Adjective
2.	class	Noun		person	Noun
	consists	Verb	5.	Kolkata	Noun
	students	Noun		big	Adjective

6.	hurrah !	Interjection	8. Teach	Verb
	they	Pronoun	you	Pronoun
	won	Verb	9. Tiger	Noun
7.	you	Pronoun	great	Adjective
	obey	Verb	strength	Noun
	parents	Noun	10. leak	Noun
			great	Adjective

EXERCISE 4

	Nouns	Kind		Nouns	Kind
1.	jury	Collective	9.	hardwork	Abstract
	prisoner	Common		discipline	Abstract
2.	noise	Abstract		sincerity	Abstract
3.	pen	Common		qualities	Abstract
	sword	Common	10.	students	Common
4.	wisdom	Abstract		class	Collective
	strength	Abstract	11.	soldier	Common
5.	ornaments	Common		award	Common
	gold	Material	12.	bouquet	Collective
6.	herd	Collective		birthday	Abstract
	cattle	Common	13.	police	Collective
	field	Common		shells	Common
7.	happiness	Abstract	14.	health	Abstract
	health	Abstract		happiness	Abstract
8.	soldier	Common	15.	cleanliness	Abstract
	arm	Common		godliness	Abstract
	battlefield	Common			

EXERCISE 5

1. regiment	2. flock	3. herd	4. mob	5. jury
6. committee	7. swarm	8. crew	9. fleet	10. Team

EXERCISE 6

1. strength	2. childhood	3. punishment	4. proposal	5. wisdom
6. truth	7. freedom	8. innocence	9. happiness	10. bravery

EXERCISE 7

Feminine	Feminine	Feminine	Feminine
1. girl	10. gentle lady	19. hostess	28. stewardess
2. boy	11. madam	20. countess	29. tigress
3. lioness	12. ewe	21. giantess	30. negress
4. hen-sparrow	13. daughter	22. duck	31. heiress
5. heroine	14. hind	23. manageress	32. conductress
6. sister	15. mother	24. jewess	33. princess
7. bitch	16. goose	25. duchess	34. poetess
8. doe	17. baroness	26. aunt	35. waitress
9. filly	18. authoress	27. witch	36. pea-hen

EXERCISE 8

	Adjective	Kind		Adjective	Kind
1.	heavy	quality	8.	every	distributive
2.	funny	quality		his	possessive
3.	empty	quality	9.	these	demonstrative
	much	quantity	10.	heavy	quality
4.	great	quality	11.	your	possessive
	precious	quality	12.	which	interrogative
5.	precious	quality	13.	whose	interrogative
	useless	quality	14.	heroic	quality
6.	stormy	quality	15.	honest	quality,
	rough	quality		sincere	quality
7.	many	quantity			
	green	quality			

EXERCISE 9

1. polite, rude
2. sour, sweet
3. sharp
4. honest
5. wise, foolish
6. honest
7. small
8. short
9. vegetarian
10. fresh
11. less
12. timely
13. all
14. these
15. what
16. new
17. every
18. good

EXERCISE 10

	Comparative	Superlative		Comparative	Superlative
1.	braver	bravest	22.	taller	tallest
2.	heavier	heaviest	23.	bolder	boldest
3.	more beautiful	most beautiful	24.	more clever	most clever
4.	uglier	ugliest	25.	kinder	kindest
5.	noisier	nosiest	26.	younger	youngest
6.	lighter	lightest	27.	greater	greatest
7.	more timid	most timid	28.	more proper	most proper
8.	wiser	wisest	29.	more learned	most learned
9.	nobler	noblest	30.	more difficult	most difficult
10.	abler	ablest	31.	more splendid	most splendid
11.	larger	largest	32.	better	best
12.	whiter	whitest	33.	more	most
13.	finer	finest	34.	more	most
14.	happier	happiest	35.	older	oldest
15.	easier	easiest	36.	blacker	blackest
16.	wealthier	wealthiest	37.	worse	worst
17.	bigger	biggest	38.	abler	ablest
18.	redder	reddest	39.	drier	driest
19.	hotter	hottest	40.	merrier	merriest
20.	thinner	thinnest	41.	higher	highest
21.	smaller	smallest	42.	sadder	saddest

EXERCISE 11

Adjective	Degree	Adjective	Degree
1. better	comparative	8. better	comparative
2. best	superlative	9. highest	superlative
3. sharper	comparative	10. hottest	superlative
4. less	comparative	11. mild	positive
5. idlest	superlative	12. most intelligent	superlative
6. unhappy	positive	13. best	superlative
happier	comparative	14. untidy	positive
7. strongest	superlative		

EXERCISE 12

1. better 2. hotter 3. best 4. most 5. cheaper
6. best 7. better 8. more 9. better 10. highest
11. happiest 12. worse, worst 13. latest 14. best.

EXERCISE 13

1. which 2. who 3. what 4. who 5. what
6. which 7. which

EXERCISE 14

1. they, them 2. it, 3. I, it 4. I, them 5. we, you, us
6. you 7. them, them, me, I, you, we

EXERCISE 15

1. myself 2. himself 3. themselves 4. herself 5. himself

EXERCISE 16

	Demonstrative Pronoun	Demonstrative Adjective		Demonstrative Pronoun	Demonstrative Adjective
1.	—	your	6.	—	this
2.	—	this	7.	this	—
3.	this	—	8.	—	such
4.	—	these	9.	such	—
5.	these	—			

EXERCISE 17

1. this 2. these 3. this 4. this 5. this
6. those 7. such 8. that

EXERCISE 18

1. any 2. some 3. all 4. none 5. one

EXERCISE 19

1. each 2. either 3. neither 4. either 5. each

EXERCISE 20

1. which 2. whom 3. which 4. whom 5. which
6. which

EXERCISE 21

1. who 2. which 3. whom 4. which 5. who
6. that 7. which 8. who 9. who 10. which

EXERCISE 22

1. who 2. who 3. who 4. which 5. who
6. who 7. which 8. who

EXERCISE 23

	Past	Past Participle		Past	Past Participle
1.	wrote	written	31.	crept	crept
2.	read	read	32.	spread	spread
3.	spoke	spoken	33.	lost	lost
4.	bathed	bathed	34.	telecast	telecast
5.	knew	known	35.	broadcast	broadcast
6.	told	told	36.	came	come
7.	heard	heard	37.	lent	lent
8.	played	played	38.	quit	quit
9.	danced	danced	39.	smelt	smelt
10.	gave	given	40.	spent	spent
11.	grew	grown	41.	thought	thought
12.	hid	hidden	42.	wept	wept
13.	forgot	forgotten	43.	burst	burst
14.	flew	flown	44.	hurt	hurt
15.	flowed	flowed	45.	let	let
16.	found	found	46.	met	met
17.	got	got	47.	paid	paid
18.	chose	chosen	48.	said	said
19.	began	begun	49.	sang	sung
20.	beat	beaten	50.	saw	seen
21.	arose	arisen	51.	held	held
22.	bore	born	52.	rang	rung
23.	bore	borne	53.	blew	blown
24.	knelt	knelt	54.	became	become
25.	won	won	55.	tore	torn
26.	put	put	56.	sold	sold
27.	felt	felt	57.	taught	taught
28.	cut	cut	58.	learnt	learnt
29.	bred	bred	59.	bought	bought
30.	shut	shut	60.	brought	brought

	Past	Past Participle		Past	Past Participle
61.	caught	caught	71.	shrank	shrunk
62.	sought	sought	72.	strove	striven
63.	refused	refused	73.	took	taken
64.	made	made	74.	swore	sworn
65.	fed	fed	75.	threw	thrown
66.	carried	carried	76.	swam	swum
67.	ran	run	77.	wore	worn
68.	shot	shot	78.	built	built
69.	shone	shone	79.	had	had
70.	shook	shaken			

EXERCISE 24

1. Intransitive	2. Transitive	3. Intransitive	4. Transitive
5. Transitive	6. Intransitive	7. Transitive	8. Intransitive
9. Transitive	10. Intransitive	11. Intransitive	12. Transitive
13. Intransitive	14. Intransitive	15. Transitive	

EXERCISE 25

	Main Verb	Auxiliary Verb		Main Verb	Auxiliary Verb
1.	singing	are	9.	hung	—
2.	flying	were	10.	making	is
3.	return	did not	11.	won	—
4.	receive	will	12.	caught	—
5.	like	does not	13.	killed	—
6.	blowing	is	14.	fired	—
7.	laid	—	15.	delivering	was
8.	discovered	—			

EXERCISE 26

1. hung	2. rose	3. discovered	4. blew	5. flows
6. laid	7. robbed	8. floats	9. quack	10. cackle
11. blow	12. brays	13. hoot	14. hiss	

EXERCISE 27

1. softly	2. fast	3. often	4. badly	5. strongly
6. down	7. very	8. never	9. now	10. there
11. luckily	12. certainly	13. bravely	14. soon	15. badly
16. angrily	17. silently	18. brutally	19. noisily	20. cruelly

EXERCISE 28

1. here	2. angrily	3. well	4. sweetly	5. there
6. hardly	7. very	8. early	9. impulsively	10. softly
11. easily	12. much	13. seldom	14. fast	

EXERCISE 29

1. to
2. to
3. from
4. of
5. of
6. for
7. to
8. of
9. to
10. to
11. at
12. on
13. on
14. to
15. of
16. for
17. of
18. on, in
19. with
20. with, on
21. to
22. about
23. for
24. with
25. against, to
26. of
27. of
28. for
29. on
30. from, with
31. of
32. on
33. of
34. in
35. of
36. to
37. to
38. by
39. at, in
40. before
41. from, to
42. from
43. of
44. for
45. since
46. of
47. into
48. with
49. by

EXERCISE 30

1. unless—Subordinating
2. after—Subordinating
3. where—Subordinating
4. if—Subordinating
5. before—Subordinating
6. if—Subordinating
7. before—Subordinating
8. until—Subordinating
9. that—Subordinating
10. than—Subordinating
11. than—Subordinating
12. whether—Subordinating
13. and—Co-ordinating
14. but—Co-ordinating
15. since—Subordinating
16. after—Subordinating
17. but—Co-ordinating
18. lest—Subordinating

EXERCISE 31

1. than
2. because
3. or
4. till
5. though
6. than
7. for
8. and
9. as
10. and
11. or
12. if
13. unless
14. but
15. if
16. whether
17. and
18. but
19. unless
20. if
21. if
22. what
23. that
24. than
25. that
26. than
27. if
28. when
29. as
30. but
31. whether, or
32. since
33. though
34. unless

EXERCISE 32

1. Ram works hard but Sham works harder.
2. If he is not ill, he will come.
3. Sohan sells not only bananas but he sells apples also.
4. Both Chirag and Hari played well.
5. Sonu plays for pleasure but Monu plays for money.
6. My father is not here nor is my mother.
7. Although he is rich yet he is not happy.
8. I respect him because he is an honest person.
9. Though I worked hard I could not pass.
10. He is slow but he is sure.
11. I shall sit and draft a letter.
12. If you don't start at once you will be late.
13. My brother went to office but my sister stayed at home.
14. Although you do not write fast yet you write well.

15. He is seriously wounded because he had met with an accident.
16. The rain stopped when I had come in.

EXERCISE 33

1. met	2. has been learning	3. knows
4. rises	5. left	6. shall have completed
7. appears	8. has not met	9. arrives/will arrive
10. are learning	11. Do, know	12. have, been working
13. had reached	14. will have left	15. comes, has not come
16. have been resting	17. has slept	18. went
19. is thinking	20. have done	21. will leave/leaves
22. went	23. had been waiting	24. grumbling
25. has been suffering.		

EXERCISE 34

1. won	2. drank	3. froze	4. forgot, said
5. got up	6. rose, sank	7. flew	8. came of
9. wrote	10. swam	11. punished	12. had been waiting
13. came	14. knew	15. had been sleeping	16. made
17. forgot	18. ran	19. felt	20. went

EXERCISE 35

1. make	2. knows	3. writes	4. bleeds
5. cuts	6. fly	7. drinks	8. hold
9. knows	10. is shining	11. is taking	12. have been waiting
13. takes	14. clings	15. flies	16. grows
17. lies	18. works	19. try, succeed	20. hides
21. are playing	22. hear	23. meets	24. lays

EXERCISE 36

Go	— (i) has gone	(ii) went	(iii) went
See	— (i) saw	(ii) seen	(iii) saw
Begin	— (i) begun	(ii) began	(iii) began
Fall	— (i) fell	(ii) fell	(iii) fallen
Bite	— (i) bitten	(ii) bit	(iii) bitten
Run	— (i) ran	(ii) had run	(iii) run
Bid	— (i) bade	(ii) bidden	(iii) bade
Tear	— (i) tore	(ii) torn	(iii) torn
Forget	— (i) forgotten	(ii) forgot	(iii) had forgotten
Catch	— (i) caught	(ii) caught	(iii) caught
Give	— (i) gave	(ii) gave	(iii) gave
Know	— (i) known	(ii) knew	(iii) has known
Teach	— (i) taught	(ii) taught	(iii) had taught

Ring	— (i) rang	(ii) rung	(iii) rung
Steal	— (i) stolen	(ii) stole	(iii) stolen
Sow	— (i) sown	(ii) sowed	
Write	— (i) written	(ii) wrote	
Eat	— (i) eaten	(ii) ate	
Say	— (i) said	(ii) said	
Fly	— (i) flown	(ii) flew	
Find	— (i) found	(ii) found	
Shoot	— (i) shot	(ii) shot/have shot	
Teach	— (i) taught	(ii) taught	

EXERCISE 37

	Verb	Active	Passive
1.	has been dismissed	—	Passive
2.	is doing	Active	—
3.	have been posted	—	Passive
4.	knew	Active	—
5.	is writing	Active	—
6.	Are telling	Active	—
7.	Do bring	Active	—
8.	was given	—	Passive
9.	was consumed	—	Passive
10.	was given	—	Passive
11.	flew	Active	—
12.	were being ploughed	—	Passive
13.	Let be switched off	—	Passive
14.	Don't go	Active	—
15.	has done	Active	—
16.	was done	—	Passive
17.	Is given	—	Passive
18.	Has returned	—	Passive
19.	Will obeyed	—	Passive
20.	is making	Active	

EXERCISE 38

1. Are your teachers obeyed by you ?
2. Many toys were bought by her.
3. Many trees were felled by storm.
4. Where was my money kept by you ?
5. Is your home work being done by you ?
6. Will all the letters be typed by her ?
7. This heavy box can be lifted by me.
8. A short leave may be got by you.
9. Were the vegetables cut by you ?
10. By whom were you taught English ?
11. Where are your clothes kept by you ?
12. How was the river crossed by you ?
13. Radios are sold here by them.
14. Could your money be got back by you ?

15. This sum cannot be solved by me.
16. All the difficult sums can be solved by her.
17. Shall I be accompanied by you ?
18. Have the soldiers been alerted by the commander ?
19. Let the door not be opened.
20. Let the rules be obeyed.
21. Is a popular serial being watched by you on television ?
22. By whom was Nagasaki attacked ?
23. Were the enemy forces defeated by our army ?
24. Your house is wished to be seen by him.
25. Was the meeting wanted to be attended by him ?
26. Will the meeting be attended by you ?
27. The sums had been solved by the students when the teacher came.
28. Let your time not be wasted.
29. Animals are loved by children.
30. He was elected captain by us.

EXERCISE 39

1. I know him.
2. What one cannot cure one must endure.
3. He has given the poor woollen clothes.
4. How can we solve this problem ?
5. Who did the work ?
6. We should not deprive the poor of their dues.
7. Do you not always disturb me ?
8. We presented him a new television.
9. The doctor prescribed different medicine.
10. The reader broadcast this news on All India Radio.
11. The judge punished all the wrong doers.
12. Did you complete the work in time ?
13. Somebody is knocking at the door.
14. Where will they hold the meeting ?
15. Can you help me in this juncture ?
16. Did the hangman hang him for no crime of his ?
17. They cut all the telephone wires.
18. Gambling ruined him.
19. Who taught you English ?
20. The police has caught all the robbers.
21. We called them cowards.
22. Who dismantled the computer ?
23. We appointed him mayor.
24. Do not shut the door.
25. Please come here.

EXERCISE 40

1. Wealth is desired by all but is acquired by some.
2. By whom was the jug broken ?
3. We saw him stealing the purse.
4. The police accused him of various offences.
5. Let the poor not be insulted.
6. Why was this letter not typed by him ?
7. They refused us admission.
8. He was elected captain of our school team by them.
9. By whom is a noise being made ?
10. What one cannot cure one must endure.
11. Will that unhappy period of my life be forgotten by me ?
12. Your teacher must be listened to by you.
13. Who switched off the T.V. ?
14. We gave him a beautiful present.
15. Mother cooked food in time.
16. I wrote no letter during the last fortnight.
17. The President administered the new ministers the oath of office and secrecy.
18. Let this letter be posted.
19. The people were spreading the rumours.
20. The police has arrested many terrorists.
21. Can you solve this sum ?
22. Obey the rules.
23. Dishonest persons are leading him.
24. We left no room unattended.
25. Has he been informed of the flash news by you ?
26. Is he known to you ?
27. He left a message for you.
28. Everyone will obey you.
29. Was he given the message by you ?

EXERCISE 41

1. He told me that he had given me much trouble.
2. The student said that they had done their home work.
3. The child told his mother that he wanted to go out.
4. The teacher told the students that he was giving them a small home work.
5. She told me that she would meet me the next day.
6. The boys said that they had completed the work.
7. He told me that he had met me in the party the previous day.
8. My father told me that he had given me some home work the previous day.
9. Mother told the child that she could not allow him to play outside.

10. He said that it might rain that day.
11. The Principal said that he was busy.
12. The soldiers said that they would do their best.
13. Sonu said that he had gone to the cinema the night before.
14. He said that he would come back the next day.
15. He said that he took exercise everyday.
16. I told my father that it might not be possible for me to solve that sum.
17. The students told the teacher respectfully that they had done their class work.
18. My mother told me that she was going out and would return after two hours.
19. The teacher told the student that he had not taken serious interest in his studies.
20. The announcer said that the train was likely to be late by four hours.
21. The Principal said that the examinations were likely to be postponed for a fortnight.
22. I told him that I had gone to his house the previous day.
23. The examiner said that any examine who took help of books would be disqualified for five years.
24. He said that most of the educational institutions had become business centres these (not those) days.
25. You said that you had had your lunch.

EXERCISE 42

1. I asked him when he would come back from the tour.
2. Mother asked her daughter if she had given him her message.
3. I asked my mother if I might go out to play.
4. He asked me if I was going to market.
5. The student asked the teacher respectfully if he might come in.
6. I asked a passerby if he could tell me the way to the nearest inn.
7. She asked me if I could accompany her to the market.
8. He asked me where I lived.
9. My friend asked me what he could do for me.
10. I asked him how he went to his office.
11. He asked on telephone if he was speaking to Mr. Anil.
12. My friend asked me if I wanted to go with him for a walk.
13. My mother asked me who taught me English.
14. She asked the guests what they would like to have.
15. I inquired if he would come back from London by next month.
16. I asked him if he liked vegetarian food.
17. He asked me where I came from.
18. The doctor asked me how I felt that day.
19. She asked me which my book was.
20. The mother asked the daughter why she was so late that night.
21. The employer asked Rakesh why he was sitting idle.
22. The poor woman asked if no one would help her.

23. I asked the guest if he liked that place.
24. I asked my mother if she believed in ghosts.
25. He asked the conductor when the bus would start.

EXERCISE 43

1. I requested him to give me his book.
2. The commander commanded the soldiers not to move forward.
3. The teacher asked the students to be quiet and listen to her.
4. The accused requested the judge respectfully to pardon him.
5. He ordered the servant to leave that room.
6. The teacher asked the student to show her his notebook.
7. The teacher asked the students to listen to her attentively.
8. The teacher asked the boys to stand up.
9. Mother advised the son to work hard if he wanted to succeed.
10. I ordered/asked him to wait till I returned.
11. He ordered the driver not to park his car there.
12. The principal ordered the peon to remove all the files from his table.
13. The doctor advised the patient to go for a walk every day.
14. The engineer ordered the worker to switch off the plant.
15. The gardener ordered the children not to pluck flowers.
16. He requested his father to give him some extra pocket money.
17. The Headmaster requested the teachers to see to it that all students did well.
18. The employer warned him to make it a habit to reach office in time.

EXERCISE 44

1. The boys exclaimed joyfully that they had taken all the wickets.
2. They exclaimed joyfully that it was a very beautiful weather.
3. He said sorrowfully that she had died a tragic death.
4. He angrily exclaimed that he had brought a great trouble to the family.
5. They exclaimed that it was a horrible sight.
6. He exclaimed that it was very cruel of the king.
7. They exclaimed that it was a bad luck.
8. He prayed to God that I might live long.
9. I said that it was a rare sight.
10. We exclaimed that it was a terrible storm.

EXERCISE 45

1. The commander said to the soldiers, "Shoot"
2. He said, "Alas! I am ruined".
3. I said to him, "Have you finished your work ?"
4. My mother said to me, "Why are you up so early today ?"
5. He inquired, "Where is the cinema hall ?"

6. The teacher said to me, "What is your name ?"
7. My friend said to me, "I am writing a book".
8. The teacher said, "I have been teaching this class for six months"
9. My aunt said to me, "Who teaches you English in the school ?"
10. She said to a passerby, "How for is the Taj Mahal Hotel ?"
11. I said to my friend, "I may not be in the town this week."
12. He said to me, "I shall visit your home soon".
13. She said to her mother, "May I go out with my friends ?"
14. The magistrate said to the accused, "I can do nothing to save you".
15. I said to him, "You have put the best efforts to accomplish the work assigned to you".
16. I said to her, "I saw you in the party a few days before".
17. She said to her mother, "Is the food ready ?"
18. I said to my servant, "I may come late today".
19. My parents said to me, "You have not come up to our expectations."
20. I said to my teacher, "When are the next examinations likely to be held ?"
21. The chairman said to the members, "Are you satisfied with the decision taken at the meeting ?"
22. She said to me, "Where do you live ?"
23. My father said to me, "Are you taking proper interest in your studies ?"
24. The students said to the teacher, "Have we to answer all the questions ?"
25. He said to the manager, "What are the working hours of the office ?"
26. I said to my friend, "When will you come back from your home town ?"
27. My servant said to me, "Sir, may I go to my house now ?"
28. She said to me, "Will you take part in the annual school function of your school ?"
29. The customer said to the shop-keeper, "What is the cost of sugar ?"
30. She said to me, "How long will it take to reach the air port ?"
31. He said to his servant, "Leave the room."
32. The employer said to him, "Be punctual"
33. He said, "What a fine weather !"
34. The boys said, "Hurrah ! we have won the match".
35. I said to him, "Please give me a glass of water".
36. He said to me, "Switch off the lights".
37. The notice said, "Beware of pickpockets".
38. She said, "What a pity ! My only son is dead."
39. The boy said, "Hurrah, my kite has soared very high in the sky"

EXERCISE 46

1. A passerby asked her if she could tell him the way to the nearest inn. She replied that she could and asked if he wanted one in which he could spend the night. The passerby said that he did not want one in which he could spend the night because he only wanted a meal.
2. The soldier said that his hour had come and he must accept death boldly.

3. He told his daughter that he was going out and asked her if she wanted to accompany him.
4. The teacher told the students that she had been teaching them for a long time but they did not seem to improve. The students replied that they would certainly show improvement. The teacher further asked when they would show improvement.
5. He ordered his servant to go to the market and bring the items given in the list. He further asked if he (the servant) had understood. The servant replied respectfully that he had understood.
6. He motivated the boy to cheer up and not to get disheartened. The boy said that he had failed. He further told the boy that nothing was lost if he had failed in the examination as there were many opportunities in life. He further asked the boy if he followed him. The boy replied respectfully that he followed him.
7. He asked me if I thought our lives were happier than those of our ancestors. I replied that I thought we had got all but we had lost our peace of mind. He said that he also thought so.
8. The mother advised the child not to desire to have the moon as it was thousands of miles away and it was not a play thing for children and no child ever got it. She further said that she could get him anything else which he wished to have.
9. The teacher asked me angrily what I was thinking and why I was not paying attention. She further said that if I did not concentrate in my lesson, she would send me to the principal who was sure to punish me. She ordered me to pay attention and stop everything else.
10. The son asked his father if he (father) was angry with him. The father replied that he was angry with him. The son asked why he was angry with him (the son). The father said that he was very late to come back home. The son said that he was sorry and promised that he would never come late again.

EXERCISE 47

1. to speak to me
2. to bring her tiffin
3. to inform him
4. to improve her handwriting
5. to come in time
6. to drink

EXERCISE 48

1. to help me
2. to watch this movie
3. to help her
4. to solve this sum ?
5. to improve discipline

EXERCISE 49

1. to drive
2. to start the work ?
3. to say
4. to eat
5. to go
6. to go

EXERCISE 50

1. to be true
2. to walk
3. to work
4. to go out
5. to be solved

EXERCISE 51

1. It is not easy to solve this sum.
2. It is unethical to swindle your friend.
3. It is impossible to live without water.
4. It is not easy to climb this hill.
5. It is not wise to fiddle with this equipment.
6. It is not a good habit to borrow money.
7. It is immoral to insult the weak.

EXERCISE 52

1. to meet you after a long time.
2. to lift this heavy box
3. to advise him
4. to be heard by the students
5. not to be pardoned
6. to defeat your rival
7. to understand your trick
8. to tease the animals

EXERCISE 53

1. burnt
2. laden
3. stealing
4. hearing
5. running
6. cheating
7. burning
8. waiting
9. escaping
10. surrounded
11. torn
12. rotten
13. having
14. carrying
15. breaking

EXERCISE 54

1. singing
2. advising
3. smoking
4. driving
5. swimming
6. obeying
7. Reading
8. singing
9. smoking
10. Quarrelling
11. playing
12. Reading
13. Giving
14. Playing
15. gambling
16. Smoking
17. eating
18. nagging
19. standing
20. basking

EXERCISE 55

1. with blue eyes
2. in need
3. made of gold
4. of green colour
5. with a grey skin
6. with blue eyes
7. of great popularity
8. of great value
9. of great valour
10. of great worth
11. always in need
12. of trials and tribulations

EXERCISE 56

1. of dark colour
2. of great height
3. act of cowardice
4. full of horror
5. of India
6. of gold
7. of bravery
8. of terrorism
9. full of noise
10. full of wit

EXERCISE 57

1. worthy
2. golden
3. useless
4. shameful
5. ill-tempered
6. blameless
7. hopeful
8. boastful
9. unlucky
10. colourless

EXERCISE 58

1. of great worth
2. of same feathers
3. without tensions
4. full of valour
5. full of colours
6. made of marble
7. full of wit
8. without any logic
9. full of tensions
10. made of gold
11. of golden feathers
12. made of beautiful design
13. of great strength

EXERCISE 59

1. in the evening
2. in a brave manner
3. In former times
4. at an early date
5. in a beautiful manner
6. in a hurry
7. to a foreign country
8. to another place
9. on top of the hill
10. into the drawing room
11. in the almirah
12. in a rude manner
13. early in the morning
14. in the party
15. in the parliament
16. in a clever manner.

EXERCISE 60

1. in a cheerful manner
2. in a rude manner
3. in an eloquent manner
4. in a nice way
5. in a hurried manner
6. in a sudden manner
7. in a fierce manner
8. at this place
9. at this moment
10. at no time
11. in an angry manner
12. at that place
13. in a kind manner
14. in a passionate manner
15. in a thorough manner

EXERCISE 61

1. carefully
2. rudely
3. violently
4. heartly
5. impudently
6. carelessly
7. courageously
8. sincerely
9. satisfactorily
10. now
11. terribly
12. later
13. lastly

EXERCISE 62

1. in the foolish manner
2. in a brave manner
3. in a wise manner
4. in a decent manner
5. in a sincere manner
6. in a wise manner
7. in the evening
8. in a strong manner
9. since my childhood
10. near the sacred river
11. in a noisy manner
12. in an angry manner
13. in a wise manner
14. at this moment
15. before the students
16. in a beautiful manner
17. in a violent manner
18. early in the morning
19. in the park
20. near the temple

EXERCISE 63

1. Early to bed
2. to win the game
3. Reading books
4. to help me in future
5. to sit in the open air
6. swimming in the hot sun
7. Getting up early
8. to meet the principal
9. to be on time ?
10. the way to the restaurant
11. ill of others
12. to harm him ?
13. Taking regular exercise
14. to go on leave

EXERCISE 64

1. to join Indian Air Force
2. to learn driving
3. to help me
4. to climb the hill
5. getting up early
6. Reading books
7. to meet you
8. to stand first in the class
9. to harm him
10. to succeed in our endeavour
11. climbing the hill
12. getting up early
13. the way to the temple ?
14. to help him ?

EXERCISE 65

1. in the bank — Adverb Pharse
2. in a rude manner — Adverb Phrase
3. to learn driving — Noun Phrase
4. the civil services examinations — Noun Pharse
5. to the top of the hill — Adverb Phrase
6. the ways of God — Noun Phrase
7. Rising early — Noun Phrase
8. in a great problem — Adjective Phrase
9. off the cage — Adverb Phrase
10. in the medieval period — Adverb Phrase
11. her work — Noun Phrase
12. in small cages — Adjective Phrase
13. of great virtues — Adjective Phrase
14. in the evening — Adverb Phrase
15. to know the secret — Noun Phrase
16. all over the place — Adverb Phrase
17. company of such persons — Noun Phrase
18. To qualify the IAS examination — Noun Phrase
19. of great patience — Adjective Phrase
20. under the Ganges since then — Adverb Phrase
21. by selling newspaper — Adverb Phrase
22. in haste — Adverb Phrase
23. in a polite manner — Adverb Phrase
24. into the examination hall — Adverb Phrase
25. of black colour — Adjective Phrase
26. with great violence — Adverb Phrase
27. of great internal strength — Adjective Phrase
28. to meet his uncle — Noun Phrase
29. at this spot — Adv. Phrase
30. in a foolish manner — Adv. Phrase
31. A man of courage — Adjective Phrase

EXERCISE 66

1. till I return — of time
2. wherever they like — place
3. had you come to me in time — of condition
4. that no one could catch him — of purpose
5. because I am studying — of reason
6. Although you worked hard — of concession
7. Since he is an honest person — of reason
8. so that he can get good marks — of purpose
9. that he fell down — of result

10. that one cannot go out — of result
11. wherever you like — of place
12. when you are free — of time
13. Even if you improve your behaviour — of supposition
14. Though we walked fast — of cencession
15. because they were very late — of reason
16. If you overeat — of condition
17. than that (area is) — of comparison
18. since I am ill — of reason
19. As the manager was not in the office — of reason
20. though she had started early — of concession
21. until he comes back — of time
22. when they came to us — of time
23. even if it suffered many casualities — of concession
24. as they were told — of comparison of manner
25. that nothing moved — of result
26. wherever I go — of place
27. As the principal entered the class room — of time
28. wherever she likes — of place
29. than he speaks — of comparison
30. that I had earned — of comparison
31. since we met — of time
32. that I could not catch him — of result
33. when the house was locked — of time
34. Lest you should slip — of condition
35. that he may eat — of purpose
36. Although he did not study much — of concession
38. If I were you — of condition
39. that we may reap — of purpose

EXERCISE 67

1. as his sister (is)
2. that she fell sick
3. as he is a noble person
4. if you work hard
5. when she was young
6. If you walk slowly
7. when I am free
8. Since he is not a good person
9. Although he is rich
10. than that (room is)
11. as I was told
12. because he is weak
13. that we can hardly hear you
14. that I cannot read it
15. than air (is)
16. as he is told
17. if he is told
18. when you like
19. that all praised him

EXERCISE 68

1. as you are kind to me
2. as good as he could do
3. that one cannot go out
4. that he could not utter any words
5. that it cannot be true
6. when he arrived

7. Although she had poor health
8. As it was very cold
9. As he has good manners
10. Although he was in adversity
11. When they saw the principal
12. If the king dies
13. As he wanted to supplement his income
14. because he has done such a hard work
15. that it cannot be climbed

EXERCISE 69

1. to help me
2. Inspite of being poor
3. on entering the classroom
4. like a snake (does)
5. to see the patient's recovery
6. not to get very good marks
7. on your recommendation
8. on your being kind to him
9. like heroes
10. since your return from London
11. At dark
12. on his coming
13. for the countrymen to live
14. Being weak
15. on hearing your strange voice

EXERCISE 70

	Adjective clause	Noun/Pronoun
1.	which he presented me	— watch
2.	who work hard	— students
3.	that wears the crown	— head
4.	which you gave her	— letter
5.	where she was born	— house
6.	which I gave you	— work
7.	when he will come	— time
8.	why he did this	— reason
9.	which you wanted to purchase	— book
10.	who help themselves	— those
11.	which is praiseworthy	— anything
12.	which is very interesting	— tale
13.	that climbs too high	— He
14.	which is lost	— time
15.	which he posted	— letter
16.	who are honest	— men
17.	who take regular exercise	— those
18.	who boast	— those
19.	who is righteous	— He
20.	which your teacher gave you	— work
21.	which he proposed	— idea
22.	which are made by God	— creatures
23.	which will lead to your ruins	— path
24.	who will harm none	— person
25.	who lead simple life	— Persons

EXERCISE 71

1. which leads to the fort
2. who has won a medal in the Olympic Games
3. which has many torn pages
4. who come late
5. which you gave me
6. which has three bed rooms
7. who are hardworking
8. which glorifies the nature
9. which has many characters
10. who has taken your book
11. which is on the ground floor
12. which were authored by Jane Austin

EXERCISE 72

1. which has industries
2. when she will arrive
3. who has courage
4. when the meeting will be held
5. which is on the higher reaches of mountain
6. when the Prime Minister will arrive
7. which leads to the cave
8. which has been built by Birlas
9. which you liked
10. who live in the remote areas

EXERCISE 73

1. purchased by him
2. working in these fields
3. with many industries
4. leading to the old fort
5. standing in the front row
6. the striking employees
7. with green jacket
8. The drunken driver
9. involved in bank robbery
10. Honest, sincere and hardworking men

EXERCISE 74

1. what I want
2. that he will pass
3. that they would not go out
4. what you have purchased
5. that you will work hard
6. what he said ?
7. that you would invite him to the party
8. what he earns
9. what the teacher said
10. that he should say such words
11. that you are teaching in this school
12. what I like most in him
13. that she left her husband
14. how long he wants to remain unmarried
15. what we say
16. that he will lose his job.
17. whether I should attend the function or not
18. that discipline and hard work bring success
19. where he has gone ?
20. what you say

EXERCISE 75

1. that he would reach in time
2. what he said
3. whether he would come
4. what has happened
5. that the employees were on strike ?
6. that he will obey you
7. what they said
8. that she has failed
9. why you want to go there
10. that a thing of beauty is a joy forever
11. whether he will help me
12. that he could not solve the sum.
13. why she came here
14. that you will prove your worth
15. that life is not a bed of roses

EXERCISE 76

1. that I shall succeed
2. that the weather will change
3. that you would arrive
4. why he failed
5. that the prisoner was guilty
6. that he was guilty
7. that he may prosper
8. that you love me
9. that his health will improve
10. that you would arrive

EXERCISE 77

1. about his passing the test
2. in my words
3. of your recovery
4. his address
5. Her dying young
6. your success
7. about his preoccupation
8. of my reaching in time
9. her obeying everyone
10. his guilt

EXERCISE 78

1. Complex — (i) She asked me (Principal clause)
(ii) Where I was going (Subordinate clause)
2. Simple sentence
3. Simple sentence
4. Compound sentence — (i) He went to market (Coordinate clause)
(ii) (he) purchased books (Coordinate clause)
(iii) and (Conjunction)
5. Complex sentence — (i) She said (Principal clause)
(ii) that she would come (Subordinate clause)
6. Complex sentence — (i) She knew (Principal clause)
(ii) that I would help her (Subordinate clause)
7. Complex sentence — (i) The answer ... was not correct (Principal clause)
(ii) which you wrote (Subordinate clause)
8. Compound sentence — (i) Some people live to eat (Coordinate clause)
(ii) Some eat to live
(iii) but (Conjunction)
9. Complex sentence — (i) The boy ... is my cousin (Principal clause)
(ii) who is standing in the corner (Subordinate clause)
10. Complex sentence — (i) He did not pass (Principal clause)
(ii) Although he worked hard (Subordinate clause)
11. Complex sentence — (i) (It) was not expected (Principal clause)
(ii) that he would cheat us (Subordinate clause)
12. Compound sentence — (i) Pay attention (Coordinate clause)
(ii) Note down the points (Coordinate clause)
(iii) and (conjunction)
13. Complex sentence — (i) A guest is not liked (Principal clause)
(ii) If he stays for a long time (Subordinate clause)
14. Compound sentence — (i) Sonu passed (Coordinate clause)
(ii) Monu failed (Coordinate clause)
(iii) but (conjunction)
15. Simple sentence

EXERCISE 79

No.	Subject		Predicate				
	Subject word	Attibute	Verb	Object	Attribute	Complement	Adverbial qualifications
1.	boys	The	are flying	kites	—	—	—
2.	She	—	wants to learn	French	—	—	—
3.	They	—	found	him	—	guilty	
4.	She	—	bought	(a) a doll (b) the girl	—	—	—
5.	father	His	is	teacher	a		
6.	stitch	(a) A (b) in time	saves	nine			
7.	attitude	His	is	—	quite	clear	—
8.	Shakespeare	(a) the (b) playwright	wrote	Othello	—	—	—
9.	They	—	elected	him	—	captain	
10.	guests	The	have arrived	—	—	—	—
11.	Students	(a) The (b) anxious to pass	worked	—	—	—	hard
12.	Birds	of same feathers	flock	—	—	—	together
13.	fire	The	spread	—	—	—	in all directions
14.	habits	Bad	die	—	—	—	hard
15.	She	—	called	me	—	—	again
16.	life	(a) The (b) Village	improved	health	his	—	—
17.	They	—	spoke	—	—	—	in a soft manner
18.	Man	(a) The (b) old	is	—	—	dead	—
19.	She	—	teaches	(a) us (b) English	—	—	—
20.	He	—	seems	—	—	worried.	
21.	nothing	—	will make	him	—	happy	—
22.	weather	the	became	—	—	clear	—
23.	We	—	saw	splinters	the	falling	—
24.	members	(a) all (b) the	appointed	him	—	Secretary	—
25.	teacher	The	evaluated	answer sheets	the	—	carefully

EXERCISE 80

No.	Sentence or clause	Kind of sentence or clause	Connective	Subject Simple subject	Attribute of subject	Verb	Object	Complement	Adverbial Qualification
1.	A The chief guest was happy	Simple sentence	—	chief guest	the	was	—	happy	—
	B he gave us presents	Simple sentence	and	he		gave	(a) us (b) presents		—
2.	A He is a hardworker	Simple sentence	—	He		is		a hard worker	
	B He succeeds in his efforts	Simple sentence	and	he		succeeds		in his efforts	
3.	A He was sure that he would succeed	Complex sentence	—	He		was		sure	
	B that he would succeed	Noun clause	that	he	—	would succeed	—	—	
	C but he failed	Simple sentence	but	he	—	failed			
4.	A He entered the house	Simple sentence	—	He	—	entered	—	—	the house
	B he greeted everyone	Simple sentence	and	he	—	greeted	everyone	—	—
	C he did not speak	Simple sentence	but	he	—	did not speak	—	—	—
5.	A He was a gentleman	Simple sentence	—	he	—	was	—	a gentleman	—
	B all loved him	Simple sentence	and	all	—	loved	him	—	—
6.	A The workers felt tired	Simple sentence	—	workers	the	felt	—	tired	
	B they went to their rest room	Simple sentence	and	they	—	went			to their rest soon
7.	A I know that he will not help you	Complex sentence	—	I	—	know	—	—	—
	B that he will not help you	Noun clause object to verb know	that	he	—	will not help	you	—	—
	C you believe otherwise	Simple sentence	but	you	—	believe	—	—	otherwise
8.	A The students worked hard	Simple sentence	—	students	the	worked	—	—	hard
	B they took the test	Simple sentence	—	they	—	took	the test	—	—
	C they passed	Simple sentence	and	they	—	passed			

EXERCISE 81

1. (i) We ...... hardly realize → Principal clause
   (ii) who are lucky enough to live in this enlightened century → Adjective clause qualifying the pronoun 'we' in No. (i)
   (iii) how our forefathers suffered from their belief in the existence of mysterious and malevolent forces → Noun clause object to verb 'realise' in No. (i)
2. (i) We tried to listen to → Principal clause
   (ii) what he said → Noun clause object to preposition 'to' in No. (i)
3. (i) The boys shall be given awards → Principal clause
   (ii) who are sitting in the front rows → Adjective clause qualifying the noun 'boys' in No. (i)
4. (i) You are sure to pass → Principal clause
   (ii) If you work hard → Adverbial clause of condition
5. (i) Everyone is sure → Principle clause
   (ii) who knows him → Adjective clause qualifying the pronoun 'everyone' in No. (i)
   (iii) that he is a good person → Noun clause
6. (i) We hope → Principal clause
   (ii) that we can convince him → Noun clause object to verb 'hope' in No. (i).
   (iii) that he is wrong → Noun clause object to verb 'convince' in No. (ii)
7. (i) The book ...... was lost → Principal clause
   (ii) that he gave me → Adjective clause qualifying the noun book in No. (i)
   (iii) when I was travelling → Adverb clause of time.
8. (i) I knew → Principal clause
   (ii) that those boisterous people would disturb all → Noun clause object to verb 'knew' in No. (i)
   (iii) who were present in the meeting → Adjective clause qualifying the pronoun 'all' in No.(ii)
9. (i) I know → Principal clause
   (ii) that hardwork, sincerity and honesty are the virtues of the righteous man → Noun clause object to verb 'know' in No. (i)
   (iii) who never treads a wrong path → Adjective clause qualifying the noun 'man' in No. (ii)
10. (i) You would not have failed → Principal clause.
    (ii) If you had studied sincerely → Adverb clause of condition.
11. (i) History says → Principal clause
    (ii) that Mirabai continued to talk to her nurse → Noun clause object to verb 'says' in No. (i)
    (iii) when she was given a glass of poison → Adverbial clause of time.
    (iv) who was standing near her → Adjective clause qualifying the noun 'nurse' in No. (ii).
    (v) as she drank it → Adverbial clause of time.

12. (i) The man is a fool → Principal clause.
    (ii) who does not think → Adjective clause qualifying the noun 'man' in No. (i)
    (iii) that the goodness of every living creature is his goodness → Noun clause object to verb 'think' in No. (ii)
13. (i) They had been only a few weeks in the organization → Principal clause.
    (ii) when it was declared → Adverbial clause of time.
    (iii) that the trainees had to leave → Noun clause object to verb 'declared' in No. (ii)
14. (i) One faces the least problems in life → Principal clause.
    (ii) who is sincere and disciplined → Adjective clause qualifying the Pronoun 'one' in No. (i).
    (iii) as these are very important traits of one's character → Adverb clause of reason.
15. (i) Men fear death → Principal clause.
    (ii) as children fear to go in dark → Adverbial clause of comparison.
16. (i) The robbers have been arrested → Principal clause.
    (ii) who broke into the bank → Adjective clause qualifying the noun 'robbers' in No. (i)
17. (i) I don't know → Principal clause
    (ii) how I should solve this sum → Noun clause object to verb 'know' in No. (i)
    (iii) which is very difficult → Adjective clause qualifying the noun 'sum' in No. (ii)
18. (i) He sent her to city → Principal clause.
    (ii) As his elder daughter was a genius → Adverbial clause of Reason.
    (iii) so that she could pursue higher studies → Adverbial clause of Purpose.
19. (i) No one helps the person → Principal clause
    (ii) who is a swindler → Adjective clause qualifying the noun 'Person' in No. (i)
    (iii) for this would lead to many problems → Adverbial clause of Reason
20. (i) The house is up for sale → Principal clause
    (ii) where you lived → Adjective clause qualifying the noun 'house' in No. (i)
21. (i) You should listen carefully to → Principal clause
    (ii) what I say → Noun clause object to preposition 'to'
22. (i) Can you tell → Principal clause
    (ii) who wrote Hamlet ? → Noun clause object to verb 'tell' in No. (i)
23. (i) They set a strong guard → Principal clause
    (ii) lest any one should escape → adverbial clause of Purpose.
    (iii) when it was dark → Adverbial clause of Time.
24. (i) I think → Principal clause
    (ii) that she has typed all the letters → Noun clause object to verb 'think' in No. (i)
    (iii) which you gave her → Adjective clause qualifying the Noun 'letters' in No. (ii)
    (iv) when she was here → Adverbial clause of time.
25. (i) The children feel very happy → Principal clause.
    (ii) when they see a rainbow → Adverbial clause of time
    (iii) as it presents a very beautiful sight → Adverbial clause of reason

26. (i) He spoke against the system → Principal clause
(ii) whenever he was angry → Adverbial clause of time
(iii) which according to him was corrupt, inefficient and bureaucratic → Adjective clause qualifying the Noun 'system' in No. (i)

27. (i) Man is sure to believe → Principal clause
(ii) who has lived life beyond fifty → Adjective clause qualifying the Noun 'man' in No. (i)
(iii) that life is not a bed of roses → Noun clause object to verb 'believe' in No. (i).

EXERCISE 82

1. a	2. the	3. an	4. the	5. a
6. a	7. an	8. a, an, a	9. an	10. an
11. the, a	12. the	13. the	14. the, the	15. the, a
16. the, the	17. the, the, the	18. a	19. an	20. the
21. a	22. a	23. a	24. the	25. a
26. the, a	27. an	28. a	29. the	30. an
31. the, the	32. the, a	33. the		

EXERCISE 83

1. *The* sun sets in *the* west.
2. Do not look *a* gift horse in *the* mouth.
3. *The* sun melts snows.
4. She is *a* poor woman.
5. He is *an* intelligent boy.
6. Have you never seen *a* camel ?
7. Draw *the* map of Delhi.
8. What *a* beautiful scene this is!
9. The river was spanned by *an* iron bridge.
10. *The* sun did not rise till then.
11. Like *a* true sportsman you should give the enemy *a* fair play.
12. There is nothing like staying at this place for comfort (×).
13. I do not use this sort of medicine (×).
14. Time makes *the* worst enemies friends.
15. I have not seen her since she was *an* infant.
16. They started late in *the* afternoon.
17. Has she been told about *the* accident ?
18. He who dies in *a* great cause becomes immortal.
19. She has not seen me since I was *a* child.
20. May I have *the* pleasure of your company ?
21. This is one of *the* best books written by Kalidas.

22. They went to church to attend mass (×)

23. Do you know *the* answers to *the* questions ?

24. Get *a* kg of ghee from *the* nearest store.

25. I have seen *a* movie when I was young.

26. Where did you buy *the* present ?

27. Who wishes to walk with me ? (×)

28. I have solved all *the* sums.

29. Carry on *the* work in my absence.

30. Ceylon is *an* island.

31. The teacher gave me *an* easy sum to solve.

32. London is on *the* Thames.

33. You have scored *the* best marks.

34. This is *the* easiest sum which all students of *the* class can solve without *the least* problem.

35. Qutab Minar is *a* famous historical monument.

36. He seems to be *a* hollow from inside.

EXERCISE 84

1. is	2. was	3. has	4. make	5. was
6. was	7. am	8. are	9. is	10. is
11. is	12. has	13. have	14. am	15. is
16. is	17. is	18. is	19. have	20. is
21. is	22. is	23. was	24. is	25. is
26. is	27. is	28. is	29. was	30. has
31. makes	32. were	33. have	34. was	35. is
36. is	37. has	38. is	39. is	40. is

EXERCISE 85

A. 1. any 2. some 3. any 4. any, any

B. 1. many 2. much 3. much 4. many

C. 1. a little 2. little 3. the little 4. few 5. a little 6. few 7. a few

D. 1. neither 2. either 3. each 4. either 5. Neither

E. 1. fewer 2. less 3. less

EXERCISE 86

1. were	2. came	3. could	4. could	5. was
6. dared	7. was	8. might	9. would	10. could
11. can	12. could	13. might	14. could	15. preaches
16. told	17. continued	18. is	19. would	20. could

EXERCISE 87

1. would	2. was	3. might	4. can	5. can
6. would	7. could	8. would	9. had	10. could
11. might	12. can	13. could	14. might	15. could

EXERCISE 88

1. came	2. was	3. was	4. may	5. makes
6. are	7. would	8. would		

EXERCISE 89

1. Adverb	2. Adjective	3. Adverb	4. Adjective	5. Adverb
6. Adjective	7. Conjunction	8. Preposition	9. Adjective	10. Verb
11. Noun	12. Preposition	13. Noun	14. Verb	15. Adjective
16. Adjective	17. Adverb	18. Conjunction	19. Adjective	20. Noun
21. Adverb	22. Preposition	23. Noun	24. Adverb	25. Adjective
26. Adverb	27. Noun	28. Preposition	29. Adjective	30. Adverb
31. Pronoun	32. Noun	33. Adverb	34. Noun	35. Adjective
36. Preposition	37. Conjunction	38. Preposition	39. Adverb	40. Adjective
41. Adjective	42. Adverb			

EXERCISE 90

1. would	2. must	3. could	4. could	5. might
6. may	7. need	8. must	9. need not	10. should
11. would	12. dare	13. will	14. used to	15. shall
16. will	17. should	18. would	19. may/might	20. will
21. could	22. ought	23. must	24. can	25. can
26. must, shall	27. shall	28. dare	29. dared	30. must
31. will	32. would	33. used to/would	34. ought to	

EXERCISE 91

1. The list is unending and we have to bring books, pencils, erasers, notebooks, compasses, maps and many other items.
2. Sir, I would like to have one-day leave.
3. Even a fool, when he remains silent, is considered wise.
4. At the stroke of the midnight hour, when the world sleeps, India will awake to life and freedom.
5. He is sincere, diligent, polite, helpful and conscientious.
6. If you work hard, you will pass.
7. At dawn, however, he goes for a walk.
8. Shakespeare, the great English playwright, lived in seventeenth century.
9. Sheela, the owner of this building, knows how the neighbours disturb everyday.

10. By hard work, honesty and dedication, he rose to great heights.
11. India, Pakistan, New Zealand and Australia will play the triangular series.
12. He lost money, friends, reputation and property.
13. It was dull, long, wearisome journey.
14. One should be polite and humble, honest and sincere.
15. Titanic, the great English ship, perished in 1912.
16. Rich and poor, wise and foolish, high and low are all mortal.
17. Come into the parlour, dear.
18. One should write quickly, neatly and accurately.
19. Indian soldiers, having defeated the enemy, returned to their camp.
20. Your behaviour, to say the least, is uncouth.
21. He could not, however, succeed in his goal.
22. It rained very heavily, and there was a terrible flood.
23. The journey was long, and the wind was heavy.
24. That he will pass, is certain.
25. People who are superstitious, say that it is unlucky to part with money on Thursday.
26. He said, 'Please give me some food".
27. When I was young, I often went on long treks.
28. India, with all your beauties, I love you.
29. Jealously, anger, pride, uncharity, cruelty, self-righteousness, touchiness, doggedness and sullenness are the ingredients of ill-temper.
30. No form of vice, not worldliness, not agreed of gold, not drunkenness itself, does more to unchristianise society than evil temper.
31. Many people, unfortunately, seem to think that Government can always pay out money quite easily and in any quantity and they forget or else they do not know that the Government can only pay out money that it has received in taxes.

EXERCISE 92

1. The mother, finding her child missing, exclaimed, "What shall I do now ?"
2. "Perhaps", said he, "I may be wrong as you say".
3. "Bring me a glass of water", he said to his servant.
4. "You have all done very badly", remarked the teacher.
5. They had played together in childhood, they had worked together when young; they were now tottering about and gossiping away in the evening of life and in a short time, they will, probably be buried together in the neigbouring churchyard.
6. King Francis was a great lover of all kinds of sport and one day he and his courtiers, noblemen and ladies sat watching wild, savage lions fighting each other in the enclosure below. Among the courtiers sat Count de Lorge beside a beautiful and lively lady of noble birth, whom he loved and hoped to marry. The lions roared and bit and tore each other with

savage fury until the king said to his courtiers, "Gentlemen, we are better up here than down there."

7. (Continued) The lady, hearing him thought she would show the king and his court how devoted her lover was to her, so she dropped her glove down among the fighting lions and looked at Count de Lorge, and smiled at him. He bowed to her and leaped down among the savage lions, without hesitation recovered the glove, and climbed back to his place. Then he threw the glove right in the lady's face. King Francis cried out, "Well and bravely done, but it was not love that made you lady set you such a dangerous thing to do but her vanity."
8. The lady was angry with her servant and said, "Why have you again disturbed me in my sleep ?" "I am sorry madam, excuse me again this time. I shall not repeat the mistake", the servant said.
9. The principal said to the students, "Where do you want to go for a picnic ?" "Either to Nehru Park or to Buddha Jaynti Park", said the students.
10. Mr. Boggis clapped one hand over his heart, staggered to the nearest chair and collapsed into it, breathing heavily. "What's the matter with you", Claud asked, "It's nothing", he gasped, "I'll be all right in a minute. Please – a glass of water. It's my heart." Best fetched him the water, handed it to him and stayed close beside him, staring down at him with a fatuous leer on his face.
11. "So, when will you come back to work ?" Feld asked him. To his surprise, Sobel burst out, "Never". Jumping up, he strode over to the window that looked out upon the miserable street. "Why should I come back", he cried. "I will raise your wages". The shoe-maker, knowing, he did not care what else to say. "What do you want from me, Sobel ?" "Nothing". "I always treated you like you were my son". Sobel vehemently denied it.
12. "Listen, he said to me, "You know the old Imam, don't you ? I saw you talking to him." "yes", I said, "I talked to him once. "My wife's ill", Khamees said, "I want the Imam to come to my house to give her an injection. He won't come, if I ask him. He doesn't like me. You go and ask". "He doesn't like me either", I said. "Never mind", Khamees insisted, "he will come if you ask him – he knows you are a foreigner. He will listen to you."

EXERCISE 93

1. He is so stupid that he cannot understand your advice.
2. Her heart was so full that she could not speak any words.
3. Our teacher taught so fast that we could not understand.
4. This watermelon is so cheap that it cannot be good.
5. He is so clever that he will see through your trick.
6. She is so proud that she will not beg,
7. The boy is so small that he cannot be beaten.
8. She is so grieved that she cannot make a statement.
9. We were so late that we could not see the whole movie.
10. Your words are so good that they don't require any testimony.

EXERCISE 94

1. No other mountain in the world is so high as the Himalayas.
2. His friend is not stronger than Robin.
3. He is better than any other boy of our class.
4. Kolkata is one of the most crowded cities in India.
5. Very few Indian emperors were as great as Ashoka.
6. Rakesh is the most intelligent boy in our class.
7. Australia is larger than any other island in the world.
8. Very few countries in the world are as rich as the U.S.A.
9. Himachal Pradesh is cooler than Punjab.
10. Bangalore is not the most beautiful city in India.
11. No other city in the world is as beautiful as Paris.
12. Ankur is not stronger than Rahul.
13. Sunil is better than any other sportsman of our school.
14. Very few girls of our school are as beautiful as Sunita.
15. No other athlete is as good as he.

EXERCISE 95

1. The brave are admired by every one.
2. Bathing is enjoyed by children.
3. What cannot be cured must be endured.
4. I was given a beautiful present by him.
5. Shall I be accompanied to the market by you ?
6. The ways of God are known to no one.
7. He was appointed captain of the school cricket team by us.
8. We shall be blamed by her.
9. Have all the letters been typed by you ?
10. By whom was the furniture bought ?
11. This hill can not be climbed by me.
12. I was seen off at the air port her her.
13. Let this bill be paid now.
14. All of us were disturbed by him.
15. Was the letter drafted by you according to the instruction you were given by him ?
16. Happiness is desired by all.
17. The shutters have been downed by the shopkeepers.
18. Had all the questions been answered by the Minister when you entered the Parliament House ?
19. Let the door be closed.

20. Let a noise not be made.
21. Was cricket being played by the boys ?
22. Have all the sums been solved by him ?

EXERCISE 96

1. The management dismissed him form the service.
2. My friend saw me off.
3. The teacher punished the late-comers.
4. Who delivered the speech ?
5. The rainbow will gladden the children.
6. The Principal praised the children.
7. Have you given him his salary ?
8. The receptionist is typing the letters.
9. Was he admonishing you ?
10. The law forbids us.
11. Did the Managing Committee appoint him Secretary ?
12. Switch off the light.
13. The widow collected the award.
14. The Commander was presenting the sword of honour to the best cadet.
15. I shall deliver the message in time.

EXERCISE 97

1. No sooner did the President enter the hall than all stood up.
2. No sooner did the rain stop than we went out.
3. No one will disagree that he is an honest person.
4. He has not performed better than you.
5. Sohil is not as strong as he.
6. He is not more disciplined than you
7. I don't care much what others say about me.
8. No one but a maniac can do such a deed.
9. No other student of our class is as good as she.
10. He owns no other wealth than these books.

EXERCISE 98

1. Everyone will admit that you are an honest person.
2. I shall remember the wrongs done to me.
3. Every body believes in your sincerity.
4. He is always late.
5. Very few persons would doubt his honesty.

6. Every one present is crying.
7. She lived a few years in London.
8. Very few would disagree with me.

EXERCISE 99

1. You can't gather grapes from thistles.
2. Everyone knows our Prime Minister.
3. I shall never forget these unhappy days.
4. Let us not waste time in useless talk.
5. No one can know the ways of God.

EXERCISE 100

1. Who can pump the ocean dry ?
2. Isn't it useless to offer advice to a person who is fool ?
3. Is this the custom we follow here ?
4. Is there anything better than complete peace ?
5. Is he the person who will listen to you ?

EXERCISE 101

1. It is a very beautiful rainbow.
2. It is a matter of shame that you have slapped your father.
3. This place gives a great sweet joy.
4. You are very weak.
5. We wish that we were young again.
6. It is really a bloody deed.
7. If I could have a draught of fresh air.
8. You are very well fitted for this work.
9. A peacock is a very wonderful bird.
10. I wish to have a little solace.

EXERCISE 102

1. What a horrible journey it was !
2. What a rash deed he has done !
3. What a beautiful scene !
4. What an unhappy life you lead !
5. What a great job she has done !

EXERCISE 103

1. He has greatly succeeded.
2. He intends to prolong his stay.
3. He has endeavoured to improve the working of this office.

4. He attempted once to pass the Civil Service Examination.
5. I incline for success.
6. We accepted all he proposed.
7. He cannot be admitted in this institution.

EXERCISE 104

1. He succeeded in doing his work.
2. It can be admitted that Gandhiji was the greatest advocate of non-violence.

EXERCISE 105

1. The accused expressed regret that his deed was full of hatred.
2. Her intelligence is equal to that of a great scholar.
3. He gets the admiration of all because of his honesty.
4. He gave a clarification that he had done a deed of guilt.

EXERCISE 106

1. The boy was joyful to me greatly.
2. It is all probable that it will rain today.
3. The boy has been greatly successful and is admired by his school-mates.

EXERCISE 107

1. You have dressed shabbily and carelessly.
2. You have not been wrongly punished by your teacher.

EXERCISE 108

1. On the hill sat the saint and he was meditating.
2. He was unhappy and he tendered his resignation.
3. He failed in the examination and it was a great surprise for me.
4. He not only owns a Rolce Royce but also owns a Mercedes Benz.
5. He was preoccupied and could not come to receive us at the railway station.
6. The weather was fine and we decided to resume our journey.
7. He had poor health but he walked a long distance.
8. There have been heavy rains and there is water-logging everywhere.
9. The boys saw the tiger coming and they climbed up a tree.
10. He possesses all knowledge but he cannot be called an educated person.
11. He had pleasant behaviour and achieved great success.
12. He did hard work but he could not succeed.
13. He took pity on the poor and helped him in every manner.
14. He took off his clothes and jumped into the river.
15. It was evening but you had not reached there.

EXERCISE 109

1. His uncle is now in London and he will go there to meet him.
2. The soldier's fire arms had been snatched and he felt helpless.
3. He heard the stranger's footsteps and he came out.
4. He is arrogant and stubborn and therefore people dislike him.
5. You are ignorant and you are following the wrong path.
6. He must not come late or we shall cancel the meeting.
7. The flood caused a havoc and many people became homeless.
8. He put his best efforts but he could not win a medal.
9. His best friend cheated him and he became hopeless.
10. He wanted to avoid being seen and he hid behind the cupboard.

EXERCISE 110

1. Inspite of being very poor, he never complained.
2. His friend having died he became depressed.
3. In spite of our running fast we could not board the train.
4. Being very poor, he had to often go without food.
5. Having killed his partner, he became the owner of the property.
6. Finding my son missing from home, I was shocked.
7. He went abroad to see his mother.
8. They rejected the proposal accepted by us.
9. Work hard to avoid failure.
10. All went to meet the film star except me.
11. He being a very disciplined person, must have started in time.
12. In spite of being rich, Madhubala was not happy.
13. Having done his M.A., he went abroad for higher studies.
14. Seeing the teacher, the students greeted him.
15. He did not reply the letter written by me.
16. Inspite of being very rich, he is not contented.

EXERCISE 111

1. The rain having stopped, we resumed our play.
2. The train having departed, we could not board it.
3. I have an unpleasant work to do.
4. Having performed his duty well, he left the place.
5. The accused having evaded arrest many times, was finally put behind bars.
6. The Principal having entered the class room, everyone rose from his seat.
7. He being a hardworker and sincere, worked exceedingly well.
8. Your doing this will make everyone go against you.
9. He did not show any progress in spite of having been taught for a long time.

10. He did not care for the commander's order to fire.
11. The movie having begun, the lights were switched off.
12. Having practised everyday, he rose to great heights.
13. He was delighted to meet his old friend after a long time.
14. The doctor having examined him, was hopeful of his recovery.
15. Being very weak, he must rest.

EXERCISE 112

1. He hoped that he would pass the examination.
2. I always think that God is present everywhere.
3. They expected that they would meet me in the party.
4. The accused confessed that he was guilty.
5. You are pleading that you are ignorant of traffic rules.
6. It is not likely that your mother will question you.
7. They overheard what we were conversing.
8. We shall be glad that you will present yourself in the function.
9. You should reveal what is true.
10. I order that you should obey him.
11. Your father will be happy to hear that you have succeeded.
12. The commander told the soldiers that they should prepare for war.
13. It is said that he is a smuggler.
14. You should listen to what I say.
15. It is said that he is a man of his word.

EXERCISE 113

1. He did this when I was present.
2. Although he had poor health, he continued his journey.
3. As he was quite late for duty, he decided not to go.
4. It is so hot that one cannot go out.
5. You should wait till he arrives.
6. I have come so that I can meet my old friends.
7. As I am unwell I can't teach you today.
8. I saw him when he was jumping the wall.
9. When he was questioned he admitted his fault.
10. As he was quite happy, he prolonged his stay.
11. As he was unhappy with the new boss, he resigned his jobs.
12. You are liked because you are straightforward.
13. This sum is so difficult that it cannot be solved.
14. I can accompany you if my father consents.
15. The boy would be happy, if he gets more pocket money.

16. I spoke as best as I could.
17. He went abroad for he wanted to meet his mother.
18. We overstayed so that we could meet the director.
19. We decided to go out because the rain had stopped.
20. The soldiers moved very slowly so that they could avoid being seen by the enemy.
21. You should come here when it is 9 O'clock.
22. She was annoyed because she was criticized.

EXERCISE 114

1. We departed when we had paid obeisance.
2. Do you know when she will arrive ?
3. We expect that every employee should work sincerely and honestly.
4. I switched on the T.V. after my mother had slept.
5. I found the pen which I had lost.
6. The exact date when Lord Rama was born is not known.
7. We can meet at any place which is convenient for you.
8. We can excuse you if we take into consideration your problems.
9. The Army General became the Head after the Prime Minister had been deposed.
10. It is not known when she will arrive.
11. Work hard if you want to prevent reappear in the test.
12. I convinced him that English Grammar was important.
13. It is not expected that a noble person will do ignoble deeds.
14. It is uncertain how long the conference will last.
15. The hope that he will arrive is little.
16. It is known to very few people who wrote Othello.
17. You can prove that you are ignorant.
18. Those who came late were punished.
19. He went to the police station when he found the car missing.

EXERCISE 115

1. The magistrate ordered the police to arrest the trouble-makers.
2. The son did not know about his mother's return.
3. I hope of good sense prevailing on you.
4. The result of your negligence was your failure.
5. The news of his departure is not true.
6. I asked him the cause of his failure.
7. The judge declared his innocence.
8. The Principal ordered punishment to the late comers.
9. The Prime Minister's departure to England has been reported.
10. Your having done a blunder is believed by everyone.
11. Tell us the meaning of your statement.

EXERCISE 116

1. An industrious man is sure to meet success.
2. He has no money to lend me.
3. This is the place of my worship.
4. I have no money to spend.
5. This boy stood first in the Board Examination.
6. This box belongs to her.
7. I told her the expected time of my return.
8. People living in this area are boisterous.
9. A man having risen by his own efforts is sure to succeed.
10. She has found her lost purse.
11. I saw a one-eyed man.
12. Do you remember your former principal ?
13. The answer given by you is irrelevant.
14. Have you nothing to offer to the deity ?
15. I regained my lost ground with the help of my friends.
16. A learned person needs no riches.
17. The smoke coming from the burnt houses is suffocating.
18. This house belongs to him.
19. I have no time to waste on useless discussion.
20. The help rendered by me to my relations should not be underestimated.

EXERCISE 117

1. Being sick I am unable to work.
2. I am annoyed at your having not obeyed your teacher.
3. You can eat to your fill.
4. He will not improve unless compelled.
5. I have achieved better than my hope.
6. The students will shout in the absence of the teacher.
7. I am too tired to work more.
8. He became depressed on hearing the result.
9. In spite of being rich he is not happy.
10. Being ill, I don't wish to go out.
11. Being rich, you can afford to spend.
12. He will meet you on hearing from us.
13. Not being able to get a better job, he accepted a lowly job.
14. The boys ran away on seeing a tiger.
15. On seeing me, you hid behind the curtain.
16. He was too lazy to succeed.

17. Being sincere, honest and disciplined, he is admired by all.
18. He is too old to walk.
19. I was surprised at your accompanying a dubious person.
20. There is no hope without life.
21. You cannot come without his consent.
22. I was very angry at being refused admission.
23. In spite of being poor he is contented.
24. I did the work to the best of my ability.
25. It was too dark to see anything.

EXERCISE 118

1. No patient is admitted without being examined.
2. It is terrible for people to cheat their best friends.
3. His arrival is doubtful.
4. He asked my age.
5. The sum is too difficult for me to solve.
6. The successful students will receive certificates.
7. His arrival is certain.
8. We insist on getting our salary today.
9. He has become too weak to walk.
10. The accused gave a graphic account of his escape.
11. The President awarded the soldiers posthumously.
12. An orphan child is pitied by all.
13. I know this from the information received by me.
14. This is the time for you to depart.
15. He went to a hill station to recover his health.
16. We continued our journey in spite of the weather having become inclement.
17. In spite of being successful he could not get good marks.
18. He makes a promise to keep.
19. The place of saint's cremation has been discovered.
20. He has no advice to offer to anyone.
21. I was lucky to escape except hurting my toe.
22. The period of his stay is uncertain.
23. Your being silent proves your guilt.
24. I owe my success to the Creator.
25. You must be a member of the club to be admitted.

EXERCISE 119

1. We went to a hill station where we enjoyed a lot.
2. I love him because he is my son.
3. You were not available when we called at your office yesterday.
4. He succeeded because he studied hard.

5. If you speak another word you shall be taught a lesson.
6. If he does not come he will inform.
7. He is putting his best efforts because he wishes to become great.
8. Although we hurried to the airport, we missed the flight.
9. If you don't do as you are told, you will repent.
10. If you sweep this area you will find the ring.
11. Although the soldier was seriously wounded, he did not lose heart.
12. The children ran away when they saw the danger.
13. I am working hard because I aim at succeeding.
14. If I did not come I would be criticized.
15. Although he is not rich, he is certainly contented.
16. If you don't improve, you will have to resign.
17. Although life is not a bed of roses yet no one wants to die.
18. He fell down when he was climbing the stairs.
19. If you take care of small things big things will take care of themselves.
20. I started at once when I received the message.
21. If you don't reach office in time you may lose your job.
22. As you have lost all your wealth, you will face problems.
23. If you step out of the house you will face serious problems.
24. The old man wanted rest because he was tired.
25. He was hanged because he was a traitor.

EXERCISE 120

1. Although you have insulted him, he will forgive you.
2. Though you have passed the examination you have not got good marks.
3. If you give me the documents I will sign them.
4. Although I told him to improve his grammar, he did not care.
5. If you take the medicine you will be all right.
6. Although he is a coward he always claims to be brave.
7. If you avoid overeating you will not fall sick.
8. Had the robber not escaped, the cop would have killed him.
9. If you send me the script, I will edit it.
10. As I don't like this person, I don't associate with him.
11. Since it is very hot, we shall not go out.
12. If you cannot pay cash, you can pay demand draft.

EXERCISE 121

1. Study seriously or you will fail.
2. You must improve your behaviour or else you cannot continue this job.
3. The rain stopped and we went out.
4. You say so and I must believe it.
5. He had started late and therefore he reached late.

6. He saw a tiger and he ran away.
7. He is brave and we admire him.
8. He is poor but he is happy.
9. The soldier fought valiantly but he was defeated.
10. You told him something and he knows it.
11. He came and we started our journey.
12. Write the letter and then show it to me.
13. You work hard but you seldom get success.
14. She was educated in a public school and there she learnt French.
15. He studied very hard and he stood first in the school.
16. She has a cousin and he speaks Latin fluently.
17. The rain started and we stopped playing.

EXERCISE 122

1. He finished his work and immediately he came here.
2. You joined politics and since then you have never been sincere.
3. You will not succeed and I think so.
4. You come and immediately we shall go.
5. She has to type all the letters and then she can go.
6. We offer good salary and we expect good results.
7. She may like anytime and then she can come.
8. He is rich but he is not arrogant.
9. She left Delhi and since then we have never heard from her.
10. We cannot admire a corrupt man but we may admire a poor man.

EXERCISE 123

1. You did not reply me for one week.
2. He not only owns a Maruti but he also owns a Fiat.
3. No sooner did the flight land than we proceeded towards the aeroplane.
4. We were surprised to find half the staff absent.
5. Circumstances compelled him to sell a big house in order to repay the loan.
6. When I was informed by a boy that the entrance test had been passed by my son, a great party was announced by me.

EXERCISE 124

1. I don't know where I have seen you before.
2. I am sure that your are innocent.
3. That you will waste your time is certain.
4. No one can doubt that he has worked sincerely.
5. I think that he has done a blunder.
6. Can anyone tell me who wrote Hamlet ?
7. That you have cheated him is the truth.

8. That he will not succeed is certain.
9. It is difficult to understand why he distrusts his best friends.
10. We expect that the chief guest will arrive in time.
11. Ask someone if it is the time for the aeroplane to land.
12. Do you deny that you disturbed me ?
13. Do you know when the function will start ?
14. The fact that he is a great statesman cannot be denied.
15. Tell us what he has done.

EXERCISE 125

1. Can you tell me the reason why you are not working sincerely ?
2. This is the college where I studied.
3. Show me the place where you were surmoned.
4. He is the boy who has defied his parents.
5. The robbers who committed the robbery yesterday have been arrested.
6. A man who was proud of his strength disliked weak persons.
7. I have many plans which will lead me to great heights.
8. I met a man who was a stranger in this city.
9. He has eaten the food which was kept for me.
10. This man who used to take drugs has become very weak.

EXERCISE 126

1. The flight landed after we had reached the airport.
2. She has been very poor since her parents died.
3. Even a child can understand this poem because it is very easy.
4. I cannot teach you today because I am not well.
5. He will be hanged for he has committed a murder.
6. Although he is poor, he is happy.
7. The boy is being honoured because he has stood first in the examination.
8. She cannot work any more as she is very tired.
9. Sonu is better than any other boy in our school.
10. He was admonished because he came late.
11. If you don't hurry, you will miss the flight.
12. When I was returning from office, I was caught in a shower.
13. When I went to your office, you were out.
14. We were puzzled when we saw some strange footmarks on the ground.
15. I did not go out because I was not well.
16. The function started when the principal arrived.
17. The clock struck four when you entered the room.
18. He studied hard so that he could get good marks.
19. You must be very tired because you had no sleep last night.
20. If a tutor calls, please ask him to wait.

21. He soon rose to great heights because he worked very hard.
22. Do not go until I dress up.
23. No body can hear you because you speak in a·very low voice.
24. No sooner did the saint leave than the house collapsed.
25. Although he studied hard, he could not get success.

EXERCISE 127

1. Nothing can describe the confusion which he felt when he was surrounded by bandits.
2. Milton did not educate his daughters in the languages because he said that one tongue was enough for women.
3. He told me that he had read Shakespeare when he was sixteen.
4. I felt better after taking the medicine because it cured my sickness.
5. It is my duty to give you orders whether you like it or not.
6. You are sure to receive your money which is due to you.
7. The decision that you will not participate in the debate is foolish because you are the best debater in our school.
8. I got very angry as I waited longer since I had asked you to be punctual.
9. This is the elephant which had gone 'must' as it killed two persons.
10. That is the man who gave me a present which was stolen.
11. It was expected that you would succeed as you had studied hard.
12. That boy is being interviewed by the reporters as he has topped the Civil Services Examination.
13. I have lost the very costly pen which was gifted to me by my father.
14. We have been told that her behaviour is very strange which we are unable to understood.
15. I was told that you stole a purse which had the owner's name written on it.
16. They despised their boss, a very arrogant person who had an authoritarian temperament.
17. At daybreak they stood on a hill which overlooked the moor.
18. The chief guest who entered the hall at 10 A.M. was received by the Principal who read the report.
19. We are happy to know that you have passed for, you deserved to pass.
20. I am very unhappy to receive your report which says that you are a lethargic and careless boy.
21. The Principal has issued orders that you will be given admission on the condition that you work hard.
22. I have got leave to go to the U.S.A. where my father is a doctor.

EXERCISE 128

1. A group of armed robbers some of whom had escaped from the prison entered the village at wee hours and looted the villagers who dared not challenge the robbers.
2. After the death of his father, he had to discontinue his studies as he had to look after his mother and two younger brothers and this made him search a job which he got but the job did not give him complete satisfaction but he was compelled to continue his job.

3. It is a golden rule that we should spend only our earning and should save a little and we should not look to any one for financial help as friends generally draw back their hand at the hour of need.
4. Most of us either live in the past or look forward to the future and the past may be glorious or otherwise and the future may have its glorious uncertainties but our optimism makes the future a dream world but we breathe and exist in the present and hope for something better and brighter to turn up.
5. Tagore's versatility who wrote poems, plays, novels and short stories and who was a great musical composer and director of stage production and who also took to painting in the last years of his life is well-known.
6. The school at Santiniketan was started in 1901 when Tagore who for the next forty years gave to the school and Visvabharati, his life and love, was forty years old and in these institutions Tagore strove to renew the ideals of a bygone age of forest hermitages, of simplicity of life, of clarity of spiritual vision, of purity of heart, of harmony with the universe.
7. He offered me help which I needed but persisted in refusing it and he left me to my fate.
8. The name of Buddha means the Awakened One who attained spiritual realization and he gives us a way based on clear knowledge and Buddhism is a system of spiritual realization in which personal realization is the starting point.
9. Man who is a child of God can become immortal through union with God but until then he wanders in the darkness of the world and he is like a spark from the fire, or a wave of the ocean but he manifests God's will perfectly when he becomes perfect.
10. The spirit of science leads to the refinement of religion which is not magic or witchcraft, quackery or superstition and is not to be confused with outdated dogmas and incredible superstitions which are hindrances and barriers and spoil the simplicity of spiritual life.
11. All religions require us to look upon life as an opportunity for self-realization and call upon us to strive incessantly and to wrest the immortal from the mortal.
12. Religion reflects both God and man and religion is a life to be lived and it is not a theory to be accepted nor is it a belief to be adhered to as it allows scope and validity to varied approaches to the Divine.
13. An author has written an interesting book in which he tells the story of his life, part of which was spent in exile from his own country where he is now absolute master.
14. She took the 'Sadhu' to her home and told him to remain there for the night and then she found him hungry and procured some fruits from outside and gave them to the 'sadhu' for supper.
15. He was a man of very haughty and arrogant temper and was treated very ungraciously by the king but was supported whole-heartedly by the people and this might be expected that he would eagerly take the first opportunity of showing his power and satiating his anger.

NOTES

NOTES